Anonymous

The Legal And Financial Lights of America

Anonymous

The Legal And Financial Lights of America

ISBN/EAN: 9783744743471

Printed in Europe, USA, Canada, Australia, Japan

Cover: Foto ©Suzi / pixelio.de

More available books at **www.hansebooks.com**

A NEW AND ORIGINAL COMPILATION OF THE MOST HONORABLE AND RELIABLE
ATTORNEYS (ONE IN EACH COUNTY);

THE LARGEST, BEST AND MOST PROMINENT BANKS (ONE
IN EACH COUNTY);

THE OFFICIAL DIPLOMATIC AND CONSULAR GUIDE OF THE U. S. THROUGHOUT
THE WORLD;

AND THE MOST COMPREHENSIVE DIGEST OF ALL COMMERCIAL LAWS OF EACH
STATE AND TERRITORY IN THE UNION;

ALL OF WHICH HAS BEEN ACCOMPLISHED FOR THE MUTUAL INTEREST AND
PROFITS OF ATTORNEYS AND BANKS, AND THE WHOLESALE
MERCHANTS AND MANUFACTURERS.

NEW YORK.
1895.

PREFACE.

FOR the first time in the history of commerce, a system has been established by which a mutual and beneficial arrangement is entered into between the wholesale Merchants and Manufacturers of the country, with a legal representative herein contained, as well as getting honest information and treatment as to the debtor class in general; also for banking facilities, in connection with said sole attorney for each county, we give the most reliable Banks in same district which are giving special time and attention to all banking business entrusted to them. The system is entirely new, and cannot fail to save hundreds and thousands of dollars per year and relieve the minds of the commercial world of many of its commercial vexations and burdens; for where one attends (in one small district) to the interest of the many from the outside, how easy, indeed, it becomes for the one to make more satisfactory and quicker settlements in case of liquidation, and the same can be made far more profitable to creditor and beneficial to its treasury, by saving expenses, per cents., costs and remaining stock. All further explanations cheerfully given by our representatives or the publishers.

In conclusion, for all international business, we also give you the official Diplomatic and Consular list of the United States throughout the world.

With this short review of our work, we feel confident that these "Lights" will be and become the greatest panacea to commerce at large.

SCHUHL & LEMAIRE,
Publishers.

AGREEMENT BETWEEN

The Wholesale Merchants' & Manufacturers' Guarantee Credit Company

AND

THE LEGAL AND FINANCIAL LIGHTS OF AMERICA.

---※---

It is agreed by The Wholesale Merchants' and Manufacturers' Guarantee Credit Company and the publishers of The Legal and Financial Lights of America, that the said members of the Wholesale Merchants' and Manufacturers' Guarantee Credit Company do, and will, uphold and encourage the said publication for divers good reasons as duly made acquainted with; and support it to the full extent, as follows:

FIRST. To be and become its annual subscribers.

SECOND. To deal directly with the attorneys contained therein in all matters pertaining to law, and judicial business in their respective counties.

THIRD. For all financial business to act directly with the banks therein furnished.

And the said publishers pledge themselves at all times, and in each edition to furnish only the most honorable and responsible attorneys and banks, one in each and every county of the United States (in larger cities, two or more as the case may necessitate).

ALL OF WHICH IS MUTUALLY CONCURRED IN BY

The Wholesale Merchants' and Manufacturers' Guarantee Credit Company

AND THE

Publishers of the Legal and Financial Lights of America,

ALABAMA.

County Seat.	County.	Name of Atty.	Name of Bank.	Cashier.
Abbeville	Henry.	J. W. Foster.	At Columbia, Bk. of Jno. T. Davis & Son.	
Andalusia	Covington.	Ed. T. Albritton.	At Luverne, Bk. of Luverne.	H. Folmar.
Ashland	Clay.	A. S. Stockdall.	See Talladega.	
Ashville	St. Clair.	E. J. Robinson.	See Gadsden.	
Athens	Limestone.	W. R. Walker.	Bk. of Athens.	C. E. Frost.
Birmingham	Jefferson.	Mountjoy & Tomlinson.	Berney Natl. Bk.	W. P. G. Harding.
Blountsville	Blount.	M. L. Ward.	See Cullman.	
Butler	Choctaw.	Vacant.	See Livingston.	
Brewton	Escambia.	Jas. M. Davison.	Bk. of Brewton.	O. F. Luttrell.
Camden	Wilcox.	P. M. Horn.	Camden Bk.	S. J. Walling, Jr.
Carrollton	Pickens.	E. D. Willett.	See Tuscaloosa.	
Centre	Cherokee.	C. Daniel.	See Jacksonville.	
Centreville	Bibb.	S. D. Logan.	At Blocton, Blocton Svgs. Bk.	J. B. Wadsworth.
Clanton	Chilton.	W. A. Collier.	See Montgomery.	
Clayton	Barbour.	A. A. Evans.	Citizens Bk.	J. E. Meadows.
Columbiana	Shelby.	D. R. McMillan.	Bk. of Gordon DuBose.	H. C. DuBose.
Cullman	Cullman.	Geo. H. Parker.	Bk. of Parker & Co.	H. C. Bounds.
Dadeville	Tallapoosa.	Jno. A. Terrell.	Tallapoosa Co. Bk	Z. J. Wright, Jr.
Daphne	Baldwin.	D. C. Anderson.	See Mobile.	
DOUPLE SPRINGS.	Winston.	P. H. Newman.	See Jasper.	
Edwardsville	Cleburne.	A. A. Hurst.	Bk. of P. A. Kowle.	
Elba	Coffee.	P. N. Hickman.	At Luverne, Bk. of Luverne.	
Eufaula	Barbour.	A. H. Merrill.	East Alabama Natl. Bk.	C. P. Roberts.
Eutaw	Greene.	Seay, Judge & DeGraffenried.	First Natl. Bk.	B. B. Barnes.
Evergreen	Conecuh.	Farnham, Crum & Newton.	See Brewton.	
Fayette	Fayette.	Jno B. Sanford.	See Jasper.	
Florence	Lauderdale.	Simpson & Jones.	First Natl. Bk.	N. C. Elting.
Fort Payne	De Kalb.	L. A. Dobbs.	Fort Payne Bk.	W. P. Hemphill.
Gadsden	Etowah.	Dortch & Martin.	First Natl. Bk.	W. G. Brockway.
Geneva	Geneva.	Chas. H. Laney.	Bk. of Geneva.	Wm. J. Hall.
Greensboro'	Hale.	A. M. Tunstall.	Bk. of Greensboro'.	J. A. Blunt.
Greenville	Butler.	Richardson & Hamilton.	Exchange Bk.	B. Steiner.
Grove Hill	Clarke.	J. T. Lackland.	See Camden.	
Guntersville	Marshall.	Lusk & Bell.	Bk. of Guntersville.	W. M. Cantrell.
Hamilton	Marion.	A. J. Stanford.	At Aberdeen, Miss.	
Hayneville	Lowndes.	Clements & Brewer.	At Montgomery.	
Huntsville	Madison.	O. R. Hundley.	First Natl. Bk.	Jos. Martin.
Jacksonville	Calhoun.	H. Lee Stevenson.	Tredegar Natl. Bk.	Geo. P. Ide.
Jasper	Walker.	W. B. Appling.	Jasper Trust Co.	Jno. A. Gravelee.
La Fayette	Chambers.	Dowdell & Duke.	Bk. of Lafayette.	J. C. Griffin.
Linden	Marengo.	Jno. C. Anderson.	At Uniontown, Plan. & Mer. Bk.	W. J. White.
Livingston	Sumter.	A. G. Smith.	Bk. of McMillan & Co.	
Luverne	Crenshaw.	M. W. Rushton.	Bk. of Luverne.	H. Folmar.
Marion	Perry.	B. M. Huey.	Marion Central Bk.	Jas. T. Fitzgerald.
Mobile	Mobile.	Fielding Vaughan.	First Natl. Bk.	C. D. Willoughby.
Monroeville	Monroe.	Thos. S. Wiggins.	At Brewton.	

ALABAMA—Continued.

County Seat.	County.	Name of Atty.	Name of Bank.	Cashier.
Montgomery	Montgomery.	Tompkins & Troy.	First Natl. Bk.	A. M. Baldwin.
Moulton	Lawrence.	W. T. Lowe.	At Decatur, First Natl. Bk.	W. W. Littlejohn.
Opelika	Lee.	W. J. Samford & Son.	First Natl. Bk.	Orrin Brown.
Ozark	Dale.	A. T. Borders.	Planters' & Merchants' Bk.	H. M. Sessions.
Prattville	Autaga.	M. A. Smith.	At Montgomery.	
Rockford	Coosa.	J. H. Parker.	At Tallapoosa.	
Russellville	Franklin.	G. C. Almond.	See Tuscumbia.	
Rutledge	Crenshaw.	A. B. Brooks.	At Luverne, Bk. of Luverne.	H. Folmar.
Scottsboro'	Jackson.	Jno. F. Proctor.	Jackson Co. Bk.	A. H. Coffey.
Seale	Russell.	J. F. Waddell.	At Union Springs.	
Selma	Dallas.	Mallory & McLeod.	City Natl. Bk.	A. G. Parrish.
Somerville	Morgan.	Wm. E. Skeggs.	At Decatur, First Natl. Bk.	W. W. Littlejohn.
St. Stephens	Washington.	Vacant.	At Mobile.	
Talladega	Talladega.	A. M. Garber.	Isbell Natl. Bk.	R. L. Ivey.
Troy	Pike.	Parks, Harmon & Gamble.	Farmers' & Merchants' Bk.	L. M. Baslinsky.
Tuscaloosa	Tuscaloosa.	Foster & Oliver.	Merchants' Natl. Bk.	Glenn Foster.
Tuscumbia	Colbert.	Kirk & Almon.	Colbert Co. Bk.	J. H. Bemis.
Tuskegee	Macon.	W. G. Brewer.	Bk. of Tuskegee.	J. H. Drakeford.
Union Springs.	Bullock.	D. S. Bethune.	Merchants' & Farmers' Bk.	J. H. Rainer, Jr.
Vernon	Lamar.	T. B. Nesmith.	At Aberdeen, Miss.	
Wedowee	Randolph.	Jas. W. Oliver.	At Roanoke, Bk. of Roanoke.	B. F. Weathers.
Wetumpka	Elmore.	W. P. Gaddis.	Bk. of M. Hohenberg & Co.	

DIGEST OF ALABAMA COMMERCIAL LAWS.

Assignments.—Every general assignment made by a debtor, by which a preference or priority of payment is given to one or more creditors over the remaining creditors, shall be and inure to the benefit of the creditors equally. No preferences.

Attachments.—Attachments may issue when defendant resides out of the State, or absconds, or secrets himself so that the ordinary process of law cannot be served on him; or is about to remove out of the State; or is about to remove his property out of the State, so that plaintiff will probably lose his debt or have to sue for it in another State; or is about fraudulently to dispose of his property; or has fraudulently disposed of his property; or has moneys, property or effects, liable to satisfy his debts, which he fraudulently withholds.

Bank Laws.—Banks of discount and deposit may be established under the general incorporation laws, but must be wound up at the end of twenty years. Depositors not claiming interest are preferred creditors in case of insolvency. Any number of persons (not less than three stockholders) may associate themselves together to establish a bank of deposit and discount; their capital stock to be not less than $50,000, of which not less than twenty per cent., and in no case less than $25,000 must be actually paid by the subscribers for stock before the filing of the declaration of incorporation. A transcript of the declaration of incorporation must also be

ALABAMA—Continued.

filed in the office of the Secretary of State, who issues to the incorporators a certificate of incorporation. A stockholder is liable for the debts of the bank only to the extent of unpaid stock. It is made an offense punishable by fine for any bank, or officer of a bank of any kind, to receive deposits when the bank or person doing such banking business is in a failing or insolvent condition. Any banker who discounts a bill or note at a greater rate than 8 per cent. cannot enforce the collection of same except as to the principal, and if any interest has been paid it must be deducted from the principal.

Exemptions.—A resident of Alabama is entitled to a homestead not exceeding in value $2,000 and in area 160 acres ; and if he leaves surviving him a widow and minor child or children, or either, during the life of the widow and minority of the child or children, such property continues exempt from levy and sale for his debts. Personal property to value of $1,000 and wages to $25 per month are also exempt.

Interest.—Legal rate is 8 per cent. In case of usurious contract where usury is pleaded, all interest forfeited and defendant recovers full costs.

Legal Holidays.—Sunday, Christmas, February 22d, July 4th, January 1st, Thanksgiving Day, Mardi-Gras, Good Friday, Birthdays of General Lee and Jefferson Davis, and Memorial Day (April 26th).

Limitation of Actions.—Judgments, twenty years ; actions founded upon any contract or writing under seal for the recovery of lands, tenements, hereditaments, or any part thereof, actions against officers. ten years ; actions on contracts in writing not under seal, for loans and upon stated or other liquidated accounts ; for use and occupation of lands ; against attorneys-at-law for failure to pay over money ; upon judgments obtained before justices of the peace of this State, six years ; for money due by open or unliquidated account, three years.

Married Women.—All property acquired by the wife before marriage, and all property acquired after marriage by gift, grant, inheritance or devise, remains her sole estate, and is liable for all debts contracted before marriage, also for articles of comfort and support of the household for which the husband would be liable.

Notarial Fees.—Protest $1.50, and fifty cents each endorser.

Notes and Bills of Exchange.—Promissory notes payable at a bank or a certain place of payment therein designated, and bills of exchange are governed by the commercial law. All other instruments payable at a bank, or other designated place of payment, are governed by the commercial law as to days of grace, protest and notice. Three days of grace allowed on commercial paper and on sight bills. If last day of grace falls on a holiday, paper is due the next business day. No acceptance valid unless in writing. Damages on protest for non-acceptance or non-payment, five per cent. This covers all charges except interest.

Stay of Executions.—On sums less than $20.00, thirty days ; over $20.00, sixty days.

Transfer of Corporation Stocks.—1. Shares of stock in corporation are personal property, transferable on the books of the corporation in such manner as is required by the By-Laws, or regulations of the corporation. 2. When the charter, By-Laws or regulations of private corporations require the transfer of the stock to be made on the books of the corporation, no transfer of stock is valid as against *bona fide* creditors, or subsequent purchasers, without notice, except from the time such transfer shall have been registered. 3. It is the duty of every corporation to

ALABAMA—Continued.

require the transfer of its stock to be made on its books ; and persons holding stock not so transferred or registered or holding any stock under hypothecation, mortgage or other lien must have the same made or registered on the books of the corporation, or upon failing to do so within fifteen days, all such transfers, hypothecations, mortgages or other liens shall be void as to *bona fide* creditors, or subsequent purchasers without notice.

ARIZONA.

County Seat.	County.	Name of Atty.	Name of Bank.	Cashier.
Flagstaff	Coconino.	T. G. Norris.	Arizona Central Bk.	J. H. Hoskins, Jr.
Florence	Pinal.	W. R. Stone.	See Phœnix.	
Globe	Gila.	P. T. Robertson.	Old Dominion Coml. Go.	A. Bailey.
Kingman	Mohave.	W. G. Blakely.	See Flagstaff.	
Phœnix	Maricopa.	Chas. F. Ainsworth.	Phœnix Natl. Bk.	A. H. Harscher.
Prescott	Yavapai.	E. M. Sanford.	Prescott Natl. Bk.	R. C. Woodruff.
St. Johns	Apache.	Geo. A. Estes.	State Bk. of Arizona.	A. F. Banta.
Solomonsville	Graham.	C. E. Moorman.	See Tucson.	
Tombstone	Cochise.	A. R. English.	See Tucson.	
Tucson	Pima.	C. W. Wright.	Arizona Natl. Bk.	M. P. Freeman.
Yuma	Yuma.	Geo. M. Knight.	See Phœnix.	

DIGEST OF ARIZONA COMMERCIAL LAWS.

Assignments.—Assignments shall provide for the distribution of all real and personal property, not exempt, among creditors in proportion to their respective claims. Preferences are void.

Attachments.—Attachments may issue when the action is on contract, express or implied, for the direct payment of money, made or payable in territory, and no security has been given for satisfaction of the payment to be rendered. It shall specify the character of the indebtedness, that same is due to plaintiff, over and above all legal set-offs or counter claims, and that demand has been made for the amount due ; or that defendant is indebted to plaintiff, stating the amount and character of debt ; that the same is due over and above all legal set-offs and counter claims, and that the defendant is a non-resident of the territory, or is a foreign corporation doing business therein ; or that an action is pending between the parties, and the defendant is about to remove his property beyond the jurisdiction of the court to avoid the payment of the judgment, and that the attachment is not sought for wrongful or malicious purposes, and the action is not prosecuted to hinder or delay any creditor of the defendant.

Bank Laws.—Banks of discount and deposit may be incorporated under the general Corporation Act. Banking business may be carried on by individuals or firms, or by corporations organized for that purpose. The Territory Auditor is ex-officio bank comptroller. Every bank and banker shall make to the bank comptroller not less than three reports each year under oath.

Exemptions.—Head of family may hold real property, selected to the value of $4,000 and $1,000 worth of personal property.

Interest.—Legal rate 7 per cent. per annum, and by contract any rate may be fixed. There is no usury law.

Legal Holidays.—Sunday, January 1, February 22, May 30, July 4, December 25, Thanksgiving, General Territorial election, or special election called by the Governor.

ARIZONA—Continued.

Limitation of Actions.—To recover real estate, three years after cause accrued; where founded on possession, two years. Three years for debt, where indebtedness is not evidenced by a contract in writing, upon stated or open accounts. All actions for which no limitation is prescribed, except to recover real estate, actions to contest wills, and to cancel a will for forgery or fraud, two years after the discovery thereof. Five years, judgment or actions for debt evidenced by, or founded upon contract in writing, made within this territory, actions upon a judgment or upon an instrument in writing executed without this territory. New acknowledgment or promise must be in writing.

Married Women.—All property of a married woman, whether acquired before or after marriage, by gift, grant, inheritance, devise or otherwise, shall remain her sole property so long as she wills. Said property is not liable for her debts or contracts unless said debts and contracts were made with special reference to its being liable.

Notarial Fees.—Protest $2.50 and 75 cents each notice.

Notes and Bills of Exchange.—All notes in writing shall be due and payable as therein expressed, and shall have the same effect and be negotiable in like manner as inland bills of exchange. The payees and indorsees of every such note payable to them or their order, and the holders of every such note payable to bearer, may maintain actions for the sums of money therein mentioned against the makers and indorsers of the same respectively in like manner as in cases of inland bills of exchange, and not otherwise. To charge a person within this territory as an acceptor on a bill of exchange, his acceptance must be in writing, signed by himself or his lawful agent. Three days of grace shall be allowed on all bills. Paper maturing on a holiday becomes due the next business day. Damages for protested bills, 10 per cent.

Stay of Executions.—Three months by giving good security,

Transfer of Corporation Stocks.—Transfer of stock shall not be valid except as between the parties thereto, until the same are regularly entered upon the books of the company, so as to show the names of the persons by whom and to whom the transfer is made, the numbers or other designation of the shares and date of the transfer.

ARKANSAS.

County Seat.	County.	Name of Atty.	Name of Bank.	Cashier.
Arkadelphia	Clark.	Murry & Kinsworthy.	Elk Horn Bk.	W. E. Barkman.
Arkansas City	Desha.	Murphy & Gates.	Desha Bk.	Henry Thane.
Augusta	Woodruff.	Stanley & Andrews.	Bk. of Augusta.	L. J. Stacy.
Batesville	Independence	Yancey & Fulkerson.	Bk. of Batesville.	Jno. Q. Wolf.
Benton	Saline.	A. D. Jones.	Saline Co. Bk.	Jno. G. Still.
Bentonville	Benton.	W. D. Mauk.	People's Bk.	Jas. M. Bohart.
Berryville	Carroll.	J. P. Fancher.	Carroll Co. Bk.	W. R. Hamilton.
Camden	Ouachita.	Smead & Powell.	Ouachita Valley Bk.	W. K. Ramsey.
Centre Point	Howard.	W. D. Lee.	At Nashville, Howard Co. Bk.	D. P. Terry.
Clarendon	Monroe.	Ewan, Manning & Lee.	Merchants' & Planters' Bk.	J. W.B.Robinson.
Clarksville	Johnson.	A. S. McKennon.	Bk. of Clarksville.	Cortis L. Pyle.
Clinton	Van Buren.	S. W. Simpson.	See Morrilton.	
Conway	Faulkner.	P. H. Prince.	Bk. of Conway.	D. R. Fones.
Corning	Clay.	G. B. Oliver.	Bk. of Corning.	W. D. Polk.
Dallas	Polk.	F. M. Reeves.	See Waldron.	
Dardanelle	Yell.	J. M. Parker.	People's Bk.	J. B. Crownover.
De Witt	Arkansas.	Gibson & Holt.	At Stuttgart, German Am. Bk.	J. W. Underwood.
Dumas	Desha.	Jas. Murphy.	See Arkansas City.	
Eldorado	Union.	Jesse B. Moore.	Bk. of Eldorado.	E. H. Smith.
EveningShade	Sharp.	Sam. H. Davidson.	See Batesville.	
Fayetteville	Washington.	Walker & Walker.	Bk. of Fayetteville.	H. L. Gregg.
Forrest City	St. Francis.	N. W. Norton.	Bk. of Eastern Arkansas.	Chas. H. Sanders.
Fort Smith	Sebastian.	Ira D. Oglesby.	First Nat'l Bk.	Jno. Valle.
Hamburg	Ashley.	Geo. W. Norman.	See Arkansas City.	
Hampton	Calhoun.	C. L. Poole.	See Camden.	
Harrisburg	Poinsett.	Jno. J. Mardis.	See Jonesborough.	
Harrison	Boone.	H. C. King.	Boone Co. Bk.	H. C. King.
Heber	Cleburne.	J. P. Wood.	See Searcy.	
Helena	Phillips.	Quarles & Moore.	First Nat'l Bk.	S. S. Faulkner.
Hot Springs	Garland.	Wood & Henderson.	Arkansas Nat'l Bk.	Chas. N. Rix.
Huntsville	Madison.	A. M. Brumfield.	Madison Co. Bk.	W. T. Brooks.
Jasper	Newton.	M. T. Briscoe.	See Harrison.	
Jonesborough	Craighead.	J. C. Hawthorne.	Bk. of Jonesboro.	S. A. Warner, Jr.
Lake Village	Chicot.	Gaines & Street.	See Monticello.	
Little Rock	Pulaski.	Ratcliffe & Fletcher.	Citizens' Bk.	J. E. England.
Lockesburg	Sevier.	Steel & Steel.	At Nashville, Howard Co.	D. P. Terry.
Lonoke	Lonoke.	Geo. Sibley.	See Little Rock.	
Magnolia	Columbia.	Stevens & Stevens.	Columbia Co. Bk.	J. C. McNeill.
Malvern	Hot Springs.	N. P. Richmond.	Bk. of Malvern.	F. M. Smith.
Marianna	Lee.	E. D. Robertson.	Lee Co. Bk.	R. H. Nall.
Marion	Crittenden.	R. F. Crittenden.	At Memphis, Tenn.	
Marshall	Searcy.	Albert Welborn.	See Yellville.	
Melbourne	Izard.	Jas. J. Baker.	See Batesville.	
Monticello	Drew.	Wood & Matthews.	Monticello Bk.	R. F. Hyatt.
Morrilton	Conway.	C. C. Reid.	Bk. of Morrilton.	W. J. Stowers.
MOUNTAIN HOME	Baxter.	M. N. Dyer.	See Yellville.	
MOUNTAIN VIEW	Stone.	Ben. F. Williamson.	See Batesville.	

ARKANSAS—Continued.

County Seat	County	Name of Atty.	Name of Bank.	Cashier.
Mount Ida	Montgomery	Watkins & Witt.	See Hot Springs.	
Murfreesboro	Pike	J. C. Pinnix.	See Prescott.	
New Louisv'le	La Fayette	King & Searcy.	Citizens' Bk.	P. E. McRae.
Newport	Jackson	Jno. W. & Jos. M. Stayton.	Bk. of Newport.	R. M. Johnson.
Osceola	Mississippi	S. S. Semmes.	Bk. of Osceola.	Jas. L. Hale.
Ozark	Franklin	W. W. & Geo. A. Mansfield.	Arkansas Valley Bk.	J. B. Carter.
Paragould	Greene	Block & Sullivan.	Greene Co. Bk.	W. H. Ritter.
Paris	Logan	Jackson & White.	Bk. of Paris.	W. R. Cherry.
Perryville	Perry	J. F. Sellers.	See Morrilton.	
Pine Bluff	Jefferson	N. T. White.	Merchants' & Planters' Bk.	F. H. Head.
Pocahontas	Randolph	P. H. Crenshaw.	At Black Rock, Bk. of Black Rock.	Jay J. Bryan.
Powhatan	Lawrence	Robert P. Mack.	At Black Rock, Bk. of Black Rock.	Jay J. Bryan.
Prescott	Nevada	C. C. Hamby.	Nevada Co. Bk.	O. B. Gordon.
Princeton	Dallas	R. T. Fuller.	At Fordyce, Bk. of Fordyce.	C. McKee.
Richmond	Little River	J. C. & H. C. Head.	At Hope, Hempstead Co. Bk.	T. H. Simms.
Rison	Cleveland	Atty. & Bk., see Pine Bluff.		
Russellville	Pope	Davis & Son.	First National Bk.	Jas. E. Battenfield
Salem	Fulton	Robert P. Maxey.	See Yellville.	
Searcy	White	Jno. T. Hicks.	People's Bk.	T. B. Paschall.
Sheridan	Grant	T. B. Morton.	See Pine Bluff.	
Star City	Lincoln	D. H. Rousseau.	See Pine Bluff.	
Texarkana	Miller	Arnold & Cook.	At Texarkana, Texas.	
Van Buren	Crawford	Miles & Miles.	Citizens' Bk.	R. E. Brown.
Vanndale	Cross	T. E. Hare.	At Wynne, Cross Co. Bk.	J. R. Perkins.
Waldron	Scott	W. W. Wallis.	See Paris.	
Warren	Bradley	W. R. Quinney.	Merchants & Planters Bk.	I. J. Adair.
Washington	Hempstead	A. B. & R. B. Williams.	See Prescott.	
Yellville	Marion	J. C. Floyd.	Bk. of Yellville.	A. S. Layton.

DIGEST OF ARKANSAS COMMERCIAL LAWS.

Assignments.—Assignments can be made of any property, real, personal or mixed, or choses in action, for the payment of debts. No preferences are allowed.

Attachments.—Attachments may issue when defendant is a foreign corporation or non-resident of the State, or has been absent from the State four months, or has departed from the State with intent to defraud his creditors, or has left the county of his residence to avoid the service of summons, or conceals himself that summons cannot be served upon him, or is about to remove or has removed his property, or a material part thereof, out of the State, not leaving enough therein to satisfy the claims of defendant's creditors, or has sold, conveyed or otherwise disposed of his property, or suffered or permitted the same to be sold, with the fraudulent intent to cheat, hinder and delay his creditors, or is about to sell, convey, or otherwise dispose of his property with such intent. But attachments will not be granted against a defendant on the ground that he is a non-resident, except in actions arising upon contract.

ARKANSAS—Continued.

Bank Laws.—Any number of persons, not less than three, may form a banking corporation. Those proposing to form such a body must elect a board of directors, a president, secretary and treasurer, and adopt articles of association, which must be filed with the Secretary of State and with the clerk of the county in which the corporation is to transact business, together with a certificate setting forth the purpose for which the corporation is formed, the amount of its capital stock, the amount paid in, the names of the stockholders, and the number of shares held by each. Stockholders are only liable for the par value of the stock respectively held by them. Reports are required to be made showing the financial condition of the bank annually to the county clerk, and by him recorded in a book kept for that purpose, and a failure to make these reports renders the president and secretary individually liable for all debts of the bank during the period of such failure.

Exemptions.—The homestead outside of any city, town or village, shall consist of not exceeding 160 acres of land, with the improvements thereon, to be selected by the owner, not to exceed in value the sum of $2,500; and in no event shall the homestead be reduced to less than eighty acres without regard to value. The homestead in any city, town, or village, shall consist of not exceeding one acre of land, with the improvements thereon, to be selected by the owner, not to exceed in value the sum of $2,500, and in no event shall such homestead be reduced to less than one-quarter of an acre of land, without regard to value. Unmarried persons are entitled to $200, and married persons and heads of families to $500 of persona property.

Interest.—Legal rate is 6 per cent., but contracts may be made for any rate not exceeding 10 per cent.; usury forfeits principal and interest.

Legal Holidays.—Sunday, July 4, Christmas and Thanksgiving, January 1, February 22, Birthday of Lee.

Limitation of Actions.—Accounts, three years; notes and sealed instruments, five years (sealed instruments executed prior to March 29, 1889, ten years); judgments, ten years. A written acknowledgment of indebtedness and promise to pay, or a part payment, revives the debt. Limitations of actions for the recovery of real estate, seven years. Suits to foreclose mortgages or trust deeds are barred, unless brought within a period of limitation fixed by law for suit on the debt or liability for the security of which they are given.

Married Women.—All property of a married women, whether acquired before or after marriage, by gift, grant, inheritance, devise or otherwise, shall remain her sole property so long as she wills. Said property is not liable for her debts or contracts, unless said debts and contracts were made with special reference to its being liable.

Notarial Fees.—Protest, $1.65; fifty cents each notice; twenty-five cents seal and postage.

Notes and Bills of Exchange.—The general rules of commercial law prevail. Notes to be negotiable must be expressed to be for value received. Three days of grace are allowed. Paper due on holidays becomes payable on the preceding day. Protests are in common form and made by notary public. Acceptances thereof must be in writing. Any person upon whom a bill of exchange is drawn and to whom the same may be delivered for acceptance, who destroys such bill, or refuses within twenty-four hours after such delivery, or within such time as the holder may allow to return the bill accepted or unaccepted to the holder is deemed to have

ARKANSAS—Continued.

accepted the same. Damages, 2 per cent. on domestic bills, and on foreign, if payable in certain named states, 4 per cent.; other points in United States, 5 per cent. Outside United States, 10 per cent. Bills of exchange protested for non-payment or non-acceptance bear interest at the rate of 10 per cent. per annum.

Stay of Execution.—Three months by giving good security.

Transfer of Corporation Stocks.—Stock of corporations can only be legally transferred by endorsement on back of stock, and by transfer on the books of the corporation, and when any stockholder shall transfer his stock, a certificate of such transfer shall forthwith be deposited with the county clerk, and no transfer of stock shall be valid as against any creditor of such stockholder until such certificate shall have been so deposited.

CALIFORNIA.

County Seat.	County.	Name of Atty.	Name of Bank.	Cashier.
Alturas	Modoc.	D. W. Jenks.	At Cedarville, Bk. of Cresslar & Bonner.	
Auburn	Placer.	Ben. B. Tabor.	Placer Co. Bk.	T. J. Nichols.
Bakersfield	Kern.	B. Brundage.	Bk. of Bakersfield.	J. J. Mack.
Bridgeport	Mono.	W. O. Parker.	See Madera.	
Colusa	Colusa.	H. M. Albery.	Colusa Co. Bk.	W. P. Harrington.
Crescent City	Del Norte.	W. A. Hamilton.	See Yreka.	
Downieville	Sierra.	Stanley A. Smith.	At Forest City, Bk. of Chas. Heintzen.	
Eureka	Humboldt.	Sevier Bros.	Randall Bnkg. Co.	J. S. Murray.
Fairfield	Solano.	G. A. Lamont.	At Vallejo, Vallejo Coml. Bk.	Jos. R. English.
Fresno	Fresno.	Geo. E. Church.	First Natl. Bk.	E. A. Walroud.
Hanford	Kings.	Newman Jones.	Farmers' & Merch. Bk.	B. A. Fassett.
Hollister	San Benito.	Briggs & Hudner.	Bk. of Hollister.	T. W. Hawkins.
Independence	Inyo.	D. W. Forbes.	See Visalia.	
Jackson	Amador.	A. C. Brown.	At Lodi, Bk. of Lodi.	F. Cogswell.
Lakeport	Lake.	M. S. Sayre.	Bk. of Lake.	W. E. Greene.
Los Angeles	Los Angeles.	Allen & Flint.	Farmers' & Merch. Bk.	J. Milner.
Madera	Madera.	F. H. Short.	Coml. Bk. of Madera.	E. H. Cox.
Mariposa	Mariposa.	L. F. Jones.	See Merced.	
Martinez	Contra Costa.	W. S. Wells.	Bk. of Martinez.	H. M. Hale.
Marysville	Yuba.	Forbes & Dinsmore.	Rideout Bk.	C. S. Brooks.
Merced	Merced.	T. C. Law.	Coml. Savg. Bk.	M. S. Huffman.
Modesto	Stanislaus.	C. C. Wright.	Modesto Bk.	J. R. Broughton.
Napa	Napa.	Denn's Spencer.	Bk. of Napa.	Henry Brown.
Nevada City	Nevada.	Fred. Searles.	Citizens' Bk.	Jno. T. Morgan.
Oakland	Alameda.	Metcalf & Metcalf.	Central Bk.	C. R. Yates.
Oroville	Butte.	J. M. McGill.	Bk. of Rideout, Smith & Co.	E. W. Fogg.
Placerville	Eldorado.	Williams & Witmer.	Bk. of A. Mierson.	Max Mierson.
Quincy	Plumas.	E. F. Hogan.	See Oroville.	
Red Bluff	Tehama.	N. P. Chipman.	Bk. of Tehama Co.	W. B. Cahoon.
Redding	Shasta.	Aaron Bell.	Bk. of Shasta Co.	C. C. Bush.
Redwood City	San Mateo.	Geo. C. Ross.	Bk. of San Mateo Co.	L. P. Behrens.
Riverside	Riverside.	Purington & Adair.	Orange Growers' Bk.	H. T. Hays.
Sacramento	Sacramento.	W. F. George.	Natl. Bk. of D. O. Mills & Co.	C. F. Dillman.
Salinas City	Monterey.	W. M. R. Parker.	Salinas City Bk.	W. S. Johnson.
San Andreas	Calaveras.	J. H. Reed.	See Stockton.	
SAN BERNARDINO	S.Bernardino.	E. E. Rowell.	Farmers' Exchange Bk.	S. F. Zombro.
San Diego	San Diego.	M. A. Luce.	Bk. of Commerce.	C. W. Jorres.
San Francisco	San Francisco	Norman H. Hurd.	Bk. of California.	Thomas Brown.
San Jose	Santa Clara.	Wilcox & Coolidge.	First Natl. Bk.	L. G. Nesmith.
SAN LUIS OBISPO	S.LuisObispo.	W. H. Spencer.	Andrews Bkg. Co	J. W. Smith.
San Rafael	Marin.	Hepburn Wilkins.	Bk. of A. P. Hotaling.	S. M. Augustine.
Santa Anna	Orange.	E. E. Keech.	First Natl. Bk.	J. A. Turner.
Santa Barbara	Santa Barbara	E. B. Hall.	Santa Barbara Co. Natl. Bk.	E. S. Sheffield.
Santa Cruz	Santa Cruz.	C. B. Younger.	City Bk.	W. D. Haslam.
Santa Rosa	Sonoma.	Rutledge & Pressley.	Santa Rosa Natl. Bk.	F. A. Brush.

CALIFORNIA—CONTINUED.

County Seat.	County.	Name of Atty.	Name of Bank.	Cashier.
Sonora	Tuolumne.	Street & Street.	See Modesto.	
Stockton	San Joaquin.	Baldwin & Thompson.	Farmers' & Merch. Bk.	C. H. Keagle.
Susanville	Lassen.	Goodwin & Goodwin.	Bk. of Lassen Co.	H. W. Meylert.
Ukiah	Mendocino.	J. A. Cooper.	Bk. of Ukiah.	Samuel Wheeler.
Ventura	Ventura.	Barnes & Selby.	Bk. of Wm. Collins & Son.	Jno. S. Collins.
Visalia	Tulare.	Daggett & Adams.	Bk. of Visalia.	C. J. Giddings.
Weaverville	Trinity.	J. B. Philbrook.	Bk. of C. W. Smith.	
Willows	Glenn.	Dudley & Long.	Bk. of Willows.	B. H. Barton.
Woodland	Yolo.	Frank E. Baker.	Bk. of Yolo.	C. W. Bush.
Yreka	Siskiyou.	Jas. F. Farraher.	Siskiyou Co. Bk.	F. E. Wadsworth.
Yuba City	Sutter.	M. E. Sanborn.	Farmers' Co-operative Union.	C. R. Boyd.

DIGEST OF CALIFORNIA COMMERCIAL LAWS.

Assignments.—An insolvent debtor may, in good faith, execute an assignment of property to one or more assignees, in trust, for the satisfaction of his creditors. A debtor is insolvent when he is unable to pay his debts from his own means as they become due. A debtor may pay one creditor in preference to another, or may give one creditor security for the payment of his demand in preference to another.

Attachments.—An attachment may issue in an action upon a contract, express or implied, for the direct payment of money, where the contract is made or payable in this State, and is not secured by any mortgage or lien upon real or personal property, or any pledge of personal property, or, if originally so secured, such security has, without act of the plaintiff or the person to whom the security was given, become valueless. In an action upon a contract, expressed or implied, against a defendant not residing in this State.

Bank Laws.—Corporations may be formed under the general laws for banking purposes. No corporation, association, or individual shall issue or put in circulation as money anything but the lawful money of the United States. Bank commissioners must annually examine the affairs of all banks. All banks are required to make semi-annual reports to the bank commissioners on the 20th of January and the 20th of July. There must be published semi-annually a statement of the capital, condition and assets of every bank or banker. Every banking corporation must keep in its office, in a place accessible to its stockholders, depositors, and creditors, a book containing a list of its stockholders, and the number of shares held by each. It must also post in a conspicuous place in its office a notice signed by the president or secretary, giving the names of the directors of the corporation and the number and value of shares held by each. The capital must be paid in money. The directors of a bank making a false statement in the above mentioned certificates shall be liable personally to the persons thereafter doing business with the bank. All foreign banking corporations must make similar statements to those required by local banks, verified by the agent or manager of the business, resident in California, and he shall be subject to the same liabilities provided against directors and officers for false statements. No bank failing to comply with the provisions of this law can prosecute any action in the courts. There is no limitation

CALIFORNIA—Continued.

of the right to sue a bank, banker, trust company, savings or loan association for money or property deposited with them.

Exemptions.—The head of a family is entitled to a homestead not exceeding $5,000; one not a head of a family to a homestead not exceeding $1,000 in value.

Interest.—Legal rate is 7 per cent. per annum, but any rate may be contracted for. There are no usury laws.

Legal Holidays.—Sunday, January 1, February 22, May 30, July 4, September 9, December 25, any public fast, Thanksgiving, Labor Day, State or General Election Day.

Limitation of Actions.—Upon a judgment and for mesne profits of real property, five years; upon any contract, obligation or liability founded upon an instrument in writing, executed in this State, four years; upon a liability created by statute other than a penalty or forfeiture, for trespass upon real property; for taking, detaining or injuring any goods or chattels, including actions for the specific recovery of personal property; for relief on the ground of fraud or mistake, and the cause of action does not accrue until the discovery of fraud or mistake, three years; upon a contract, obligation or liability not founded upon an instrument of writing, or founded upon an instrument of writing executed out of this State, two years.

Married Women.—No special law.

Notarial Fees.—Protest $4.00, and $1.00 for each endorser additional.

Notes and Bills of Exchange.—Bills of exchange and promissory notes, bank notes, checks, bonds, and certificates of deposit are negotiable instruments. Paper maturing on a holiday becomes payable the business day after. Days of grace not allowed. Acceptances must be in writing by the drawee or by an acceptor for honor, and may be made by the acceptor writing his name across the face of the bill with or without other words. The acceptance of a bill of exchange by a separate instrument binds the acceptor to one, who, upon the faith thereof, has the bill for value or other good consideration. The protest of a notary under his hand and official seal, is *prima facie* evidence of the facts contained therein. A bill of exchange, if accepted with the consent of the owner by a person other than the drawee, or an acceptor for honor, becomes, in effect, the promissory note of such person, and all prior parties thereto are exonerated. If a promissory note, payable on demand or at sight, without interest, is not duly presented for payment within six months from its date, the indorsers thereof are exonerated, unless such presentation is excused.

Stay of Executions.—It is within the power of the court to grant a stay for a reasonable time.

Transfer of Corporation Stocks.—By endorsement, delivery and transfer on books of corporation.

COLORADO.

County Seat.	County.	Name of Atty.	Name of Bank.	Cashier.
Akron	Washington.	Muntzing & Skelton.	Bk. of Akron.	R. H. Northcott.
Aspen	Pitkin.	E. C. Stimson.	First Natl. Bk.	Thos. G. Lyster.
Boulder	Boulder.	B. M. Williams.	First Natl. Bk.	W. H. Thompson.
Breckenridge	Summit.	W. M. Clark.	Engle Bros. Exchange Bk.	Geo. Engle.
Buena Vista	Chaffee.	G. K. Hartenstein.	Bk. of Buena Vista.	A. C. Wallace.
Burlington	Kit Carson.	T. J. Edwards.	Bk. of Burlington.	Chas. E. Paris.
Canon City	Fremont.	Chas. D. Bradley.	First Natl. Bk.	A. M. Hawley.
Castle Rock	Douglas.	A. G. Webster.	See Denver.	
Central City	Gilpin.	Chas. Withrow.	First Natl. Bk.	F. H. Messinger.
CHEYENNE WELLS	Cheyenne.	Chas. H. Farrell.	Cheyenne Co. Bk.	W. L. Patchen.
Colorado Springs	El Paso.	H. M. Black.	First Natl. Bk.	J. A. Hayes.
Conejos	Conejos	J. W. Hughes.	At Alamosa, First Natl. Bk.	Wm. F. Boyd.
Cortez	Montezuma.	C. W. Blackmer.	At Dolores, Jno.J.Harris & Co.'s Bk.	
Del Norte	Rio Grande.	E. F. Richardson.	Bk. of Del Norte.	J. G. Huntington.
Delta	Delta.	King & Robertson.	Delta Co. Bk.	E. L. Kellogg.
Denver	Arapahoe.	Benedict & Phelps.	American Natl. Bk.	H. Evans.
Durango	La Plata.	Russell & Ritter.	First Natl. Bk.	Wm. P. Vaile.
Fair Play	Park.	Chas. A. Wilkin.	At Alma, Bk. of Alma.	J. H. Singleton.
Fort Collins	Larimer.	Robinson & Love.	First Natl. Bk.	G. A. Webb.
Fort Morgan	Morgan.	Wm. A. Hill.	State Bk. of Ft. Morgan.	Jno. T. Ross.
Georgetown	Clear Creek.	A. D. Bullis.	Bk. of Georgetown.	H. Seifried.
Glenwood Springs	Garfield.	J. T. Shumate.	First Natl. Bk.	J. H. Fessler.
Golden	Jefferson.	W. A. Dier.	Bk. of Woods.	Wilson & Rubey.
GRAND JUNCTION	Mesa.	W. S. Wallace.	First Natl. Bk.	J. F. McFarland.
Greeley	Weld.	McCreery & Todd.	Greeley Natl. Bk.	Chas. H. Wheeler.
Gunnison	Gunnison.	T. C. Brown.	First Natl. Bk.	E. P. Shove.
Hahn's Peak	Rout.	R. G. Wallace.	At Craig, Bk. of Craig.	C. A. Seymour.
Holyoke	Phillips.	W. D. Kelsey.	Farmers & Merchants Bk.	S. Z. Peck.
Hot Sulphur Springs	Grand.	Morrison & Filius.	See Georgetown.	
Hugo	Lincoln.	James Reeves.	See Denver.	
Julesburg	Sedgwick.	J. S. Carnahan.	Citizens' Bk.	E. D. Hamilton.
Kiowa	Elbert.	See Castle Rock.	See Denver.	
Lake City	Hinsdale.	Chas. McDougal.	Miners & Merchants Bk.	Henry Derst.
La Junta	Otero.	Fred. A. Sabin.	La Junta State Bk.	M. Z. Farwell.
Lamar	Prowers.	C. C. Goodale.	First Natl. Bk.	W. C. Gould.
Las Animas	Bent.	Allen M. Lambright.	Bent Co. Bk.	P. G. Scott.
Leadville	Lake.	John A. Ewing.	Carbonate Natl. Bk	Geo. W. Trimble.
Meeker	Rio Blanco.	M. T. Ryan.	Bk. of Meeker.	A. C. Monlton.
Montrose	Montrose.	Sherman & Twitchell.	First Natl. Bk.	E. L. Osborn.
Ouray	Ouray.	Story & Stevens.	Miners & Merchants Bk.	E. J. Bent.
PAGOSA SPRINGS	Archuleta.	See Durango.	See Durango.	
Pueblo	Pueblo.	Chas. E. Gast.	First Natl. Bk.	R. F. Lytle.
Red Cliff	Eagle.	C. K. Phillips.	See Leadville.	
Rico	Dolores.	J. H. Pulliam.	Rico State Bk.	T. F. Neeley.
Saguache	Saguache.	Chas. B. Phillips.	Saguache Co. Bk.	Chas. Tarbell.

COLORADO—Continued.

County Seat.	County.	Name of Atty.	Name of Bank.	Cashier.
San Luis	Costilla.	See Trinidad.	See Walsenburg.	
Sheridan Lake	Kiowa.	J. S. Booker.	Citizens Bk.	J. H. Slater.
Silver Cliffs	Custer.	H. Townsend.	At Westcliffe, Bk. of H. H. Tompkins & Co.	G. B. Beardsley.
Silverton	San Juan.	Edgar Buchanan.	First Natl. Bk.	J. H. Werkhelser.
Springfield	Baca.	J. W. White.	See Lamar.	
Sterling	Logan.	H. D. Hinkley.	Logan Co. Bk.	L. T. Gillett.
Telluride	San Miguel.	S. R. Fitzgerald.	Bk. of Telluride.	W. E. Wheeler.
Trinidad	Las Animas.	W. B. Morgan.	First Natl. Bk.	H. J. Alexander.
Walsenburg	Huerfano.	J. A. J. Valdes.	Bk. of Fred. Walsen.	P. E. Moss.
Wason	Mineral.	M. S. Beale.	At Creede, First Natl. Bk.	J. E. Black.
Yuma	Yuma.	Barnes & Muntzing.	Bk. of Yuma.	B. F. Durham.

DIGEST OF COLORADO COMMERCIAL LAWS.

Assignments.—Assignments must be made for the benefit of all creditors. No preferences are allowed.

Attachments.—Suit may be brought by attachment on overdue accounts and overdue paper for the direct payment of money, and where the defendant is a non-resident of this State, and in certain other cases, and upon debts not yet due where fraud on the part of the defendant alleged and proven; but the plaintiff must give bond in double the amount claimed for all damages in case the suit was improvidently commenced.

Bank Laws.—Any number of persons, not less than three, may establish a bank of discount and deposit, and savings bank, or a trust, deposit and security association in this State under the general corporation laws of the State. Capital stock must not be less than $30,000, fifty per cent. to be paid in before opening, and the balance within one year thereafter. Shareholders in all banks in this State are held individually liable for all obligations of the bank, in double the amount of the par value of the stock owned by them respectively.

Exemptions.—Every householder, being the head of a family, is entitled to a homestead exempt from execution and attachment, not exceeding the value of $2,000. The homestead may consist of a house and lots in any town or city, or a farm of any number of acres not exceeding the homestead value. Also personal property, tools, etc., to the value of $500; persons not heads of families are entitled to $300 of tools, working animals and stock in trade.

Interest.—Legal rate is 8 per cent. per annum, but parties may contract for any other or higher rate. There are no usury laws.

Legal Holidays.—Sunday, January 1, February 22, May 30, July 4, December 25, Thanksgiving, Labor Day, and Saturday afternoons during June, July and August.

COLORADO—Continued.

Limitation of Actions.—All actions on contracts, judgments of courts of record, for arrears of rent, for waste or trespass on land, replevin, all actions which would have been on the case at common law, must be commenced within six years. Actions for a balance upon an open account in six years after the last item. Limitations apply to set off as well as demand. In actions accruing outside the State on contracts, sealed instruments or judgments more than six years before the commencement of the the action the statute of limitation may be pleaded in bar.

Married Women.—A married woman may acquire and hold real and personal property independently of her husband, and not subject to his debts. She may sue and be sued in her own name, and convey her separate estate without the husband joining in the deed. The right of dower is abolished.

Notarial Fees.—Protest, $1.75, and for notices fifty cents each.

Notes and Bills of Exchange.—Bills of exchange, notes, etc., are assignable by indorsement, and the assignee may maintain the same kind of an action against the maker as could have the payee. A non-negotiable note cannot be made. No maker of any note, bond, etc., shall be allowed to allege payment to the payee made after notice of assignment as a defense against the assignee. Three days' grace on bills of exchange and notes by contract. None on sight drafts or checks. Paper maturing on holiday is payable the day previous. Protest necessary on bills of exchange drawn in this State upon non-residents. Damages for non-acceptance or non-payment, 10 per cent.

Transfer of Corporation Stocks.—The shares of stock shall not be less than $1.00, nor more than $100 each, and shall be deemed personal property, and transferable as such in the manner provided by the By-Laws. Transfers and pledges of stock must be entered upon the books of the company. The practice is to endorse transfer on back of stock, and also to note transfer on books of the company.

CONNECTICUT.

County Seat.	County.	Name of Atty.	Name of Bank.	Cashier.
Bridgeport	Fairfield.	Hollister & Kelsey.	First Natl. Bk.	O. H. Brothwell.
Brooklyn	Windham.	H. C. Atwood.	Brooklyn Savings Bk.	C. A. Potter.
Hartford	Hartford.	Hyde, Joslyn & Gilman.	Aetna Natl. Bk.	A. Spencer, Jr.
Litchfield	Litchfield.	Jno. T. Hubbard.	First Natl. Bk.	Chas. E. Wilson.
Middletown	Middlesex.	Arthur B. Calef, Jr.	First Natl. Bk.	E. G. Camp.
New Haven	New Haven.	Morris & Tyler.	Natl. Tradesmen's Bk.	W. T. Fields.
New London	New London.	Chas. W. Butler.	Natl. Bk. of Commerce.	Geo. B. Brest.
Tolland	Tolland.	Edwin S. Argard.	Savings Bk. of Tolland.	F. T. Newcomb.

DIGEST OF CONNECTICUT COMMERCIAL LAWS.

Assignments.—Assignments in insolvency are made to an assignee.

Attachments.—Attachments are by mesne or foreign process. They are made upon the personal or real property of defendant, or upon his body if the cause of action permits it. Wages to the extent of $50 are exempt from attachment.

Bank Laws.—Banks cannot be organized in this State except by special charter of the Legislature. There are two Bank Commissioners, appointed by the Governor, with the advice and consent of the Senate; and they have full power to at any time visit each bank and examine its affairs, and are required so to do twice in each year These commissioners make annual reports to the Legislature concerning the condition of each bank.

Exemptions.—Homestead to the value of $1,000 is exempt, if declaration to hold it as such is recorded. Of the property of any one person, his necessary apparel and bedding and household furniture necessary for supporting life; arms, military equipments, uniforms, or musical instruments owned by any member of the militia for military purposes; and pension moneys received from the United States, while in the hands of the pensioner; implements of the debtor's trade; his library; not exceeding $500 in value; cattle, poultry, etc, not to exceed $325 in value; certain specified family stores; the horse of any practicing physician or surgeon, of a value not exceeding $200 and buggy; one boat used in the business of planting or taking oysters or clams, or shad, with the sails, tackle, rigging, and implements used in said business, not exceeding in value $200; one sewing machine in use; one pew in church in use, and lots in burying ground, appropriated by its owner for the burial place of any person or family; so much of any debt which has accrued by reason of the personal services of the debtor as shall not exceed $50.

Interest.—Legal rate is 6 per cent. No penalty for usury.

Legal Holidays.—Sunday, January 1, February 22, May 30, July 4, Labor Day, Thanksgiving, December 25, Fast Day.

Limitation of Actions.—Actions upon writings under seal, or non-negotiable promissory notes, must be brought within seventeen years; upon simple contract within six years. But persons legally incapable of bringing an action at the time of the

CONNECTICUT—Continued.

accruing of the right of action, may bring the same at any time, in the case of specialties, within four years, and in the case of simple contracts, within three years, after becoming legally capable. Actions founded on express contract (other than actions of book debt) not in writing, must be brought within three years. Actions upon negotiable notes, fraudulently obtained, must be brought within one year after notice of the fraud, or six months after maturity.

Married Women.—A married woman may make contracts in her own name, buy goods, and give notes in settlement for purchases which will be binding upon her separate estate, real or personal, if these contracts and purchases are made for the benefit for herself, her family, or her estate.

Notarial Fees.—Protest $1.00 and twenty-five cents for each notice, also postage and travel.

Notes and Bills of Exchange.—Promissory notes made payable to order or bearer for the payment of money only, are negotiable. No days of grace, unless specified, are allowed on non-negotiable notes, or on paper payable at sight, or on demand. Paper maturing on a holiday becomes due the day preceding. A negotiable promissory note payable on demand is regarded as dishonored, if unpaid four months after date. Demand and reasonable notice are necessary to bind endorsers. Damages for protested bills, foreign, are from 2 to 8 per cent. according to location of state where protested. Protests of inland bills of exchange and promissory notes, protested without this state, shall be *prima facie* evidence of the facts therein stated.

Transfer of Corporation Stocks.—By endorsement on the back of stock, and by transfer on the books of the corporation. A transfer by simple endorsement would be good as between the parties, but until its transfer on the books of the corporation, it is liable to attachment in suit against the original holder.

DELAWARE.

County Seat.	County.	Name of Atty.	Name of Bank.	Cashier.
Dover	Kent.	James Pennewill.	First National Bk.	J. H. Bateman.
Georgetown	Sussex.	E. R. Paynter.	Farmers' Bk.	W. F. Tunnell.
Wilmington	New Castle.	L. C. Vandegrift.	Union Natl. Bk.	Jno. H. Danby.

DIGEST OF DELAWARE COMMERCIAL LAWS.

Assignments.—Voluntary assignments for the benefit of creditors may be made. No preferences are allowed.

Attachments.—A writ of domestic attachment may issue against an inhabitant of this State when the defendant cannot be found and proof satisfactory to the court of the cause of action, or upon affidavit made by the plaintiff or some other credible person and filed with the prothonotary that the defendant is justly indebted to the plaintiff in a sum exceeding fifty dollars, and has absconded from the place of his usual abode or gone out of the State with intent to defraud his creditors or to elude process, as it is believed. A writ of foreign attachment may issue against any person not an inhabitant in this State after the return to a summons or capias issued or delivered to the sheriff or coroner ten days before the return thereof and showing that the defendant cannot be found and proof satisfactory to the court of the cause of action ; or upon affidavit made by the plaintiff or some other credible person and filed with the prothonotary that the defendant resides out of the State, and is justly indebted to the said plaintiff in a sum exceeding fifty dollars.

Bank Laws.—There is no general banking act and but one State bank, which was chartered by the Legislature in 1807. There are no official examinations, and the bank is merely required to make a yearly report of its condition to the Governor of the State. Banking companies can only be formed by special act of the Legislature, and the holders of stock therein are taxed at the rate of one-fourth of one per centum on the cash value of each share of capital stock.

Exemptions.—No homestead law. Personal property, etc., to value of $75 is exempt, depending upon the county in which the debtor resides. In addition to the above, personal property, not exceeding in value $200, is exempt from execution process where debtor is the head of a family. In some of the counties the amount does not exceed $150. Wages are exempt from execution attachment in New Castle county.

Interest.—Legal rate, 6 per cent. Usury forfeits principal and interest. If any bank incorporated by any law of this State shall engage in any transaction the amount of profit of which shall exceed the rate of 1 per cent. for sixty days, such bank shall be deemed and taken to have forfeited its charter, and the directors or managers of the bank shall be guilty of a misdemeanor, and shall be fined at the discretion of the court.

Legal Holidays.—Sunday, Christmas, January 1, February 22, July 4, May 30, Thanksgiving, Labor Day.

DELAWARE—Continued.

Limitation of Actions.—No action of trespass, replevin, detinue, no action of debt not found upon a record or specialty, no action of account, no action of assumpsit, nor action on the case can be brought after expiration of three years from the occurring of the cause of action. When the cause of action arises from a promissory note, bill of exchange or an acknowledgment of the party of a subsisting demand, the action may be commenced at any time within six years from the accruing of such action. All actions for the recovery of real property may be brought within twenty years from the occurring of such cause of action.

Married Women.—No special law.

Notarial Fees.—Protest $1.25 and twenty cents each notice.

Notes and Bills of Exchange.—All checks, notes, drafts or inland bills of exchange, payable without time or at sight, are due and payable on presentation without grace. Three days grace is allowed on notes and bills, none on sight drafts. Notes due on a holiday must be paid the business day next preceding. To hold indorser, note must be duly presented, and notice of dishonor given to indorser.

Stay of Execution.—On judgments for want of affidavit of defense; six months if security be given within twenty days after judgment.

Transfer of Corporation Stocks.—Certificates of stock are deemed personal property, and are transferable on the books in such a manner as the by-laws provide. Transfers as collateral security must be so entered upon the books.

DISTRICT OF COLUMBIA.

| County Seat. | County. | Name of Atty. | Name of Bank. | Cashier. |
| Washington | ..Washington. | Gordon & Gordon. | Central Natl. Bk. | A. B. Ruff. |

DIGEST OF DISTRICT OF COLUMBIA COMMERCIAL LAWS.

Assignments.—Voluntary assignments for the benefit of creditors may be made at common law, except that no preferences are allowed. No bankruptcy or involuntary assignment law in force.

Attachments.—Writs of attachment are issued when defendant is a non-resident of the District; or evades the service of ordinary process by concealing himself, or withdrawing from the District temporarily ; or that he has removed, or is about to remove, some of his property from the District, so as to defeat just demand against him, or has assigned, disposed of, secreted, or is about to assign, dispose of, or secrete property with intent to defraud his creditors.

Bank Laws.—There is no statutory provision regulating banks, private or other, except that savings banks may be incorporated under the general statute, and when so incorporated they may continue for twenty years.

Exemptions.—No homestead law. In addition to wearing apparel, etc., household furniture to the value of $300, implements of debtor's trade or business to the value of $200, stock for carrying on business to amount of $200, one horse, harness and cart, wagon or dray, and earnings of married men or heads of families, not to exceed $100 per month.

Interest.—Six per cent. per annum is the legal rate ; parties may agree in writing for any interest not exceeding 10 per cent. The penalty for usury is forfeiture of the whole of the interest, which may be recovered by corporation or person paying same by suit brought within a year after such unlawful interest has been paid.

Legal Holidays.—Sunday, January 1, February 22, July 4, Labor Day, Thanksgiving, Christmas, Inauguration Day, and every Saturday afternoon and Decoration Day.

Limitation of Actions.—Actions to recover usurious interests must be brought within one year ; actions upon simple contract, book debt or account, detinue and replevin, and for trespass for injuries caused by negligence, must be brought within three years ; actions on contracts under seal and on judgments must be brought within twelve years ; to foreclose mortgage or deed of trust within twenty years.

Notarial Fees.—Protest, $1.50, and twenty-five cents for each notice.

Notes and Bills of Exchange.—Law-merchant is in force as to presentation, indorsement, protest, etc. Three days' grace allowed on all commercial paper except checks and sight drafts. Paper maturing on a holiday is payable on business day previous. Inland bills of exchange and promissory notes, as well as foreign bills of exchange, may be protested by notaries public.

Transfer of Corporation Stocks.—By endorsement on the back of stock and by a transfer on the books of the corporation.

FLORIDA.

County Seat.	County.	Name of Atty.	Name of Bank.	Cashier.
Apalachicola	Franklin.	W. F. Farley.	See Tallahassee.	
Arcadia	De Soto.	E. B. Carlton.	Bk. of Simmons, Carlton & Co.	R. E. Whidden.
Bartow	Polk.	Wilson & Wilson.	Polk Co. Natl. Bk.	Warren Taylor.
Blountstown	Calhoun.	A. P. Higgins.	See Marianna.	
Bristol	Liberty.	W. B. Sheppard.	See Marianna.	
Bronson	Levy.	J. C. Sale.	See Gainesville.	
Brooksville	Hernando.	W. S. Jennings.	Brooksville State Bk.	
Braidentown	Manatee.	J. H. Humphries.	At St. Petersburg, St. Petersburg State Bk.	H. A. Bishop.
Cerro Gordo	Holmes.		See Vernon.	
Crawfordville	Wakulla.	N. R. Walker.	See Tallahassee.	
Dade City	Pasco.	J. A. Hendley.	Bk. of Pasco Co.	W. I. Porter.
De Funiak Springs	Walton.	D. Campbell.	See Vernon.	
De Land	Volusia.	Stewart & Bly.	Volusia Co. Bk.	F. E. Bond.
Fernandina	Nassau.	Baker & Drew.	First Natl. Bk.	R. C. Cooley.
Gainesville	Alachua.	Horatio Davis.	First Natl. Bk.	H. E. Tayler.
Green Cove	Clay.	P. C. Fisher.	See Starke.	
Inverness	Citrus.	A. C. Clark.	See Ocala.	
Jacksonville	Duval.	B. B. Archibald.	Natl. Bk. St. of Florida.	T. P. Denham.
Jasper	Hamilton.	B. B. Blackwell.	Bk. of Blackwell & Co.	
Key West	Monroe.	E. O. Locke.	First Natl. Bk.	Geo. L. Lowe.
Kissimmee	Osceola.	E. G. Beggs.	Osceola Co. State Bk.	P.A.Vans. Agnew
Lake City	Columbia.	W. M. Ives.	Bk. of Wm. R. Bush.	
Live Oak	Suwannee.	H. B. Blackwell.	Live Oak Bk.	H. M. Wood.
Maclenny	Baker.	See Lake City.	See Lake City.	
Madison	Madison.	A. Patterson.	See Monticello.	
Marianna	Jackson.	F. B. & J. H. Carter.	Bk. of W. J. Daniel & Co.	W. H. Milton, Jr.
Miami	Dade.	See Palm Beach.	At Palm Beach, Dade Co. St. Bk.	Geo. L. Braming.
Milton	Santa Rosa.	C. J. Perrenot.	See Pensacola.	
Monticello	Jefferson.	D. A. Finlayson.	Jefferson Co. St. Bk.	R. F. Smith.
Myers	Lee.	R. Mickle.	At Punta Gorda, Punta Gorda Bk.	Jno.H.Farrington
New Troy	Lafayette.	John Miller.	See Live Oak.	
Ocala	Marion.	W. S. Bullock.	Merchants' Natl. Bk.	H. C. Wright.
Orlando	Orange.	Beggs & Palmer.	First Natl. Bk.	Jas. L. Giles.
Palatka	Putnam.	R. W. Davis.	East Florida S. & Tr. Co.	E. S. Crill.
Pensacola	Escambia.	Wm. Fisher.	First Natl. Bk.	J. S. Leonard.
Perry	Taylor.	Jno. M. Gornto.	See Monticello.	
Quincy	Gadsden.	P. W. White.	Quincy State Bk.	Geo. D. Munroe.
St. Augustine	St. Johns.	W. W. Dewhurst.	First Natl. Bk.	H. Gaillard.
Starke	Bradford.	L. R. Rhodes.	Bradford Co. Bk.	N. W. Hackett.
Sumterville	Sumter.	J. C. Longley.	At Leesburg, Bk. of Leesburg.	Yager Bros.
Tallahassee	Leon.	Henderson & Raney.	First Natl. Bk.	W. C. Lewis.
Tampa	Hillsboro'.	P. O. Knight.	Exchange Natl. Bk.	J. B. Anderson.
Tavares	Lake.	Alex. St. Clair Abrams.	Bk. of Tavares.	C. H. Newell.
Titusville	Brevard.	Minor S. Jones.	Indian River State Bk.	Wm. M. Brown.
Vernon	Washington.	Wm. B. Jones.	See Marianna.	

FLORIDA—Continued.
DIGEST OF FLORIDA COMMERCIAL LAWS.

Assignments.—Assignments may be made by deed and recorded in the clerk's office of the county in which the property is situated. Not valid unless in writing and providing for an equal disposition of all assignor's property, both real, personal or mixed, except such as is by law exempt from levy and sale among his creditors.

Attachments.—Attachments may issue when defendant is removing or about to remove either himself or his property without the limits of the State or the judicial circuit in which he resides, or lives without the limits of the State, or is secreting or fraudulently disposing of his property, or that he will fraudulently dispose of his property before judgment can be obtained against him, or conceals himself so as to avoid service of process.

Bank Laws.—Banking corporations may be established by five or more persons, in any incorporated town or city having 3,000 or more inhabitants with a capital of not less than $50,000. In towns of not less than 3,000 inhabitants the capital may, with the Comptroller's approval, be not less than $15,000. Savings banks may not have less than $20,000 capital. Banks are formed as other corporations are, and cannot begin business until authorized by the Comptroller. The Comptroller of the State may inspect and supervise the business of the bank, and inspect and examine its books, papers, documents, minutes, and everything pertaining to the acts of the bank. Banks are required to make a semi-annual return to the State Comptroller of resources and liabilities, and advertise in January of each year amount of stock, property and contractual indebtedness. Before organization 50 per cent. of the capital stock must be paid in cash ; 10 per cent. each month thereafter. Stockholders are individually liable to the extent of their stock at the par value thereof, in addition to the amount invested in said shares. Directors must be citizens of the United States and own ten shares of stock of $100 per share. The Comptroller with the aid of the courts, winds up the affairs of insolvent banks.

Exemptions.—Real property to the extent of not exceeding 160 acres outside of any incorporated town or city, and not to exceed one-half an acre within the limits of any such town or city, is exempt from forced sale, together with $1,000 worth of personal property to every person who is the head of a family residing in this State ; and money due to such person for personal labor or services is exempt from garnishment or attachment.

Interest.—Legal rate is 8 per cent., but parties can stipulate for any rate not exceeding ten. Usury forfeits entire interest.

Legal Holidays.—Sunday, January 1, February 22, July 4, Labor Day, December 25, any General Election Day, Thanksgiving, June 3.

Limitation of Actions.—For the recovery of real estate within seven years of the commencement of the adverse possession of the defendant. Upon a judgment or decree of any court of record of Florida within twenty years ; upon foreign judgments within seven years, and upon any contract, obligation or liability upon a writing under seal. Within five years upon any writing not under seal ; within three years upon an action upon a liability created by statute other than a penalty or a forfeiture. For trespass to real property ; for taking, detaining or injuring any goods or chattels, and for the specific recovery of personal property ; an action for relief on the ground of fraud ; an action upon a contract, obligation or liability not founded upon an instrument of writing, except an action upon an open account for

FLORIDA—Continued.

goods, wares and merchandise, within two years. On an open account for goods, wares and merchandise sold and delivered, and for an article charged in a store account shall not be barred until four years.

Notarial Fees.—Protest $2.00.

Notes and Bills of Exchange.—Notes and bills of exchange are subject to rules of the common law generally, except that maker and indorser cannot be sued in one action, nor can acceptor and drawer. Three days' grace are allowed on all paper except sight drafts. Paper maturing on holidays is payable business day preceding. Five per cent. damages are allowed on protested foreign commercial paper.

Transfer of Corporation Stocks.—Transfers are governed by the By laws of each corporation.

GEORGIA.

County Seat.	County.	Name of Atty.	Name of Bank.	Cashier.
Abbeville	Wilcox.	E. F. Strozier.	At Cordele, 1st Natl. Bk.	F. J. Blvins.
Albany	Dougherty.	Wooten & Wooten.	First Natl. Bk.	J. S. Davis.
Alpharetta	Milton.	Thomas L. Lewis.	See Canton.	
Americus	Sumter.	Jas. Dodson.	Bk. of Sumter.	W. C. Furlow.
Appling	Columbia.	D. C. Moore.	See Augusta.	
Athens	Clarke.	Erwin & Cobb.	Natl. Bk. of Athens.	James White.
Atlanta	Fulton.	B. F. & C. A. Abbott.	Atlanta Natl. Bk.	C. E. Currier.
Augusta	Richmond.	Jos. R. Lamar.	Georgia R. R. Bk.	C. G. Goodrich.
Bainbridge	Decatur.	Donaldson & Hawes.	Bainbridge State Bk.	E. J. Perry.
Baxley	Appling.	J. I. Carter.	See Jesup.	
Blackshear	Pierce.	A. B. Estes, Jr.	Blackshear Bk.	A. P. Brandley.
Blairsville	Union.	W. E. Chandler.	See Morganton.	
Blakely	Early.	R. H. Powell & Son.	Bk. of Blakely.	Jno. W. Wade.
Brunswick	Glynn.	Goodyear, Kay & Brantley.	Natl. Bk. of Brunswick.	J. H. Smith.
Buchanan	Haralson.	W. P. Robinson.	At Bremen. Bk. of G. R. Hamilton & Co.	
Buena Vista	Marion.	Geo. P. Munro.	Buena Vista Loan & Sav. Bk.	J. W. Roberts.
Butler	Taylor.	W. E. Steed.	Peoples Bkg. Co.	T. H. Frierson.
Calhoun	Gordon.	W. R. Rankin.	Bk. of Calhoun.	O. U. Starr.
Camilla	Mitchell.	Spence & Bennett.	Bk. of Camilla.	C. R. Twitty.
Canton	Cherokee.	Geo. R. Brown.	Bk. of Canton.	Jno. B. Richards.
Carnesville	Franklin.	W. R. Little.	See Hartwell.	
Carrollton	Carroll.	Adamson & Jackson.	Carrollton Bk.	J. B. E. Brown.
Cartersville	Bartow.	Jno. W. Akin.	First Natl. Bk.	J. H. Vivion.
Cedartown	Polk.	Irwin & Bunn.	Commercial Bk.	R. O. Pitts.
Clarkesville	Habersham.	C. H. Sutton.	See Demorest, Bk. of Demorest.	A. Hampton.
Clayton	Rabun.	J. W. Merritt.	See Demorest, Bk. of Demorest.	A. Hampton.
Cleveland	White.	J. J. Kimsey.	See Demorest, Bk. of Demorest.	A. Hampton.
Clinton	Jones.	R. V. Hardeman.	See Macon.	
Clyde	Bryan.	A. P. Smith.	See Savannah.	
Colquitt	Miller.	C. C. Bush.	See Blakely.	
Columbus	Muscogee.	C. E. Battle.	Third Natl. Bk.	J. W. Murphy.
Conyers	Rockdale.	Gleaton & Maddox.	Bk. of Jno. H. Almand.	W. J. Eakes.
Covington	Newton.	J. M. Pace.	Clark Banking Co.	J. G. Lester.
Crawfordville	Talliaferro.	H. M. Holden.	See Greensboro'.	
Cumming	Forsyth.	H. L. Patterson.	At Flowery Branch, Bk. of G. H. Stidham.	
Cusseta	Chattaho'chee	Z. A. Littlejohn.	See Columbus.	
Cuthbert	Randolph.	Arthur Hood.	Bk. of Cuthbert.	Ed. McDonald.
Dahlonega	Lumpkin.	Price & Charters.	See Morganton.	
Dallas	Paulding.	W. K. Fielder.	See Atlanta.	
Dalton	Whitfield.	R. J. & J. McCamy.	First Natl. Bk.	Price Peak.
Danielsville	Madison.	R. H. Kimbrew.	See Jefferson.	
Darien	McIntosh.	F. S. Bander.	Darien Bk.	F. S. Bander.
Dawson	Terrell.	J. G. Parks.	Dawson Natl. Bk.	F. E. Clark.
Dawsonville	Dawson.	James M. Bishop.	See Canton.	
Decatur	DeKalb.	H. C. Jones.	See Atlanta.	

THE LEGAL AND FINANCIAL LIGHTS OF AMERICA.

GEORGIA—Continued.

County Seat.	County.	Name of Atty.	Name of Bank.	Cashier.
Douglas	Coffee.	M. O'Brien.	See Way Cross.	
Douglasville	Douglas.	W. T. Roberts.	Douglasville Bkg. Co.	H. T. Cooper.
Dublin	Laurens.	P. L. Wade.	Dublin Bkg. Co.	Jas. H. Finn.
Eastman	Dodge.	E. A. Smith.	Citizens' Bkg. Co.	J. B. Caldwell.
Eatonton	Putnam.	W. B. Wingfield.	Middle Georgia Bk.	B. W. Hunt.
Elberton	Elbert.	Jos. N. Worley.	Bk. of Elberton.	L. M. Heard.
Ellaville	Schley.	Chas. R. McCrory.	See Americus.	
Ellijay	Gilmer.	J. C. Allen.	See Morganton.	
Fairburn	Campbell.	Roan & Golightly.	See Atlanta.	
Fayetteville	Fayette.	R. T. Dorsey.	See Atlanta.	
Forsyth	Monroe.	Berner & Bloodworth.	W. H. Head Bkg. Co.	R. P. Brooks.
Fort Gaines	Clay.	John D. Rambo.	Bk. of Ft. Gaines.	J. E. Paulin.
Franklin	Heard.	W. H. Daniel.	At Hogansville, Mer. & Far. Bk.	J. F. Mobley.
Gainesville	Hall.	H. H. Dean.	State Bkg. Co.	W. S. Williams.
Georgetown	Quitman.	Jno. W. Lee.	See Cuthbert.	
Gibson	Glascock.	B. F. Walker.	See Sandersville.	
Greenville	Merriweather.	Terrell & Terrell.	Greenville Bkg. Co.	Wm. T. Revill.
Greensboro'	Greene.	Jas. B. Park, Jr.	Bk. of E. A. Copelan.	C. E. Monfort.
Griffin	Spaulding.	J. S. Boynton.	City Natl. Bk.	J. G. Rhea.
Hamilton	Harris.	See Columbus.	See Columbus.	
Hartwell	Hart.	A. G. McCurry.	Hartwell Bk.	S. W. Peck.
Hawkinsville	Pulaski.	A. C. Pate.	Hawkinsville Bk. & Tr. Co.	E. J. Henry.
Hiawassee	Towns.	W. G. Blackwell.	See Morganton.	
Hinesville	Liberty.	Ben. A. Way.	See Savannah.	
Homer	Banks.	A. C. Moss.	See Gainesville.	
Homerville	Clinch.	R. W. Yates.	See Way Cross.	
Irwinton	Wilkinson.	J. W. Lindsey.	See Macon.	
Irwinville	Irwin.	Wooten & Wooten.	At Cordele, First Natl. Bk.	F. J. Bivins.
Isabella	Worth.	J. G. Polhull.	See Albany.	
Jackson	Butts.	Wright & Beck.	Jackson Bkg. Co.	L. D. Watson.
Jasper	Pickens.	J. W. Henley.	See Canton.	
Jefferson	Jackson.	J. C. Turner.	Jefferson Bkg. Co.	J. C. Turner.
Jeffersonville	Twiggs.	J. D. Jones.	See Macon.	
Jesup	Wayne.	S. R. Harris.	Merchants & Farmers Svgs. Bk.	W. H. Whaley.
Jonesboro'	Clayton.	C. W. Hodnett.	See Atlanta.	
Knoxville	Crawford.	W. S. Blasingome.	At Fort Valley, Ex. Bk.	A. D. Skellie.
La Fayette	Walker.	Copeland & Drew.	See Summerville.	
La Grange	Troup.	F. M. Longley.	La Grange Bkg. & Tr. Co.	J. T. Johnson
LAWRENCEVILLE	Gwinnett.	S. J. Winn & Son.	See Atlanta.	
Leesburg	Lee.	H. L. Long & Son.	See Albany.	
Lexington	Oglethorpe.	W. M. Howard.	Bk. of Arnold & Stewart.	Chas. M. Hunter.
Lincolnton	Lincoln.	C. R. Strother.	See Augusta.	
Louisville	Jefferson.	Phillips & Phillips.	Bk. of Louisville.	L. R. Farmer.
Lumpkin	Stewart.	R. F. Watts.	Bk. of Stewart Co.	W. L. Madre.
Macon	Bibb.	Bacon & Miller.	Exchange Bank.	J. W. Cabaniss.
Madison	Morgan.	Foster & Butler.	Bk. of Madison.	H. T. Shaw.
Marietta	Cobb.	Sessions & Sessions.	Marietta Tr. & Bk. Co.	J. T. Anderson.
McDonough	Henry.	Wm. T. Dicken.	See Jackson.	
McRae	Telfair.	Eason & Swain.	See Eastman.	

GEORGIA—Continued.

County Seat.	County.	Name of Atty.	Name of Bank.	Cashier.
Milledgeville	Baldwin.	Chas. P. Crawford.	Milledgeville Bkg. Co.	B. T. Bethune.
Monroe	Walton.	B. S. Walker.	Bk. of Monroe.	J. R. Radford.
Monticello	Jasper.	J. D. Kilpatrick.	Bk. of Monticello.	M. S. Benton.
Morgan	Calhoun.	J. J. Beck.	Bk. of J. J. Beck.	
Morganton	Fannin.	O. R. Dupree.	Bk. of B. Crawford.	
Moultrie	Colquitt.	E. A. Milligan.	See Quitman.	
MOUNT VERNON	Montgomery.	H. W. Carswell.	See Savannah.	
Nashville	Berrien.	Peeples & Alexander.	See Way Cross.	
Newnan	Coweta.	Freeman & Wright.	Newnan Natl. Bk.	J. S. Hollinshead.
Newton	Baker.	Wooten & Wooten.	See Albany.	
Oglethrope	Macon.	Edwards & Grier.	Bk. of Lofley, Greer & Co.	
Perry	Houston.	C. C. Duncan.	Perry Loan & Savgs. Bk.	J. D. Martin.
Preston	Webster.	J. B. Hudson.	At Richland, Bk. of Richland.	O. V. Lamar.
Quitman	Brooks.	C. M. Hitch.	Bk. of Quitman.	C. M. Hitch.
Reidsville	Tattnall.	H. J. McGee.	See Savannah.	
Ringold	Catoosa.	A. T. Hackett.	See Dalton.	
Rome	Floyd.	Fouche & Fouche.	First Natl. Bk.	B. I. Hughes.
Sandersville	Washington.	Evans & Evans.	Bkg. House of Louis Cohen.	H. Bashinsky.
Savannah	Chatham.	Charlton,MacKall&Anderson	Southern Bk., State of Georgia.	James Sullivan.
Sparta	Hancock.	Robert H. Lewis.	Bk. of R. A. Graves.	Jno. D. Walker.
Springfield	Effingham.	S. S. Pitman.	See Savannah.	
Spring Place	Murray.	C. W. King.	See Dalton.	
Statenville	Echols.	W. S. West.	See Valdosta.	
Statesboro'	Bullock.	Groover & Johnston.	Bk. of Statesboro'.	H. S. Blitch.
St. Mary's	Camden.	Goodyear, Kaly & Brantley.	See Savannah.	
Summerville	Chatooga.	Jas. M. Bellah.	Bk. of Commerce.	N. K. Bitting.
Swainsboro'	Emanuel.	Williams & Brannen.	See Louisville.	
Sylvania	Screven.	W. V. Taylor.	At Millen, Bk. of Millen.	H. E. Cary.
Talbotton	Talbot.	J. M. Matthews.	Peoples' Bk.	C.W. Kimbrough.
Thomaston	Upson.	J. A. Cotton.	Farmers' & Mer. Bk.	T. M. Matthews.
Thomasville	Thomas.	Macintyre & Macintyre.	Bk. of Thomasville.	B. H. Wright.
Thomson	McDuffie.	John T. West.	Bk. of Thomson.	Jas. T. Neal.
Traders Hill	Charlton.	See Way Cross.	See Way Cross.	
Trenton	Dade.	J. G. & D. H. Clark.	See Chattanooga, Tenn.	
Valdosta	Lowndes.	W. H. Griffin.	Citizens' Bk. of Valdosta.	C. W. Lamar.
Vienna	Dooly.	Handerson & Harvard.	Bk. of Vienna.	W. C. Hamilton.
Warrenton	Warren.	James Whitehead.	Bk. of Warrenton.	J. A. Allen.
Washington	Wilkes.	M. M. & M. P. Reese.	Washington Ex. Bk.	J. R. Dyson.
Watkinsville	Oconee.	R. M. Jackson.	See Athens.	
Way Cross	Ware.	Leon A. Wilson.	First Natl. Bk.	J. E. Wadley.
Waynesboro'	Burke.	Lawson & Scales.	Bk. of Waynesboro'.	W. E. Jones.
Wrightsville	Johnson.	A. F. Daley.	At Tennille, Farm. & Merch. Bk.	Jno. A. McCrary.
Zebulon	Pike.	J. S. Pope.	At Barnesville, New South Savgs. Bk.	G. E. Huguley.

GEORGIA—Continued.

DIGEST OF GEORGIA COMMERCIAL LAWS.

Assignments.—Transfers or assignments of real or personal property by insolvent debtors are fraudulent and null and void as against creditors, where any trust or benefit is reserved to the assignor or any person for him.

Attachments.—Attachments may issue where the debtor resides out of the State ; or where he is actually removing, or is about to remove, without the limits of the county ; or where he absconds ; or where he conceals himself ; or where he resists legal arrest ; or where he is causing his property to be removed beyond the limits of the State ; or where he is disposing of, or threatens to dispose of, or conceal his property liable to the payment of his debts, or make a fraudulent lien thereon to avoid the payment of his debts.

Bank Laws.—State banks must be chartered by legislative enactment. There is a general law for their incorporation, approved October 21, 1891. Their stockholders are liable for all their debts to the extent of unpaid subscriptions, but are further and additionally liable to depositors in an amount equal to the face value of their respective shares of stock. In some special charters passed before the general law, the "double liability clause" is made to apply to all the debts of the bank. The State Treasurer is *ex-officio* examiner of State banks, and it is the duty of this officer to examine all State banks at least once a year. All State banks must make quarterly statements under oath to the State bank examiner and publish same in local papers at their own expense.

Exemptions.—The head of every family, or the guardian or trustee of a family of minor children, every aged or infirm person, or person having the care and support of dependent females of any age, is entitled to have a homestead set apart on realty or personalty, or both, to the value, in the aggregate, of $1,600. No judgment, execution or decree may be enforced against the property so set apart as a homestead, including improvements made thereon, from time to time, except for taxes, for the purchase money of the same, for labor done thereon, for material furnished therefor, or for the removal of encumbrances thereon. The right of homestead may be waived in writing as against any particular debt, except as to wearing apparel and $300 worth of household and kitchen furniture and provisions. The homestead may not be alienated or incumbered, but it may be sold by the debtor and his wife, if any, jointly, with the sanction of the Judge of the Superior Court where the debtor resides, or the land is situated, the proceeds to be re-invested upon the same uses.

Interest.—Legal rate, except on contracts specifying another rate, is 7 per cent. and no more than 8 per cent. per annum may be contracted for, even by written instrument. The penalty in cases where usury is contracted for, is the forfeit of the excess above legal interest, and where the title to any property has been conveyed as security for the usurious debt, such title is absolutely void.

Legal Holidays.—Sunday, February 22, April 26, July 4, Labor Day, December 25, Thanksgiving, General Lee's Birthday, January 1 and 19.

Limitation of Actions.—Suits on bonds and other instruments under seal, should be brought within twenty years from the accrual of the right of action. Suits on promissory notes and other similar contracts in writing must be brought within seven years from maturity of such contract. Suits on open accounts, contracts not in writing, should be brought within four months.

GEORGIA—Continued.

Married Women.—All property of the wife in possession at the time of marriage, or afterwards acquired by her, is her separate property, and not liable for the payment of any debts, defaults, or contracts of the husband.

Notarial Fees.—Protest, $3.00.

Notes and Bills of Exchange.—Bills of exchange and promissory notes made for the purpose of negotiation, or intended to be negotiated at any chartered bank, and which are not paid at maturity, must be protested in order to bind the endorser. Notice of non-payment and of protest, or non-payment, or non-acceptance, must be given to the endorser within a reasonable time, either personally, or by post. It will not be necessary to protest in order to bind the endorser, except in the following cases: Where the paper is made payable on its face, at a bank or banker's office. Where it is discounted at a bank or banker's office. Where it is left at a bank or banker's office for collection. In all such cases, days of grace must be allowed, and the last day of grace is the day of maturity. No days of grace are allowed on sight papers. When paper matures on a holiday, it is payable the day before, unless two holidays come together, when paper due on the second one becomes due the day after. Accommodation endorsers, sureties and endorsers, may be sued in the same county and in the same action, with the maker, drawer or acceptor. Bills of exchange must be accepted in writing to bind acceptor. In this State a contract to pay attorney's fees cannot be collected unless a defense is filed and not sustained.

Stay of Executions.—Execution issued from the Superior Court may be stayed for sixty days upon good security.

Transfer of Corporation Stocks.—Transfer on the back of stock is good between the parties and those taking with notice. Transfer on the books of the corporation binds all parties regardless of notice.

IDAHO.

County Seat.	County.	Name of Atty.	Name of Bank.	Cashier.
Albion	Cassia.	Chas. Cobb.	See Pocatello.	
Bellevue	Logan.	V. Bierbower.	See Halley.	
Blackfoot	Bingham.	Stewart & Dietrich.	Bk. of C. Bunting & Co.	
Boise City	Ada.	Geo. H. Stewart.	Boise City Natl. Bk.	Alfred Eoff.
Caldwell	Canyon.	Jno. C. Rice.	First Natl. Bk.	W. R. Sebree.
Challis	Custer.	L. H. Johnston.	At Halley.	
Halley	Alturas.	R. F. Butler.	First Natl. Bk.	F. H. Parsons.
Idaho City	Boise.	W. H. Dunton.	Boise County Bk.	E. W. Barry.
Lewiston	Nez Perces.	Jas. E. Babb.	First Natl. Bk.	E. W. Eaves.
Malad City	Oneida.	D. C. McDougall.	Bk. of J. N. Ireland & Co.	C. Jones.
Mount Idaho	Idaho.	J. H. Forney.	At Grangeville, Bk. of Grangeville.	W. Scott.
Moscow	Latah.	R. T. Morgan.	First Natl. Bk.	F. N. Gilbert.
MOUNTAIN HOME	Elmore.	W. C. Howie.	Elmore Co. Bk.	J. W. Campbell.
Murray	Shoshone.	H. S. Gregory.	Bk. of North Idaho.	Albert Johnson.
Paris	Bear Lake.	Robert S. Spence.	At Montpelier, Bk. of Montpelier.	G. C. Gray.
Pocatello	Bannock.	Eden & Warner.	First Natl. Bk.	M. C. Senter.
Rathdrum	Kootenai.	Henry Melder.	Exchange Bk.	W. A. Hart.
Salmon City	Lemhi.	R. P. Quarles.	See Dillon, Montana.	
Silver City	Owyhee.	C. M. Hayes.	See Mountain Home.	
St. Anthony	Fremont.	P. Averitt.	First Bk. of Fremont Co.	S. R. Findley.
Weiser	Washington.	J. W. Ayers.	Bk. of Weiser.	C. J. Selwyn.

DIGEST OF IDAHO COMMERCIAL LAWS.

Assignments.—An insolvent debtor owing debts exceeding $300, and having been resident of county for six months, may be discharged of his debts by executing an assignment of all his property, real and personal. No preferences are allowed.

Attachments.—Attachment may issue on affidavit stating that defendant is indebted to plaintiff (specifying net amount) and that plaintiff is non-resident of State and that the attachment is not sought and the action is not prosecuted to hinder, delay or defraud any creditor of the defendant.

Bank Laws.—There is no statute law relating to banks. No charters can be granted to banks except by the Legislature and no provision is made for the supervision of banks or bankers by any State official or otherwise.

Exemptions.—The homestead, consisting of a quantity of land and a dwelling house thereon, with its appurtenances, not exceeding the value of $5,000, to be selected by the husband or wife, or both, or by other head of a family, and not exceeding $1,000 if claimant is not the head of a family. Office furniture and library, $100, necessary household and kitchen furniture, and provisions for family for three months; certain farm animals, etc., with food for three months; tools and implements of husbandry up to $200. Libraries of professional men, and team used by a laborer or teamster, are also exempt.

THE LEGAL AND FINANCIAL LIGHTS OF AMERICA.

IDAHO—Continued.

Interest.—Legal rate 10 per cent. Parties may agree in writing for 18 per cent. Above that rate usurious. Usury penalty, forfeiture of 10 per cent. per year of the principal to the school fund and loss of all interest.

Legal Holidays.—Sunday, January 1, February 22, May 30, July 4, December 25, Thanksgiving, General Territorial Election, or Special Election held by the Governor.

Limitation of Actions.—Six years on actions on judgments and to recover mesne profits. Five years on action for real estate and on written contracts. Four years on actions on contracts not in writing and accounts. Three years on actions for trespass on real property, taking, detaining or injuring goods or chattels, for recovery of personal property, and for relief on account of fraud or mistake and for statutory penalty.

Married Women.—No special law.

Notarial Fees.—Protest $3, recording 50 cents, and $1 for each notice.

Notes and Bills of Exchange.—Commercial paper becomes negotiable by being executed and delivered, and is made negotiable by endorsement, what is called "in blank." The protest of a notary, under his hand and official seal, of a bill of exchange or promissory note, for non-acceptance or non-payment, stating the presentment for acceptance or payment and the non-acceptance or non-payment thereof, the service of and mode of giving notice to parties, and the reputed residence of the parties. is made by our statute *prima facie* evidence of the facts contained therein. Damages for protested bills: Domestic, 15 per cent.; foreign, 30 per cent. Days of grace are not allowed on either bills or notes. Paper maturing on a holiday becomes payable the day previous.

Transfer of Corporation Stocks.—Whenever the capital stock of any corporation is divided into shares, and certificates therefor are issued, such shares of stock are personal property, and may be transferred by endorsement, by the signature of the proprietor, or his attorney or legal representative, and delivery of the certificate; but such transfer is not valid except between the parties thereto until the same is so entered upon the books of the corporation, so as to show the name of the parties by and to whom transferred, the number and designation of the shares, and the date of the entry. Corporations may, by by-laws, provide that no transfer of its stock shall be made upon its books until all indebtedness to the corporation of the person in whose name the stock stands, whether for assignment, calls or otherwise, is paid.

ILLINOIS.

County Seat.	County.	Name of Atty.	Name of Bank.	Cashier.
Albion	Edwards.	H. J. Strawn.	Edwards Co. Bk.	E. M. Pace.
Aledo	Mercer.	Pepper & Scott.	Bk. of A. M. Byers & Co.	Wm. N. Graham.
Belleville	St. Clair.	Barthel & Farmer.	First Natl. Bk.	Casimir Andel.
Belvidere	Boone.	R. W. Wright.	Peoples Bk.	John Greenlee.
Benton	Franklin.	Spiller & Hart.	Exchange Bk.	W. R. Ward.
Bloomington	McLean.	Livingston & Bach.	National State Bk.	A. B. Hoblit.
Cairo	Alexander.	Green & Gilbert.	City Natl. Bk.	J. S. Alsthorpe.
Cambridge	Henry.	Turner & Street.	First Natl. Bk.	Henry White.
Carlinville	Macoupin.	M. L. Keplinger.	Bk. of C. H. C. Anderson.	John C. Anderson
Carlyle	Clinton.	P. W. Brown.	Schlafley Bros.	J. F. Keshner.
Carmi	White.	P. A. Pearce.	First Natl. Bk.	T. W. Hall.
Carrollton	Greene.	Henry T. Rainey.	Greene Co. Natl. Bk.	Ornem Pierson.
Carthage	Hancock.	Sharp & Berry Bros.	Hancock Co. Natl. Bk.	Chas. S. De Hart.
Charleston	Coles.	A. J. Fryer.	Second Natl. Bk.	Felix Johnston.
Chester	Randolph.	H. Clay Horner.	First Natl. Bk.	John D. Gerlach.
Chicago	Cook.	Ferguson & Goodnow. Runyan & Runyan.	The Bankers Natl. Bk. First Natl. Bk.	John C. Craft. R. J. Street.

Clinton	De Witt.	Moore & Warner.	De Witt Co. Natl. Bk.	E. S. Nixon.
Danville	Vermillion.	Edwin Winter.	First Natl. Bk.	C. L. English.
Decatur	Macon.	Albert G. Webber.	Natl. Bk. of Decatur.	D.O.McReynolds.
Dixon	Lee.	A. K. Truesdell.	Dixon Natl. Bk.	C. H. Hughes.
Edwardsville	Madison.	C. N. Travous.	J. A. Brickett & Son.	H. E. Brickett.
Effingham	Effingham.	Wright Bros.	First Natl. Bk.	J. Partridge, Jr.
ELIZABETHTOWN	Hardin.	J. Q. A. Ledbetter.	Warford's Bk.	Wm. P. Warford.
Fairfield	Wayne.	R. D. Adams.	Bank of Fairfield.	E. E. Creps.
Freeport	Stephenson.	H. C. Hyde.	First Natl. Bk.	A. Bidwell.
Galena	Jo Daviess.	E. L. Bedford.	Galena Natl. Bk.	Walter Ford.
Galesburg	Knox.	Williams, Lawrence & Williams	Galesburg Natl. Bk.	J. H. Losey.
Geneva	Kane.	W. J. Brown.	Bk. of Geneva.	Gaunt & Field.
Golconda	Pope.	Rose & Sloan.	Pope Co. Bk.	E. B. Clark.
Greenville	Bond.	Thomas G. Parker.	Holles & Sons.	
Hardin	Calhoun.	Thomas J. Selby.	See Grafton, Grafton Bk.	E. Meysenburg.
Harrisburgh	Saline.	Boyer & Thompson.	First Natl. Bk.	F. T. Joyner.
Havana	Mason.	Wallace & Lazey.	Havana Natl. Bk.	N. C. King.
Hennepin	Putnam.	William H. Casson.	Putnam Co. Bk.	W. C. Patterson.
Hillsborough	Montgomery.	Edward Lane.	Hillsborough Natl. Bk.	Luther M. Beck.
Jacksonville	Morgan.	Charles A. Barnes.	Jacksonville Natl. Bk.	C.W.Fitzsimmons
Jerseyville	Jersey.	Joseph S. Carr.	Natl. Bk. of Jerseyville.	Edward Cross.
Joliet	Will.	John T. Donahoe.	Joliet Natl. Bk.	Robert T. Kelly.
Jonesboro	Union.	Karraker & Lingle.	Bank of Jonesboro.	H. W. Karraker.
Kankakee	Kankakee.	Wheeler & Hunter.	The City Natl. Bk.	H. M. Stone.
Lacon	Marshall.	Barnes & Barnes.	First Natl. Bk.	W. H. Ford.

THE LEGAL AND FINANCIAL LIGHTS OF AMERICA. 37

ILLINOIS—Continued.

County Seat.	County.	Name of Atty.	Name of Bank.	Cashier.
LAWRENCEVILLE	..Lawrence.	Gee & Barnes.	Lawrenceville Bk.	McCleave & Barnes.
Lewiston	......Fulton.	H. W. Masters.	Lewiston Natl. Bk.	W. H. Rhodes.
Lincoln	.........Logan.	James T. Hobild.	Lincoln Natl. Bk.	P. E. Kuhl.
Louisville	.....Clay.	J. A. Barnes.	Farmers & Merchants Bk.	G. B. McCollum.
Macomb	........McDonough.	Sherman & Tunnicliff.	Union Natl. Bk.	B. F. McLean.
Marion	.........Williamson.	Clemens & Warder.	Bk. of Marion.	O. H. Burnett.
Marshall	.......Clark.	Graham & Tibbs.	Dulaney Natl. Bk.	H. B. Dulaney.
McLEANSBORO'	....Hamilton.	T. M. Eckley.	Peoples Bk.	J. H. Miller.
Metamora	......Woodford.	A. R. Rich.	Metamora Bk.	P. & D. Schertz.
METROPOLIS CITY	.Massac.	R. W. McCartney.	First Natl. Bk.	W. H. Armstrong.
Monmouth	....Warren.	Grier & Stewart.	Natl. Bk. of Monmouth.	W. B. Young.
Monticello	.....Piatt.	C. A. Tatman.	First Natl. Bk.	O. W. Moore.
Morris	..........Grundy.	E. Sanford.	Grundy Co. Natl. Bk.	J. C. Carr.
Morrison	......Whiteside.	F. D. Ramsay.	First Natl. Bk.	A. J. Jackson.
Mound City	...Pulaski.	L. M. Bradley.	First State Bk.	J. A. Waugh.
Mt. Carmel	....Wabash.	S. R. Putname.	First Natl. Bk.	H. T. Goddard.
Mt. Carroll	.....Carroll.	R. E. Eaton.	First Natl. Bk.	O. P. Miles.
Mt. Sterling	...Brown.	E. S. Parry.	First Natl. Bk.	C. H. Turner.
Mt. Vernon	...Jefferson.	Charles H. Patton.	Mt. Vernon Bk.	C. D. Ham & Co.
MURPHYSBORO'	...Jackson.	J. H. Martin.	City Natl. Bk.	John G. Hardy.
Nashville	......Washington.	Forman & Watts.	Washington Co. Bk.	Louis Krughoff.
Newton	........Jasper.	T. J. Fithian.	Peoples Bk.	O. S. Scott.
Olney	...........Richland.	R. B. Witcher.	Olney Bank.	J. H. Sensenan.
Oquawka	.....Henderson.	Ross Cooper.	Bk. of Robert Moir & Co.	
Oregon	........Ogle.	H. A. Smith.	First Natl. Bank.	Charles Schneider
Ottawa	.........La Salle.	D. McDougall.	Natl. City Bank.	E. C. Allen, Jr.
Paris	............Edgar.	R. L. McKinlay.	First Natl. Bk.	R. G. Sutherland.
Paxton	.........Ford.	F. L. Cook.	First Natl. Bk.	A. S. Bushnell.
Pekin	...........Tazewell.	Graff & Rider.	Farmers Natl. Bk.	C. H. Turner.
Peoria	.........Peoria.	McCulloch & McCulloch.	Merchants Natl. Bk.	G. H. Littlewood.
Petersburgh	..Menard.	S. H. Blane.	First Natl. Bk.	J. M. Robbins.
Pinckneyville	.Perry.	W. K. Murphy.	Murphy, Wall & Co.	Allen Ozburn.
Pittsfield	.......Pike.	Matthews,Higbee & Grigsby.	Farmers State Bk.	Ross Matthews.
Pontiac	........Livingston.	George Torrence.	Natl. Bk. of Pontiac.	Joseph Spiro.
Princeton	......Bureau.	R. M. Skinner.	First Natl. Bk.	H. C. Roberts.
Quincy	..........Adams.	Hamilton & Woods.	Ricker Natl. Bk.	George E. Ricker.
Robinson	......Crawford.	Jones & Newlin.	Robinson Bk.	C. H. Steel.
Rockford	......Winnebago.	William Lathrop.	Rockford Natl. Bk.	W. F. Woodruff.
Rock Island	..Rock Island.	Sweeney & Walker.	Peoples Natl. Bk.	C. Hellpenstell.
Rushville	......Schuyler.	P. E. Mann.	Bank of Schuyler Co.	J. M. Patterson.
Salem	...........Marion.	L. M. Kagy.	Salem Natl. Bk.	Thos. S. Marshall
Shawneetown	Gallatin.	Carl Roedel.	First Natl. Bk.	Wm. D. Phile.
Shelbyville	....Shelby.	Moulton, Chafee & Headen.	First Natl. Bk.	J. W. Powers.
Springfield	....Sangamon.	Patton & Hamilton.	First Natl. Bk.	Howard K.Weber
Sullivan	........Moultrie.	W. G. Cochran.	Merchants and Farmers State Bk.	James A. Steele.
Sycamore	......DeKalb.	Carnes & Dunton.	Sycamore Natl. Bk.	Charles E.Walker
Taylorville	....Christian.	W. M. Provine.	First Natl. Bk.	E. R. Wright.
Toledo	...........Cumberland.	W. S. Everhart.	Bk. of Toledo	Willis Bros.

THE LEGAL AND FINANCIAL LIGHTS OF AMERICA.

ILLINOIS—Continued.

County Seat.	County.	Name of Atty.	Name of Bank.	Cashier.
Toulon	Stark.	Miles A. Fuller.	Exchange Bk.	Burge & Dewey.
Tuscola	Douglas.	C. Eckhart.	First Natl. Bank.	W. H. Land.
Urbana	Champaign.	White & Dobbins.	First Natl. Bk.	A. F. Fay.
Vandalia	Fayette.	W. M. Fogler.	Farmers & Merchants Bk.	Edward L. Wahl.
Vienna	Johnson.	William A. Samm.	First Natl. Bk.	D.W.Whittenberg
Virginia	Cass.	R. W. Mills.	Farmers Natl. Bk.	J. T. Robertson.
Waterloo	Monroe.	J. W. Rickert.	State Bk. of Waterloo.	George Pinkel.
Watseka	Iroquois.	Kay & Kay.	First Natl. Bk.	Geo.C.Harrington
Waukegan	Lake.	Francis E. Clarke.	First Natl. Bk.	Charles F. Wiard.
Wheaton	DuPage.	E. H. Gary.	See Geneva.	
Winchester	Scott.	J. M. Riggs.	Bk. of Neat, Condit & Croup.	
Woodstock	McHenry.	D. T. Smiley.	Farmers Exchange Bk.	M. D. Hoy & Son.
Yorkville	Kendall.	John Fitzgerald.	Yorkville Bk.	R. N. Newton.

DIGEST OF ILLINOIS COMMERCIAL LAWS.

Assignments.—Any debtor may make an assignment for the benefit of his creditors. No preferences are allowed.

Attachments.—Attachment may issue where the debtor is a non-resident of the State ; conceals himself so that he cannot be served with process, has left the State, or is about to depart from the State with the intention of having his effects removed, or is about to remove his property from the State, or has, within two years preceding the filing of the affidavit required, fraudulently conveyed, or assigned, his effects, or a part thereof, or has, within two years prior to the filing of such affidavit, fraudulently concealed or disposed of his property, or is about fraudulently to conceal, assign or otherwise dispose of his property, or where the debt sued for was fraudulently contracted on the part of the debtor, provided the statements of the debtor, which constitute the fraud, have been reduced to writing and signed by the debtor.

Bank Laws.—Associations may be formed to do a general banking business (except the issuing of bills to circulate as money), including loans on personal and real estate security, and accepting and executing trusts. The capital required is, in cities of 5,000 population or under, $25,000 ; between 5,000 and 10,000 population, $50,000 ; between 10,000 and 50,000 population, $100,000 ; 50,000 population and upwards, $200,000. Impairment of capital must be made good on notice from the State Auditor. The stock being fully subscribed, a meeting of the stockholders on not less than three days' notice, shall be held, at which the number of directors shall be determined, and they elected. The directors thereupon organize and elect officers, make by-laws, and arrange for the transaction of business. They are required to take an oath of fealty to the association and observance of the Banking Act. Upon complying with these provisions, the auditor makes examination, and if satisfied that capital has been paid in, issues a certificate of organization upon payment of reasonable expenses. This certificate must be filed in the office of Recorder of Deeds of the county where the bank is organized, and upon recording such certifi-

ILLINOIS—Continued.

cate the association may proceed to business. Stockholders are severally liable for all engagements of the association to an amount equal to their respective stockholdings, at par value, in addition to the amount invested in their share of stock. Reports under oath of president or cashier shall be made on call of the auditor at least once in three months, showing resources and liabilities in detail, which reports shall be published in some newspaper of the place where the bank is located. At least once a year the auditor shall cause an examination of the bank to be made by a suitable person not a stockholder, officer, or employee of the bank, who shall make a detailed report of his examination, and shall have power to examine officers, employees, or agents on oath. There is no provision of law for the inspection of private banking firms not organized under the statutes.

Exemptions.—Every householder having a family is entitled to a homestead, valued at $1,000, and such exemption continues to the survivor after the death of husband or wife, so long as he or she occupies it, and to the children until the youngest is twenty-one years old. In addition, there is allowed to every person, necessary wearing apparel, etc., and $100 worth of other property selected by the debtor. If the debtor is the head of a family, and resides with the same, he is allowed $300 worth in addition, to be selected by him. But such selection cannot be made from any money or wages due. Of wages there are $50 exempt from garnishment to any one who is the head of a family residing with the same. Wages to amount of $50 earned within six months are preferred debts in cases of insolvency of debtor owing such wages.

Interest.—Legal rate is 5 per cent., 7 per cent. may be contracted for on all written contracts. The penalty for usury is forfeiture of the entire interest.

Legal Holidays.—Sunday, January 1, February 12, February 22, May 30, July 4, Election Day, Labor Day, December 25, Thanksgiving.

Limitation of Actions.—All actions for the recovery of possession of real property must be commenced within twenty years. Actions on unwritten contracts, express or implied, or on awards of arbitration, or for recovery of damages for an injury done to property, real or personal, or to recover the possession of personal property or for damages for the detention or conversion thereof, and in all civil actions not otherwise provided for must be commenced within five years next after the cause of action accrued. Actions on bond, promissory notes, bills of exchange, written leases, written contracts or other evidences of indebtedness in writing, must be commenced within ten years after the cause of action accrued.

Married Women.—May contract, sue, and be sued as feme sole; may hold property, personal and real, in their own name and right, and not subject to husband's debts; may employ husband as agent to transact their business.

Notarial Fees.—Protest $1.50, with twenty-five cents per notice additional.

Notes and Bills of Exchange.—Any note, bond, bill or other instrument in writing made payable to any person named as payee therein, shall be assignable by indorsement thereon, under the hand of such person, and of his assignees, in the same manner as bills of exchange are, so as to absolutely transfer and vest the property thereof in each and every assignee successively. It is essential to the negotiability of promissory notes, bills, bonds and other instruments in writing for the payment of money or other articles of personal property by endorsement, that they be payable absolutely and unconditionally—not depending on any contingency, either in

THE LEGAL AND FINANCIAL LIGHTS OF AMERICA.

ILLINOIS—Continued.

regard to the use of the fund out of which payment is to be made, or as to the parties by whom or to whom the payment is to be made. Any note, bond, bill or other instrument in writing made payable to the bearer, may be transferred by delivery thereof, and an action may be maintained thereon in the name of the holder thereof ; every endorser of such instrument shall be held as a guarantor of payment unless otherwise expressed in the endorsement. Whenever any bill of exchange, drawn or endorsed within this State, and payable without the United States, is duly protested the drawer or endorser thereof shall pay said bill, with legal interest, from the time such bill ought to have been paid, and 10 per cent. damages in addition, together with the costs and charges of protest. If any bill of exchange, drawn upon any person or body politic or corporate, out of this State, but within the United States, for the payment of money, shall be duly presented for acceptance or payment, and protested, it shall be payable, with legal interest from the time such bill ought to have been paid, until paid, together with costs and charges of protests. No promissory note, check, draft, bill of exchange, order, or other negotiable or commercial instrument payable at sight or on demand, or on presentment, shall be entitled to days of grace. Notes maturing on holidays are payable the day previous. All other bills of exchange, drafts, or promissory notes, shall be entitled to the usual days of grace.

Stay of Execution.—No stay laws, only such as the court orders.

Transfer of Corporation Stocks.—By transfer on the books of the corporation.

INDIAN TERRITORY.

County Seat.	County.	Name of Atty.	Name of Bank.	Cashier.
Ardmore	Chickasaw.	Johnson, Cruce & Cruce.	First Natl. Bk.	Don Lacy.
Atoka	Creek.	Merrill & John.	See South McAllister	
Chickasha	Pickens.	Chas. M. Fechhelmer.	Bk. of Chickasha	J. A. Bohart.
Chickasaw	Chickasaw.	See Chickasha.	See Chickasha.	
Duncan	Pickens.	Wolverton & Rodgers.	Duncan Bk.	J. T. Jeanes.
Marlow	Pickens.	See Ardmore.		
Minco	Pontotoc.	E. E. Wilson.	Bk. of Minco	H. B. Johnson.
Muscogee	Creek.	Shepherd, Grove & Shackelford.	First Natl. Bk.	C. N. Warth.
Paul's Valley.	Pickens.	L. C. Andrews.	Bk. of Paul's Valley	J. D. Imboden, Jr.
Purcell	Pontotoc.	J. F. Sharp.	Chickasaw Natl. Bk.	A. D. Hawk.
Ryan	Chickasaw.	See Duncan.	Bk. of Ryan	J. E. Ledbetter.
So. McAllister.	Chickasaw.	Fannin & Fannin.	South McAllister Bk.	Joe Hillman.
Tahlequah	Cherokee.	Wm. F. Rasmus.	Bk. of Tahlequah	L. C. Ross.
Vinita	Cherokee.	W. H. Kornegay.	First Natl. Bk.	H. C. Cook.
Wynnewood	Pontotoc.	J. T. Planton.	Bk. of Wynnewood	J. F. Beeler.

DIGEST OF INDIAN TERRITORY COMMERCIAL LAWS.

Assignments.—Assignments can be made of all the property or a part thereof. Any creditor or creditors may be preferred.

Attachments.—Attachments may be made when the action is against one absent from the Territory for more than four months when his residence is in the Territory; has left his residence to avoid the service of summons ; is about to, or has removed his property, or a material part thereof, out of the Territory, not leaving enough therein to satisfy plaintiff's claim ; conceals himself; has sold his property with the fraudulent intent to cheat, hinder, or delay his creditors in the collection of their debts, or is about to do so.

Bank Laws.—No bank laws.

Exemptions.—The personal property of any resident of the Indian Territory who is not married or the head of a family, in specific articles to be selected by such resident, not exceeding in value the sum of $200 in addition to his wearing apparel, provided that no property shall be exempt from execution for debts contracted for the purchase money therefor while in the hands of vendee. Of a married person or head of a family, in specific articles to be selected by such resident, not exceeding in value the sum of $500 in addition to his or her wearing apparel and that of his or her family, shall be exempt on debt or contract.

Interest.—Legal rate, 6 per cent. By contract, not exceeding 10 per cent. Contracts in excess of 10 per cent. are void as to principal and interest.

Legal Holidays.—Sunday, January 1, February 22, July 4, Thanksgiving, Christmas, Fast Day, Birthday of Lee.

INDIAN TERRITORY—Continued.

Limitation of Actions.—All actions of debt founded on contract or liability not in writing; all actions of account, and the like, founded on any contract or liability, expressed or implied, three years. Action on promissory notes and other instruments in writing not under seal, must be commenced within five years, and not after; actions on bonds, writings under seal and judgments and decrees, must be commenced within ten years.

Notarial Fees.—Protest, seventy-five cents. Noting, fifty cents. Registration, forty cents. Certificate, fifty cents. Each notice, fifty cents.

Notes and Bills of Exchange.—Bills and notes are governed by the law-merchant. The general rules of commercial law on these subjects prevail. Notes to be negotiable must be expressed to be for value received. A stipulation for fixed attorney's fees does not render paper non-negotiable ; but are not recoverable. Paper maturing on a holiday becomes payable the day before. Protests are the common form, and are made by notaries public. Acceptances must be made in writing. If the drawee destroy or retain the bill, is taken as having accepted it. The statutes fix in detail the damages to be awarded the holder of a bill in case of non-acceptance or non-payment. Protested bills bear interest at the rate of ten per cent. per annum.

Transfer of Corporation Stocks.—No law.

INDIANA.

County Seat.	County.	Name of Atty.	Name of Bank.	Cashier.
Albion	Noble.	Levi W. Welker.	Bk. of Albion	F. B. Clapp.
Anderson	Madison.	Chipman, Keltner & Hendee.	Natl. Exchange Bk.	J. L. Forkner.
Angola	Steuben.	Croxton & Powers.	Steuben Co. Bk.	H. K. Scott.
Auburn	De Kalb.	D. Y. Husselman.	Farmers Bk.	A. C. Robbins.
Bedford	Lawrence.	W. H. Martin.	Citizens Bk.	J. R. Vorls.
Bloomfield	Greene.	Cavins & Cavins.	Bloomfield Bk.	O. W. Shryer.
Bloomington	Monroe.	Duncan & Batman.	First Natl. Bk.	W. E. Woodburn.
Bluffton	Wells.	Wilson & Todd.	Studebaker Bk.	J. S. Gilliland.
Boonville	Warrick.	Hatfield & Hemenway.	Boonville Natl. Bk.	J.P.Weyerbacher.
Brazil	Clay.	George A. Knight.	First Natl. Bk.	C. S. Andrews.
Brookville	Franklin.	Jones & Jones.	Brookville Bk.	Goodwin & Shirk.
Brownstown	Jackson.	Applewhite & Applewhite.	Peoples State Bk.	H. A. Burrel.
Cannelton	Perry.	Chas. A. Weathers.	Commercial Bk.	S. L. May.
COLUMBIA CITY	Whitley.	James S. Collins.	Bk. of F. H. Foust & Co.	
Columbus	Bartholomew.	Stansifer & Baker.	First Natl. Bk.	L. K. Ong.
Connersville	Fayette.	McKee, Little & Frost.	First Natl. Bk.	Q. A. Mount.
Corydon	Harrison.	W. N. & R. J. Tracewell.	Bk. of Corydon	W. B. Slemons.
Covington	Fountain.	Nebeker & Simms.	Citizens State Bk.	Sampeon Reed.
CRAWFORDSVILLE	Montgomery.	Brush & Snyder.	Citizens Natl. Bk.	C. Goltra.
Crown Point	Lake.	J. Kopelike.	First Natl. Bk.	W. C. Murphey.
Danville	Hendricks.	Cofer & Hadley.	First Natl. Bk.	M. Carter.
Decatur	Adams.	R. K. Irwin.	Old Adams Co. Bk.	R. K. Allison.
Delphi	Carroll.	Gould & Eldridge.	Citizens Bk.	J. A. Shirk.
Evansville	Vanderburgh	Alex. Gilchrist.	Old National Bk.	Henry Reis.
Fort Wayne	Allen.	John F. Rodabaugh.	Hamilton Natl. Bk.	John Mohr, Jr.
Fowler	Benton.	Fraser & Isham.	Bk. of Benton Co.	Lee Dinwiddie.
Frankfort	Clinton.	J. C. Farber.	Farmers Bk.	D. A. Coulder.
Franklin	Johnson.	T. W. Woollen.	Franklin Natl. Bk.	E. C. Miller.
Goshen	Elkhart.	W. L. Stonex.	City Natl. Bk.	C. J. Garvin.
Greencastle	Putnam.	Silas A. Hays.	Central Natl. Bk.	M. D. Bridges.
Greenfield	Hancock.	S. A. Wray.	Greenfield Bkg. Co.	M. Chandler.
Greensburg	Decatur.	William A. Moore.	Third Natl. Bk.	W. W. Bonner.
Hartford City	Blackford.	J. A. Bonham.	Citizens Bk.	E. M. Stahl.
Huntington	Huntington.	I. G. Smith.	First Natl. Bk.	Sarah F. Dick.
Indianapolis	Marion.	Robert N. Lamb.	Indiana Natl. Bk.	Edward B. Porter.
Jasper	Dubois.	Wm. A. Traylor.	Dubois Co. State Bk.	Frank Joseph.
JEFFERSONVILLE	Clark.	M. Z. Stannard.	First Natl. Bk.	H. E. Heaton.
Kendland	Newton.	Cummings & Darroch.	Bk. of Kendland	Smart & Rider.
Knox	Stark.	H. A. Woodward.	Farmers Bk.	F. P. Whitson.
Kokomo	Howard.	Blackildge & Shirley.	Citizens Natl. Bk.	G. E. Bruner.
La Fayette	Tippecanoe.	J. D. Gougar.	Merchants Natl. Bk.	C. Murdock.
La Grange	La Grange.	O. L. Ballou.	Natl. Bk. of La Grange	J. I. Norris.
La Porte	La Porte.	S. E. Williams.	First Natl. Bk.	R. E. Morrison.
LAWRENCEBURGH	Dearborn.	Thompson & Colt.	Citizens Natl. Bk.	W. D. H. Hunter.
Leavenworth	Crawford.	J. H. Weathers.	Citizens Bk.	R. H. Willett.
Lebanon	Boone.	Dutch & Higgins.	Lebanon Natl. Bk.	E. T. Lane.
Liberty	Union.	L. H. Stanford.	Union Co. Natl. Bk.	H. Husted.

INDIANA—Continued.

County Seat.	County.	Name of Atty.	Name of Bank.	Cashier.
Logansport	Cass.	Winfield & Taber.	Logansport State Bk.	W. C. Thomas.
Madison	Jefferson.	Vanosdal & Francisco.	First Natl. Bk.	Thos. A. Pogue.
Marion	Grant.	George G. Wharton.	First Natl. Bk.	A. B. Morrison.
Martinsville	Morgan.	Jordan & Matthews.	Citizens Natl. Bk.	W. D. Frazee.
Monticello	White.	Chas. C. Spencer.	Citizens Bk.	W. E. McLean.
Mount Vernon	Posey.	E. M. Spencer.	Mt. Vernon Bkg. Co.	E. D. Owen.
Muncie	Delaware.	C. E. Shipley.	Delaware Co. Natl. Bk.	C. H. Church.
Nashville	Brown.	See Columbus.		
New Albany	Floyd.	Alex. Dowling.	First Natl. Bk.	J. A. Hutton.
New Castle	Henry.	John M. Morris.	Citizens State Bk.	D. W. Kinsey.
Newport	Vermillion.	Conley & Sawyer.	Bk. of R. H. Nixon	
Noblesville	Hamilton.	Shirts & Kilbourne.	Citizens State Bk.	E. Shirts.
Paoli	Orange.	W. J. Throop.	Orange Co. Bk.	A. B. Ham.
Peru	Miami.	Mitchell & McClintic.	First Natl. Bk.	R. A. Edwards.
Petersburgh	Pike.	E. P. Richardson.	Citizens State Bk.	Byron Prenton.
Plymouth	Marshall.	Chas. P. Drummond.	First Natl. Bk.	Jas. A. Gilmore.
Portland	Jay.	S. W. Haynes.	Peoples Bk.	W. M. Haynes.
Princeton	Gibson.	Buskirk & Brady.	Peoples Natl. Bk.	W. P. Welborn.
Rensselaer	Jasper.	M. F. Chilcote.	Bk. of A. McCoy & Co.	E. L. Hollingsworth.
Richmond	Wayne.	R. A. Jackson.	Second Natl. Bk.	J. B. Dougan.
Rising Sun	Ohio.	Coles & Hall.	Natl. Bk. of Rising Sun	J. N. Perkins.
Rochester	Fulton.	Holman & Stephenson.	Rochester Bk.	A. C. Copeland.
Rockport	Spencer.	E. L. Boyd.	Farmers Bk.	E. M. Payne.
Rockville	Parke.	Maxwell & Maxwell.	Park Bk.	F. H. Stark.
Rushville	Rush.	Smith & Cambern.	Rushville Natl. Bk.	Edwin Payne.
Salem	Washington.	Alspaugh & Lawler.	Bk. of Salem	J. F. Persise.
Scottsburgh	Scott.	Jewett & Shea.	Scott Co. Bk.	W. M. Whitson.
Shelbyville	Shelby.	Love & Morrison.	First Natl. Bk.	John A. Young.
Shoals	Martin.	R. L. Ross.	Martin Co. Bk.	J. L. Passel.
South Bend	St. Joseph.	Lucius Hubbard.	First Natl. Bk.	C. A. Kimball.
Spencer	Owen.	J. H. Fowler.	Exchange Bk.	F. H. Freeland.
Sullivan	Sullivan.	John T. Hays.	Farmers State Bk.	Wake Glies.
Terre Haute	Vigo.	Harry J. Baker.	First Natl. Bk.	B. McCormick.
Tipton	Tipton.	Gifford & Gifford.	Tipton Co. Bk.	E. H. Sbirk.
Valparaiso	Porter.	A. D. Bartholomew.	Farmers Natl. Bk.	G. F. Bartholemew
Vernon	Jennings.	Benjamin F. Tweedy.	First Natl. Bk.	John S. Morris.
Versailles	Ripley.	F. M. Thompson.	Versailles Bk.	F. M. Laws.
Vevay	Switzerland.	G. S. Pleasants.	First Natl. Bk.	Albert G. Craig.
Vincennes	Knox.	L. A. Meyer.	German Natl. Bk.	George R. Alsop.
Wabash	Wabash.	W. G. Sayre.	First Natl. Bk.	F. W. Morse.
Warsaw	Kosciusko.	John D. Wideman.	Lake City Bk.	S. Bitner.
Washington	Daviess.	J. W. Ogden.	Peoples Natl. Bk.	R. C. Davis.
Williamsport	Warren.	C. V. McAdams.	Warren Co. Bk.	A. H. Haun.
Winamac	Pulaski.	Spangler & Son.	Bk. of Winamac	W. S. Huddleston
Winchester	Randolph.	J. W. Thompson.	Farmers & Merchants Bk.	T. F. Moorman.

INDIANA—Continued.

DIGEST OF INDIANA COMMERCIAL LAWS.

Assignments.—Any debtor may make a general assignment of all property in trust for the benefit of *bona fide* creditors. The assignor is not forbidden to make preferences to *bona fide* creditors, provided the preferences be made before the deed of assignment and in no way co-ordinate with it. The assignor is not relieved from his debts.

Attachments.—Attachment may issue where the defendant is a foreign corporation or a non-resident; where the defendant is secretly leaving the State, or has left it, with intent to defraud his creditors; where the defendant so conceals himself that summons cannot be served upon him; where he is removing, or about to remove, his property subject to execution, or a material part thereof, out of the State, not leaving enough to satisfy the plaintiff's claim; where he has sold or otherwise disposed of his property subject to execution, or suffered or permitted it to be sold with the fraudulent intent to cheat, hinder, or delay his creditors; where he is about to sell, convey, or otherwise dispose of his property subject to execution with such intent.

Bank Laws.—Any number of persons, not less than five, may entitle themselves to a charter as a bank of discount and deposit. The capital stock must not be less than $25,000 divided into shares of the value of $100 each. There must not be less than three directors, elected by the stockholders. These directors shall elect one of their number as president, and shall also elect a cashier, who must give bond for the faithful discharge of his duties. A corporation so formed may begin business as soon as 50 per cent. of its capital stock shall have been actually paid in; and it shall have all the powers incident to the business of banking, except the issuing of bank notes. A bank may purchase such real estate as may be necessary for use in its business, or which may be taken by mortgage or conveyance in payment of debts; but all property not required in transacting its business must be resold within five years. Stockholders are individually liable for the debts of the bank to the extent of the par value of the stock. The auditor of the State with the approval of the governor, shall, as often as he deems proper, appoint a suitable person, or more than one, to make an examination of the affairs of all banks established under the general banking law. The examiner so appointed must make a full detailed report of the condition of each bank to the State Auditor. Banks must also make at least five reports annually to the Auditor of State, verified by the president, or cashier or other managing agent, showing, in detail, the resources and liabilities of the institution.

Exemptions.—There is no homestead law. An exemption of $600 on any contract liability is allowed to resident householders. One month's wages is exempt from garnishment and on proceedings supplemental to execution while the employment lasts. There is no exemption as against mechanic's liens, purchase money liens and taxation. The right of exemption cannot be waived by contract.

Interest.—Legal rate is 6 per cent., but parties may contract in writing for 8 per cent. Where a contract calls for usurious interest, it is void only as to the interest in excess of 6 per cent.

Legal Holidays.—Sunday, January 1, February 22, May 30, July 4, December 25, public fast, Thanksgiving, National and State Election Days, and Labor Day.

INDIANA—Continued.

Limitation of Actions.—On accounts and contracts not in writing: for use, rents and profits of real property, and relief against frauds, six years; upon promissory notes, bills of exchange and other written contracts for the payment of money, ten years; upon contracts in writing other than those for the payment of money on judgments of courts of record, and for the recovery of the possession of real estate, twenty years.

Married Women.—By a recent act a married woman may (since May 31, 1879) buy, sell or transfer her separate personal property, as if sole; may carry on any trade, business or service, and her separate personal property is liable for the same.

Notarial Fees.—Protest, $1.25, and twenty-five cents for each notice.

Notes and Bills of Exchange.—Promissory notes payable to order or bearer at a bank in this State, and bills of exchange, are governed by the law-merchant. Promissory notes not payable at a bank are subject to any set off maker may have against payee, or any subsequent holder, accruing before notice of assignment. On these, maker must be exhausted before endorser can be sued. Protest is not necessary to hold endorsers of such notes; but, to hold them, maker must be sued at first term of court after maturity, unless it can be shown that he was insolvent at the time of such maturity. Three days of grace are allowed on all bills of exchange payable within the State, whether sight or time bills. Paper maturing on a holiday becomes payable the day preceding. Damages for protest on bills upon any person at any place out of this State, but within the United States, 5 per cent.; on bills drawn upon any person at any place without the United States, 10 per cent.

Stay of Executions.—On sums of six dollars, thirty days; over six and under twelve dollars, sixty days; over twelve and under twenty dollars, ninety days; over twenty and under forty dollars, one hundred and twenty days; over forty and under one hundred dollars, one hundred and fifty days; over one hundred dollars, one hundred and eighty days.

Transfer of Corporation Stocks.—By transfer on the books only for bridge, canal, insurance and steam packet companies. In all other corporations stock is transferred in any manner provided by the by-laws.

IOWA.

County Seat.	County.	Name of Atty.	Name of Bank.	Cashier.
Adel	Dallas.	White & Clark.	Adel State Bk.	T. J. Caldwell.
Afton	Union.	Sullivan & Sullivan.	Citizens Bk.	L. W. McLennan.
Albia	Monroe.	J. C. Mabry.	First. Natl. Bk.	T. D. Lockman.
Algona	Kossuth.	George E. Clark.	First Natl. Bk.	Wm. K. Ferguson.
Allison	Butler.	Craig, Ray & Hyde.	Bk. of Allison.	J. W. Ray.
Anamosa	Jones.	Sheean & McCarn.	Anamosa Natl. Bk.	C. S. Millard.
Atlantic	Cass.	Willard & Willard.	Atlantic Natl. Bk.	F. M. Nichols.
Audubon	Audubon.	Nash & Phelps.	First Natl. Bk.	F. S. Watts.
Bedford	Taylor.	Jackson & M ller.	Bedford Bk.	Ed. E. Cass.
Bloomfield	Davis.	Carruthers & Rominger.	State Bk. of Bloomfield	John R. Wallace.
Boone	Boone.	S. R Dyer.	City Bk.	C. J. A. Ericson.
Burlington	Des Moines.	Blake & Blake.	Natl. State Bk.	John J. Fleming.
Carroll	Carroll.	W. R. Lee.	First Natl. Bk.	R. E. Coburn.
Centerville	Appanoose.	Vermilion & Valentine.	First Natl. Bk.	J. A. Bradley.
Chariton	Lucas.	J. A. Penick.	First Natl. Bk.	F. R. Crocker.
Charles City	Floyd.	Reiniger & Lloyd.	Citizens Natl. Bk.	F. B. Miner.
Cherokee	Cherokee.	M. Wakefield.	Cherokee State Bk.	E. D. Huxford.
Clarinda	Page.	H. E. Pa-slow.	Clarinda Natl. Bk.	II. R. Spry.
Clarion	Wright.	Ladd & Rogers.	First Natl. Bk.	U. B. Tracy.
Clinton	Clinton.	George B. Phelps.	Clinton Natl. Bk.	C. C. Coan.
Concord	Hancock.	John F. Thompson.	See Britt, Commercial Bk.	E. P. Healy.
Corning	Adams.	W S. Hefling.	First Natl. Bk.	Chas. C. Norton.
Corydon	Wayne.	Miles & Steele.	Farmers & Merchants Bk.	F. M. Smith.
COUNCIL BLUFFS	Pottaw'tam.ie	Finley Burke	Citizens State Bk.	Chas. R. Hannan.
Cresco	Howard.	H. T Reed	First Natl. Bk.	C. A. Crawford.
Dakotah	Humboldt.	P. Finch	See Humboldt, Peoples Bk.	J. W. Foster.
Davenport	Scott.	J. A. Hanley	Citizens Natl. Bk.	E. S. Carl.
Decorah	Winneshiek.	R. F. B. Portman	First Natl. Bk.	E. R. Baker.
Denison	Crawford.	Shaw & Kuehnle	Bk. of Denison.	W. R. Barber.
Des Moines	Polk.	Park & Odell	Valley Natl. Bk.	R. A. Crawford.
Dubuque	Dubuque.	R. W. Stewart	First Natl. Bk.	U. E. Guernsey.
Eldora	Hardin.	Huff & Ward	Hardin Co. Bk.	Ellis D. Robb.
Elkader	Clayton.	D. D. Murphy	Elkader State Bk.	Chas. Johnson.
Emmettsburg	Palo Alto.	Kelly & Kelly	Palo Alto Co. Bk.	W. J. Brown.
Estherville	Emmet.	C. W. Crim	First Natl. Bk.	J. P. Kirby.
Fairfield	Jefferson.	Leggett & McKemy	First Natl. Bk.	B. S. McElhinny.
Forrest City	Winnebago.	C. L. Nelson	First Natl. Bk.	W. O. Hanson.
Fort Dodge	Webster.	Robert M. Wright	First Natl. Bk.	E. H. Rich.
Fort Madison	Lee.	Casey & Stewart	German American Bk.	H. D. McCoom.
Glenwood	Mills.	E. B. Woodruff	Mills Co. Natl. Bk.	A. C. Sabin.
Greenfield	Adair.	J. A. Storey	Citizens Bk.	A. P. Littleton.
Grundy Centre	Grundy.	Rea & Wood	Grundy Co. Natl. Bk.	H. S. Beckman.
Guthrie Centre	Guthrie.	E. R. Sayles	Guthrie State Bk.	E. C. Lane.
Hampton	Franklin.	John W. Luke	Citizens State Bk.	T. J. B. Robinson
Harlan	Shelby.	Byers & Lockwood	Shelby Co. Bk.	M. K. Campbell.
Ida Grove	Ida.	Warren & Johnston	Ida Co. Savings Bk.	C. J. Seldensticker
Independence	Buchanan.	Lake & Harmon	First Natl. Bk.	R. M. Campbell.
Indianola	Warren.	Lacy & Hatfield	Warren Co. Bk.	Wm. Buxton, Jr.

THE LEGAL AND FINANCIAL LIGHTS OF AMERICA.

IOWA—Continued.

County Seat.	County.	Name of Atty.	Name of Bank.	Cashier.
Iowa City	Johnson.	Baker & Ball	Citizens Saving & Trust Co.	Geo. W. Koontz.
Jefferson	Greene.	Russell & Toliver	Greene Co. State Bk.	M. M. Head.
Keosauqua	Van Buren.	Mitchell & Sloan	Keosauqua State Bk.	Jno. L. Therme.
Knoxville	Marion.	J. D. Gamble	Marion Co. Natl. Bk.	O. L. Wright.
Le Mars	Plymouth.	Strubble Bros. & Hart	First Natl. Bk.	G. L. Verull.
Leon	Decatur.	Harvey & Parrish	Exchange Bk.	J. N. Clark.
Logan	Harrison.	L. R. Bolter & Sons	State Savings Bk.	W. H. Johnson.
Manchester	Delaware.	Morris & Dunham	First Natl. Bk.	M. F. Le Roy.
Maquoketa	Jackson.	W. C. Gregory	Exchange Bk.	John L. Sloane.
Marengo	Iowa.	Hedges & Rumple	First Natl. Bk.	Q. P. Reno.
Marion	Linn.	D. E. Voris	Farmers & Merchants State Bk.	E. J. Esgate.
Marshalltown	Marshall.	Binford & Snelling	First Natl. Bk.	T. J. Fletcher.
Mason City	Cerro Gordo.	Blythe, Markley & Smith	City Natl. Bk.	A. H. Gale.
Montezuma	Poweshiek.	W. R. Lewis	First Natl. Bk.	G. W. Kieruff.
Mount Ayr	Ringgold.	R. H. Spencer	Citizens Bk.	Clyde Dunning.
Mt. Pleasant	Henry.	W. S. Withrow	Natl. State Bk.	Jas. T. Whiting.
Muscatine	Muscatine.	Richman & Burk	Hershey State Bk.	L. G. Burnett.
Nevada	Story.	George W. Dyer	First Natl. Bk.	W. F. Swayze.
New Hampton	Chickasaw.	J. R. Bane	First Natl. Bk.	T. Donovan.
Newton	Jasper.	A. M. Harrah	First Natl. Bk.	E. E. Lyday.
Northwood	Worth.	J. R. Smith	Worth Co. State Bk.	Henry T. Toye.
Onawa	Monona.	Oliver Bros. & Tillson	Onawa State Bk.	C. H. Huntington.
Orange City	Sioux.	Wm. Hutchinson	Northwestern State Bk.	A. Van der Meide.
Osage	Mitchell.	Eaton & Clyte	Osage Natl. Bk.	J. W. Annis.
Osceola	Clark.	John Chaney	Iowa State Bk.	F. W. Haskins.
Oskaloosa	Mahaska.	George C. Morgan	Oskaloosa Natl. Bk.	E. K. Himes.
Ottumwa	Wapello.	Wm. McNett	First Natl. Bk.	M. B. Hutchinson
Pocahontas	Pocahontas.	W. C. Roiston	State Bk. of Pocahontas	T. F. McCartan.
Primghar	O'Brien.	O. H. Montzheimer	First Natl. Bk.	Geo. R. Slocum.
Red Oak	Montgomery.	J. McJunkin	Red Oak Natl. Bk.	Paul P. Clark.
Rock Rapids	Lyon.	E. C. Roach	First Natl. Bk.	E. L. Partch.
Rockwell City	Calhoun.	Stevenson & Lavender	Security Bk.	Edw. W. Burch.
Sac City	Sac.	W. H. Hart	First Natl. Bk.	H. H. Allison.
Sibley	Osceola.	G. W. Lister	First Natl. Bk.	H. L. Emmert.
Sidney	Fremont.	George E. Draper	Metelman & Frazer	W. T. Frazer.
Sigourney	Keokuk.	C. H. Mackey	Keokuk Co. State Bk.	S. W. Brunt.
Sioux City	Woodbury.	J. H. & C. M. Swan	Security Natl. Bk.	F. M. Case.
Spencer	Clay.	Richardson, Buck & Kirkpatrick	First Natl. Bk.	David Painter.
Spirit Lake	Dickinson.	A. W. Osborne	First Natl. Bk.	John W. Cravens.
Storm Lake	Buena Vista.	Henry F. Galpin	First Natl. Bk.	A. H. Weitt.
Tipton	Cedar.	S. S. Wright	First Natl. Bk.	W. J. Moore.
Toledo	Tama.	Struble & Stiger	Toledo State Bk.	W. A. Dexter.
Vinton	Benton.	Whipple & Zollinger	Farmers Loan & Trust Co.	C. O. Harrington.
Wapello	Louisa.	H. O. Weaver	Wapello State Sav. Bk.	W. H. Colton.
Washington	Washington.	C. C. Patterson	Washington Natl. Bk.	John A. Yonng.
Waterloo	Black Hawk.	Franklin C. Platt	First Natl. Bk.	F. J. Eighmey.
Waukon	Allamakee.	J. F. Dayton	Citizens State Bk.	W. E. Beddow.

IOWA—Continued.

County Seat.	County.	Name of Atty.	Name of Bank.	Cashier.
Waverly	Bremer.	Gipson & Dawson	State Bk.	Louis Case.
Webster City	Hamilton.	George Wambach	Farmers Natl. Bk.	J. H. Shipp.
West Union	Fayette.	Einsworth & Einsworth	Bk. of West Union	F. Y. Whitmore.
Winterset	Madison.	Steele & Robbins	Citizens Natl. Bk.	W. J. Cornell.

DIGEST OF IOWA COMMERCIAL LAWS.

Assignments.—No general assignment of property by an insolvent, or in contemplation of insolvency, for the benefit of creditors, shall be valid unless it be made for the benefit of all his creditors in proportion to the amount of their respective claims. No preference is allowed to any creditor.

Attachments.—Attachments may issue when the defendant is a foreign corporation, or acting as such, or is a non-resident of the State; or is about to remove his property out of the State without leaving sufficient remaining for the payment of his debts; or has disposed of his property, in whole or in part, with intent to defraud his creditors; or is about to dispose of his property with intent to defraud his creditors; or has absconded, so that the ordinary process cannot be served upon him; or is about to remove permanently out of the county, and has property therein not exempt from execution, and that he refuses to pay or secure the plaintiff; or is about to remove permanently out of the State, and refuses to pay or secure the debt due the plaintiff; or is about to remove his property, or a part thereof, out of the county with intent to defraud his creditors; or is about to convert his property, or a part thereof, into money for the purpose of placing it beyond the reach of his creditors; or has property or rights in action which he conceals; or the debt is due for property obtained under false pretences.

Bank Laws.—Any number of persons may be incorporated for the transaction of the banking business, under the general incorporation laws of the State, but such association must have the word "State" incorporated and made a part of the name of the corporation, and any association not incorporated, partnership or individual, engaged in banking business, is prohibited from embracing or including in the name of such association, partnership or individual, the word "State." The capital of such banks must not be less than $50,000, except in cities or towns having a population of 3,000 or less, where they may be organized with a paid up capital of not less than $25,000. Stockholders are responsible to the amount of their stock over the stock held. In case of insolvency, bill holders are to be preferred. Suspension of specie payment is not permitted. The General Assembly, by a two-thirds vote, may amend or appeal any law, and no special or exclusive privileges may be given. A full and accurate statement, verified by the oath of the president or vice-president, or cashier, or two directors, must be made quarterly to the Auditor of the State. The Auditor may cause to be made four examinations per year of each bank. Corporations, to be known as savings banks, may be formed under acts applying only to such banks, for the purpose of receiving on deposit the savings and funds of others, and preserving and safely investing the same, and paying interest or dividends thereon; and any number of persons, not less than five, may

IOWA—Continued.

organize such savings banks with a paid up capital stock of not less than $10,000 in cities or towns of 10,000 inhabitants or under, and a paid up capital stock of not less than $50,000 in cities of over 10,000 inhabitants.

Exemptions.—The homestead must embrace the house used as a home by the owner thereof; and if he has two or more houses thus used by him at different times and places he may select which he may retain as his homestead. It may contain one or more lots or tracts of land, with the buildings thereon, and other appurtenances, subject to the limitations below set forth, but must in no case embrace different lots and tracts unless they are contiguous, or unless they are habitually and in good faith used as a part of the same homestead. If within a town plat it must not exceed one-half acre in extent, and if not within a town plat, it must not embrace in the aggregate more more than forty acres. When thus limited, if in either case its value be less than $500, it may be enlarged until its value reaches that amount. It must not embrace more than one dwelling house, or any other buildings except such as are properly appurtenant to the homestead as such; but a shop or other building situated thereon, and really used and occupied by the owner in the prosecution of his own ordinary business, and not exceeding $300 in value, may be deemed appurtenant to such homestead. It is liable for taxes accruing thereon, is subject to mechanics' liens, for work, labor or material done or furnished exclusively for the improvement of the same, and may, after all other property is exhausted, be sold on execution for debts contracted prior to its acquisition, except when purchased with pension money. A conveyance or encumbrance of a homestead by the owner is of no validity unless the husband or wife, if the owner be married, concur in and sign the same joint instrument. Personal property exempt includes tools, instruments, library, necessary team, etc., of mechanic, farmer, teacher, or professional man; wearing apparel, household and kitchen furniture, $200; certain farm animals and necessary food for six months. Foregoing relates only to residents being heads of families; unmarried persons and non-residents being only entitled to retain their own clothing and trunks, save and except pensioners. Where debtor is a printer, the printing press and types, furniture and material up to $1,200 are exempt. Earnings of debtor within ninety days of levy are exempt.

Interest.—Legal rate is 6 per cent. Parties may contract in writing for 8 per cent. Usury forfeits all interest and costs and 10 per cent of contract to school fund.

Legal Holidays.—Sunday, January 1, May 30, July 4, the first Monday in September, December 25, Thanksgiving, and Labor Day.

Limitation of Actions.—On unwritten contracts, those brought for injuries to property, or for relief on the ground of fraud in cases heretofore solely cognizable in a court of chancery, and all other actions not otherwise provided for in this respect, within five years. Those founded on written contracts, on judgment of any courts except those courts provided for in the next subdivision, and those brought for the recovery of real property, within ten years. Those founded on judgments of a court of record, whether of this State or any of the United States, or of the federal courts of the United States, within twenty years.

Married Women.—A married woman may own property in her own right, and manage, sell, convey and devise the same to the same extent as the husband can property belonging to him. Neither husband or wife are liable for the separate debts of

IOWA—Continued.

each other; with the expenses of the family and education of the children are chargeable upon the property of both husband and wife, or either of them, and in relation thereto they may be sued jointly or separately.

Notarial Fees.—Protest $1.75 and twenty-five cents additional for each notice.

Notes and Bills of Exchange.—Upon all negotiable bills or notes payable within the State, grace is allowed, and notice of non-acceptance, or non-payment, or both, is required according to the rules of commercial law. Paper falling due on holidays is payable the preceding day. Damages allowed on protested paper, 3 to 5 per cent. To hold indorser, note must be duly presented, payment refused, and indorser notified. Open accounts are assignable. Defense to non-negotiable paper and accounts accrued after notice in writing of assignment to maker invalid as against assignee, providing that if negotiable paper be obtained by fraud, the holder thereof shall recover no greater sum than he paid with interest and cost.

Stay of Executions.—On sums of less than $100 including costs, three months; over $100, six months. All judgments on which stay is taken shall bear interest at the rate of 10 per cent. per annum.

Transfer of Corporation Stocks.—The transfer of shares is not valid, except as between the parties thereto, until it is regularly entered on the books of the company, so as to show the name of the person by and to whom transferred, the numbers or other designation of the shares and the date of the transfer; but such transfer shall not in any way exempt the person making it from any liability of said corporation created prior thereto. The books of the company must be so kept as to show intelligibly the original stockholders, their respective interests, the amount paid on their shares and all transfers thereof; and such books, or a correct copy thereof, so far as the items mentioned in this section are concerned, shall be subject to the inspection of any person desiring the same.

THE LEGAL AND FINANCIAL LIGHTS OF AMERICA.

KANSAS.

County Seat.	County.	Name of Atty.	Name of Bank.	Cashier.
Abilene	Dickinson.	C. S. Crawford	Citizens Bk.	T. H. Malott.
Alma	Wabaunsee.	J. B. Barnes	Alma State Bk.	L. Paleneke.
Anthony	Harper.	George R. Snelling	First Natl. Bk.	P. G. Walton.
Ashland	Clark.	H. J. Bone	Farmers & Stockgrowers Bk.	A. M. Van Laningham.
Atchison	Atchison.	Henry Ellston	First Natl. Bk.	S. A. Frazier.
Atwood	Rawlins.	J. C. Cole	Rawlins Co. Bk.	B. D. Hensley.
Belleville	Republic.	T. M. Noble	Natl. Bk. of Belleville.	D. D. Bramwell.
Beloit	Mitchell.	A. E. Ellis	Beloit State Bk.	M. M. Rowley.
Burlington	Coffee.	G. E. Manchester	Peopels Natl. Bk.	A. P. Brigham.
Cimarron	Gray.	T. H. Reeve	Cimarron Bk.	C. S. Warner.
Clay Center	Clay.	F. L. Williams	First Natl Bk.	P. P. Kehoe.
Colby	Thomas.	Joseph A. Gill	Thomas. Co. Bk.	W. S. Ferguson.
Coldwater	Comanche.	W. J. Jackson	Comanche Co. State Bk.	J. M. Lobaugh.
Columbus	Cherokee.	W. R. Cowley	Cherokee Co. Bk.	H. A. La Rue.
Concordia	Cloud.	Caldwell & Ellis	First Natl. Bk.	W. W. Bowman.
Cottonwood Falls.	Chase.	Johnston Bros.	Chase Co. Natl. Bk.	W. W. Sanders.
Council Grove	Morris.	Bertram & Nicholson	Farmers & Drovers Bk.	A. Moser, Jr.
Dighton	Lane.	J. S. Simmons	First Natl. Bk.	F. W. King.
Dodge City	Ford.	M. W. Sutton	Bk. of Dodge City.	E. F. Kellogg.
Eldorado	Butler.	Reddem & Schumacher	Farmers & Merchants Natl. Bk.	E. C. Ellet.
Ellsworth	Ellsworth.	Ira E. Lloyd	Central Natl. Bk.	G. T. Tremble.
Emporia	Lyon.	L. B. Kellogg	First Natl. Bk.	D. M. Davis.
Erie	Neosho.	J. L. Denison	Bk. of Erie.	C. C. Dutoon.
Eureka	Greenwood.	W. S. Marlin	First Natl Bk.	Ira P. Nye.
Fort Scott	Bourbon.	Perry & Crain	Bk. of Ft. Scott.	C. F. Martin.
Fredonia	Wilson.	S. S. Kirkpatrick	Wilson Co. Bk.	J. D. Allen.
Garden City	Finney.	H. F. Mason	First Natl. Bk.	D. R. Menke.
Garnett	Anderson.	Walter Latimer	First Natl. Bk.	Ed. L. Foster.
Girard	Crawford.	Brown & Russel	First Natl. Bk.	J. T. Leonard.
Gove	Gove.	R. C. Jones	Exchange Bk.	G. A. Jones.
Goodland	Sherman.	Hoyt Andrews	Sherman Co. Bk.	J. M. Jordan.
Great Bend	Barton.	Swartz & Smith	J. V. Brinkman Co. Bk.	Louis Zutavern.
Greensburgh	Kiowa.	T. E. Dempey	See Pratt.	
Hays City	Ellis.	A. J. Bryant	Bk. of Hays City.	L. G. Little.
Hiawatha	Brown.	James Falloon	Morrill & Janes Bk.	C. D. Lamme.
Hill City	Graham.	H. M. Baldwin	Farmers & Merchants Bk.	H. W. Robinson.
Holton	Jackson.	J. H. Lowell	State Bk. of Holton.	A. Dunn, Jr.
Howard	Elk.	John Marshall	First Natl. Bk.	C. F. Plowman.
Hoxie	Sheridan.	M. A. Chambers	Sheridan Co. Bk.	P. G. Walker.
Hugoton	Stevens.	Wm. O'Conner	See Meade.	
Hutchinson	Reno.	Hettinger Bros.	First Natl. Bk.	E. L. Meyer.
Independence	Montgomery.	Ziegler & Ziegler	Commercial Natl. Bk.	G. T. Guernsey.
Iola	Allen.	Campbell & Hawkins	Bk of Allen Co.	H. M. Miller.
Jetmore	Hodgeman.	W. S. Kenyon	First State Bk.	C. E. Wilson.
Johnson	Stanton.	A. B. Reeves	See Syracuse	
Junction City	Geary.	Humphrey & Laundy	First Natl. Bk.	C. W. Strickland.
Kansas City	Wyandotte.	Miller & Morris	Wyandotte Natl. Bk.	C. W. Trickett.

THE LEGAL AND FINANCIAL LIGHTS OF AMERICA. 53

KANSAS—Continued.

County Seat.	County.	Name of Atty.	Name of Bank.	Cashier.
Kingman	Kingman.	Hay & Hay	First Natl. Bk.	A. C. Tredick.
Kinsley	Edwards.	F. D. Smith	Kinsley Bk.	F. B. Hine.
La Crosse	Rush.	H. L. Anderson	First Natl. Bk.	H. L. Baker.
Lakin	Kearney.	M. G. Kelso	Kearney Co. Bk.	B. B. Bacon.
Larned	Pawnee.	W. H. Vernon	First Natl. Bk.	O. F. Norwood.
Lawrence	Douglass.	S. O. Thacher	Lawrence Natl. Bk.	W. L. Howe.
Leavenworth	Leavenworth.	W. C. Hook	Leavenworth Natl. Bk.	Edward Carroll.
Leoti	Wichita.	J. S. Caldwell	First State Bk.	I. B. Martin.
Lincoln	Lincoln.	C. B. Daughters	Lincoln State Bk.	Frank F. Chase.
Lyndon	Osage.	J. H. Stavely	Peoples State Bk.	A. L. Wilson.
Lyons	Rice.	Jones & Jones	Lyons Exchange Bk.	J. H. Eble.
McPherson	McPherson.	Grattam & Grattam	First Natl. Bk.	A. E. Dwelle.
Manhattan	Itiley.	John E. Hessin	First Natl. Bk.	G. S. Murphy.
Mankato	Jewell.	G. H. Bailey	Bk. of Mankato	J. P. Fair.
Marion	Marion.	H. A. McLean.	First State Bk.	C. H. Curtsi.
Marysville	Marshall.	J. A. Broughten	Exchange Bk.	Chas. D. Schmidt.
Meade	Meade.	Bodle & Bodle	Stockgrowers & Farmers Bk.	O. Hamilton.
MEDICINE LODGE	Barbour.	G. M Martin	Citizens State Bk.	F. B. Chapin.
Minneapolis	Ottawa.	Rees & Tomlinson	Citizens Natl. Bk.	J. W. Smith.
Mound City	Linn.	James D. Snoddy	Farmers & Merchants Bk.	H. C. Reese.
Ness City	Ness.	Thomas Berry	First Natl. Bk.	C. L. Rogers.
Newton	Harvey.	Bowman & Bucher	First Natl. Bk.	A. B. Gilbert.
Norton	Norton.	L. H. Wilder	First Natl. Bk.	F. S. Hazelton.
Oakley	Logan.	K. E. Wilcockson	Bk. of Oakley.	H. F. Gressler.
Oberlin	Decatur.	Bertram & McElroy	Oberlin Natl. Bk.	Otis L. Benton.
Olathe	Johnson.	Parker & Hamilton	First Natl. Bk.	J. L. Price.
Osborne	Osborne.	Robinson & McBride	First Natl. Bk.	Grover Walker.
Oskaloosa	Jefferson.	Marshall Gephard	Jefferson Co. Bk.	M. L. Critchfield.
Oswego	Labette.	Nelson Case	Labette Co. Bk.	J. M. Berry.
Ottawa	Franklin.	Wm. H. Clark.	Peoples Natl. Bk.	Peter Shiras.
Paola	Miami.	John C. Sheridan	Miami Co. Natl. Bk.	Wm. Crowell.
PHILLIPSBURGH	Phillips.	C. L. Lewis	First Natl. Bk.	W. D. Granger.
Pratt	Pratt.	Thompson & Apt	First Natl. Bk.	G. Corlander.
Richfield	Morton.	G. P. Craddock	See Meade	
Russell	Russell.	Sutton & Russell	Russell State Bk.	Albert Yoxall.
Salina	Saline.	Milliken & Musser.	Natl. Bk. of America	Frank Hageman-
Santa Fe	Haskell.		See Cimarron	
Scott	Scott.	Travis Morse	Bk. of Scott City	S. C. Grable.
Sedan	Chautauqua.	Hill, Fitzpatrick & McGuire.	First Natl. Bk.	J. T. Bradley.
Seneca	Nemaha.	S. K. Woodworth	State Bk. of Seneca	John A Gilchrist.
SharonSprings	Wallace.	W. S. Roark	Bk. of Sharon Springs	
Smith Center	Smith.	L. C. Uhl	First Natl. Bk.	J. D. Mossman.
Springfield	Seward.	W. A. Flush	See Meade	
St. Francis	Cheyenne.	Thomas F. Eagan	Bk. of St. Francis	W. C. Willits.
St. John	Stafford.	Moseley & Dixon	St. John State Bk.	Howard Gray.
Stockton	Roks.	W. B. Ham	Exchange Bk.	E. J. Williams.
Syracuse	Hamilton.	George Getty	Bk. of Syracuse	W. F. Reed & Co.
Topeka	Shawnee.	J. D. McFarland	Bk. of Topeka	J. W. Thurston.
Tribune	Greeley.	W. M. Glenn	Bk. of Tribune	C. E. Wightman.

THE LEGAL AND FINANCIAL LIGHTS OF AMERICA.

KANSAS—Continued.

County Seat.	County.	Name of Atty.	Name of Bank.	Cashier.
Troy	Doniphan.	C. C. Camp	Bk. of Troy	H. L. Boder.
Ulysses	Grant.	J. W. Jordan	At Lakin, Kearney Co. Bk.	B. B. Bacon.
Wa Keeney	Trego.	W. E. Saum	Wa Keeney State Bk.	R. C. Wilson.
Washington	Washington.	Charles Smith	Washington Natl. Bk.	J. S. Alspaugh.
Wellington	Sumner.	W. W. Schwinn	Wellington Natl. Bk.	W. H. Burks.
Westmoreland	Pottawatomic	Smith & Badgley	First Natl. Bk.	Warren Anthony.
Wichita	Sedgwick.	Campbell & Dyer	Fourth Natl. Bk.	J. M. Moore.
Winfield	Cowley.	J. C. Pollock	Winfield Natl. Bk.	Wm. E. Otis.
Yates Center	Woodson.	J. E. Wirick	Yates Center Bk.	H. H. Winter.

DIGEST OF KANSAS COMMERCIAL LAWS.

Assignments.—Assignments may be made for the benefit of all creditors, without preference.

Attachments.—An attachment will be issued when the defendant is a foreign corporation or a non-resident of the State (but in this case for no other claim than a demand arising upon contract, judgment or decree, unless the cause of action arose wholly within the limits of this State); where the defendant has absconded with the intent of defrauding his creditors; where the defendant has left the county of his residence to avoid the service of his summons; or so conceals himself that a summons cannot be served upon him; or is about to remove his property, or a part thereof, out of the jurisdiction of the court; or is about to convert his property, or a part thereof, into money for the purpose of placing it beyond the reach of his creditors; or has property or rights in action which he conceals; or has assigned, removed or disposed of, or is about to dispose of his property, or a part thereof; or fraudulently contracted the debt or incurred the debt, liability or obligation.

Bank Laws.—Any five or more persons in this State may organize themselves into a banking association, and shall be permitted to carry on the business of receiving money on deposit and to allow interest thereon, giving to the person depositing credit therefor; and of buying and selling exchange, gold, silver, coin, bullion, uncurrent money, bonds of the United States, of the State of Kansas, and of the city, county and school district in which any association shall be organized; of loaning money on real estate and personal security, at a rate of interest not to exceed the legal rate allowed to banks; and of discounting negotiable notes and notes not negotiable. The name selected for such bank shall not be the name of any other bank doing business in the State. The capital stock shall not be less than $50,000, of which half must be paid in before commencing business and not less than 10 per cent. each month thereafter until all is paid. Capital may be increased, the increase to be paid in full. Twenty per cent. of deposits must be kept on hand or on deposit with solvent banks, at least half of which must be in cash on hand. Not more than 12 per cent. of capital and surplus shall be loaned to one debtor. Officers criminally liable for receiving deposits when bank is insolvent. Dividends can only be paid out of net profits after deducting bad debts. Private banks are subjected to the provisions of the law. The Bank Commissioner or deputy must make examination of each bank at least once a year. Four reports per annum are required and the Commissioner may call for others. The reports are practically the same as those required of national banks. Refusal to comply with the law forfeits charter.

KANSAS—Continued.

Exemptions.—One hundred and sixty acres farming land or one acre in incorporated city, with all improvements thereon, while occupied by family of owner, cannot be alienated, except by joint consent of husband and wife. No exemption for purchase money or for improvements erected on homestead. Every person being the head of a family shall have exempt personal property not exceeding $500; cattle, implements, etc., not exceeding $300; grain, meat, vegetables, groceries, etc., for the family for one year; the tools and implements of any mechanic, minor, or other person, and in addition thereto stock-in-trade not exceeding $400 in value, library, implements, and office furniture of any professional man. Residents, not the head of a family, have tools, implements, and stock-in-trade up to $400 exempt from execution.

Interest.—Six per cent. May contract in writing for 10; if more than 10 per cent. is contracted for, double the excess of 10 per cent. is forfeited. Usury does not affect *bona fide* holder of negotiable paper without notice, but after payment double the excess paid may be recovered back of person originally exacting the usury, if suit be brought within ninety days after maturity of such paper.

Legal Holidays.—Sunday, January 1, May 30, July 4, December 25, Public Fast and Thanksgiving, Labor Day.

Limitation of Actions.—An action upon any agreement, contract or promise in writing, within five years. An action on a contract not in writing, express or implied, on a liability created by statute other than a forfeiture or a penalty, within three years. An action for trespass upon real property for taking, detaining or injuring personal property, including replevin, for injury to the rights of another, not hereinafter enumerated, for relief on the ground of fraud, within two years; in case of fraud, cause of action does not accrue until discovery of the fraud.

Married Women.—The property, real and personal, which any woman in this State may own at the time of her marriage, or which may come to her otherwise than by her husband, shall remain her sole and separate property, and not to be subject to the disposal of her husband or liable for his debts. A woman may, while married, sue and be sued in the same manner as if she were unmarried.

Notarial Fees.—Protest, $1.50.

Notes and Bills of Exchange.—All bonds, notes, and bills of exchange, foreign and inland, drawn for any sum or sums of money, and made payable to any person or bearer shall be negotiable by indorsement thereon if payable to order, and by delivery if payable to bearer, so as to absolutely transfer and vest the property thereof in each and every indorsee or holder, successively. No person or persons, bank or body corporate, residing or doing business within the limits of this State, can be held liable for protest damages on any bond, note or bill protested for non-acceptance or non-payment. All bonds, notes and bills of exchange, except bank checks and sight drafts made negotiable, shall be entitled to three days' grace. Paper maturing on a holiday becomes due on the day previous.

Stay of Executions.—In Justice Courts, by filing bond, on twenty dollars and under, thirty days; twenty to fifty dollars, sixty days; fifty to one hundred dollars, ninety days; over one hundred dollars, one hundred and twenty days.

Transfer of Corporation Stocks.—Shares of stock may be transferred by endorsement, on the books of the company, or as prescribed by the by-laws. The mere assignment and delivery of stock certificates does not divest the tranferrer of individual liability until the stock sold has been transferred on the books of the corporation.

THE LEGAL AND FINANCIAL LIGHTS OF AMERICA.

KENTUCKY.

County Seat.	County.	Name of Atty.	Name of Bank.	Cashier.
Albany	Clinton.	S. C. Hardin	See Somerset	
Barboursville	Knox.	John Dishman	Bk. of John A. Black	
Bardstown	Nelson.	John D. Wickliffe	Bk. of Wilson & Muir	Eugene Wilson.
Bardwell	Carlisle.	J. A. Ray	Bardwell Deposit Bk.	H. H. Loving.
Beattyville	Lee.	G. W. Gourley	See Richmond	
Bedford	Trimble.	W. F. Peak	Bedford Loan & Dep. Bk.	W. R. Logan.
Benton	Marshall.	J. W. Dyens	Bk. of Benton	Solon L. Palmer.
Booneville	Owsley.	J. M. Sebastien	See Richmond	
BOWLING GREEN	Warren.	John M. Galloway	Potters Bk.	J. E. Potter.
BRANDENBURGH	Meade.	J. W. Lewis	Meade Co. Deposit Bk.	J. L. Fairleigh.
Brookville	Bracken.	H. P. Willis	Bracken Co. Bk.	Y. Alexander.
Brownsville	Edmundson.	A. A. Sturgeon	Bk. at Smiths Grove, Deposit Bk.	E. Bland.
Burkesville	Cumberland.	M. O. Allen	Bk. of Cumberland	J. A. Dixon.
Burlington	Boone.	F. Riddell	Bocne Co. Dep. Bk.	J. C. Revill.
Cadis	Trigg.	R. A. Burnett	Trigg Co. Farmers Bk.	E. R. Street.
Calhoun	McLean.	Wm. B. Noe	Bk. of Calhoun	A. L. Moseley.
CAMPBELLSVILLE	Taylor.	J. R. Robinson	Bk. of Campbellsville	John N. Turner.
Campton	Wolfe.	Joseph C. Lykins	At Clay City, Clay City Natl. Bk.	J. F. Cox.
Carlisle	Nicholas.	H. Kennedy	Deposit Bk.	F. E. Congleton.
Carrollton	Carroll.	E. C. Smith	First Natl. Bk.	John M. Giltner.
Cattlesburgh	Boyd.	Thomas R. Brown	Cattlesburgh Natl. Bk.	James Trimble.
Clinton	Hickman.	George W. Griffey	Clinton Bk.	J. M. Ringo.
Columbia	Adair.	H B. Miller	Bk. of Columbia.	J. Coffey.
Covington	Kenton.	Chas. S. Furber	Citizens Natl. Bk.	Wm. G. Allen.
Cynthiana	Harrison.	Blanton & Berry	Natl. Bk. of Cynthiana	J. S. Withers.
Danville	Boyle.	R. P. Jacobs	Boyle Natl. Bk.	II. G. Sanifer.
Dixon	Webster.	F. M. Baker	Dixon Bk.	C. A. Davis.
Eddyville	Lyon.	T. J. Watkins	Farmers Bk.	M. P. Molloy.
Edmonton	Metcalf.	J. C. Muncie	See Columbia	
ELIZABETHTOWN	Hardin.	S. H. Bush	Bk. of Elizabethtown	W.C.Montgomery
Elkton	Todd.	H. G. Petrie	Farmers & Merchants Bk.	S. H. Perkins.
Falmouth	Pendleton.	L. T. Applegate	Falmouth Dep. Bk.	J. E. Bohennon.
Flemingburg	Fleming.	W. G. Dearing	Fleming Co. Farmers Bk.	John W. Heflin.
Frankfort	Franklin.	John W. Rodman	State Natl. Bk.	C. E. Hoge.
Franklin	Simpson.	Walker & Walker	Simpson Co. Bk.	A. T. Bradley.
Frenchburg	Menifee.	J. H. Williams	See Mt. Sterling	
Georgetown	Scott.	James Y. Kelly	First Natl. Bk.	W. G. Abbett.
Glasgow	Barren.	Boles & Duff	First Natl. Bk.	W. B. Smith.
Grayson	Carter.	Frank Powers	Commercial Bk.	A. T. Henderson.
Greensburgh	Green.	Jeff. Henry	Greensburgh Dep. Bk.	B. W. Penick.
Greenup	Greenup.	B. E. Roe	Farmers & Merchants Bk.	J. E. Pollock.
Greensville	Muhlenburgh	W. A. Wickliffe	First Natl. Bk.	Edgar D. Martin.
HARDINSBURGH	Breckenridge.	Morris Eskridge	Bk. of Hardinsburgh	M. H. Beard.
Harlan	Harlan.	W. F. Hall	See Pineville	
Harrodsburg	Mercer.	Bell & Bell	First Natl. Bk.	H. C. Bohom.
Hartford	Ohio.	Taylor & McHenry	Bk. of Hartford	John C. Riley.
Hawesville	Hancock.	T. B. White	Hancock Dep. Bk.	W. S. Thomas.

THE LEGAL AND FINANCIAL LIGHTS OF AMERICA.

KENTUCKY—Continued.

County Seat.	County.	Name of Atty.	Name of Bank.	Cashier.
Hazard	Perry.	J. H. Combes	See Manchester	
Henderson	Henderson.	Yeaman & Lockett	Planters State Bk.	David Banks.
Hickman	Fulton.	B. T. Davis.	Hickman Bk.	W. C. Johnson.
Hindman	Knott.	Tyne & Adams	See Pikeville	
Hodgenville	La Rue.	D. H. Smith	La Rue Co. Dep. Bk.	J. W. Muir, Jr.
Hopkinsville	Christian.	Petree & Downer	City Bk.	W. T. Tandy.
Hyden	Leslie.	John L. Dixon	See Manchester	
Inez	Martin.	J. S. Patton	See Pikeville.	
Irvine	Estill.	V. P. Smith	See Richmond	
Jackson	Brethitt.	D. S. Hobson	At Clay City, Clay City Natl. Bk.	J. F. Cox.
Jamestown	Russell.	Jas. F. Montgomery	See Columbia	
La Grange	Oldham.	A. T. Ladd	Oldham Bk.	J. T. Wilson.
Lancaster	Garrard.	Wm. Hearndon	Citizens Natl. Bk.	B. F. Hudson.
LAWRENCEBURGH	Anderson.	F. R. Feland	Lawrenceburgh Bk.	J. M. Johnson.
Lebanon	Marion.	Sam. T. Spaulding	Marion Natl. Bk.	J. M. Knott.
Leitchfield	Grayson.	G. W. Stone	Grayson Co. Bk.	G. W. Long.
Lexington	Fayette.	Thornton & Kerr	Phoenix Natl. Bk.	J. W. Rodes.
Liberty	Casey.	Silas Adams	See Campbellsville	
London	Laurel.	W. S. Jackson	First Natl. Bk.	R. M. Jackson.
Louisa	Lawrence.	Alex. Lackey	Bk. of Louisa	G. R. Vinson.
Louisville	Jefferson.	Barnett, Miller & Barnett	Union Natl. Bk.	L. O. Cox.
McKee	Jackson.	W. H. Clark	See Richmond	
Madisonville	Hopkins.	Waddill & Nunn	Bk. of John G. Morton	W. C. Morton.
Manchester	Clay.	J. H. Garrard	Bk. of Manchester	R. C. Ford.
Marion	Crittenden.	James & James	Marion Bk.	Thos. J. Yandell.
Mayfield	Graves.	W. W. Robertson	Bk. of Mayfield	R. A. Mayes.
Maysville	Mason.	Cochran & Sons	First Natl. Bk.	W. W. Ball.
Monticello	Wayne.	Joseph Bertram	Monticello Bkg. Co.	W. L. Baker.
Morehead	Rowan.	John R. Powers	See Mt. Sterling	
Morganfield	Union.	Adair & Morton	Peoples Bk.	W. M. Morgan.
Morgantown	Butler.	W. A. Helm	Morgantown Dep. Bk.	John M. Carson.
Mt. Olivet	Robertson.	J. J. Osborne	Mt. Olivet Dep. Bk.	A. S. Rice.
Mount Sterling	Montgomery.	J. Grand, R. H. Winn	Mt. Sterling Natl. Bk.	Pierce Winn.
Mount Vernon	Rock Castle.	C. C. Williams	See Stanford	
Munfordville	Hart.	H. W. Curle	Hart Co. Dep. & Tr. Co.	George D. Mintz.
Murry	Calloway.	T. P. Cook	Bk. of Murry.	W. P. Gatlin.
New Castle	Henry.	J. D. Carroll	Bk. of New Castle.	J. W. Mathews.
Newport	Campbell.	Will H. Lyons	First Natl. Bk.	T. B. Younteey.
Nicholasville	Jesamine.	J. S. Bronaugh & Son	Farmers Ex. Bk.	B. M. Arnett.
Owensboro'	Daviess.	Sweeney, Ellis & Sweeney	Owensboro' Natl. Bk.	Lawson Reno.
Owenton	Owen.	E. E. Settle	Farmers Natl. Bk.	J. Holbrook.
Owingsville	Bath.	R. Gudgell & Son	Farmers Bk.	H. S. Goodpaster.
Paducah	McCracken.	Greer & Reed	First Natl. Bk.	T. A. Baker.
Paintsville	Johnson.	J. P. Wells	See Louisa	
Paris	Bourbon.	Mann & Ashbrook	Agricultural Bk.	Henry Spears.
Pikeville	Pike.	Connolly & Connolly	Bk. of Pikeville	L. J. Williamson
Pineville	Bell.	D. B. Logan	First Natl. Bk.	J. R. Rice.
Prestonburg	Floyd.	F. A. Hopkins	The Bk. of Josephine	A. J. Davidson.

KENTUCKY—Continued.

County Seat.	County.	Name of Atty.	Name of Bank.	Cashier.
Princeton	Caldwell.	Wm. Marble	First Natl. Bk.	Edward Garrett.
Richmond	Madison.	J. A. Sullivan	Madison Natl. Bk.	C. D. Chenault.
Russelville	Logan.	S. R. Crewdson	Logan Co. Bk.	H. B. Caldwell.
Salyersville	Magoffin.	T. J. Arnett	See Prestonburg	
Sandy Hook	Elliott.	M. M. Redwine	See Louisa	
Scottsville	Allen.	J. J. Gatewood	See Franklin	
Shelbyville	Shelby.	T. J. Beard	Citizens Bk.	J. C. Burnett.
SHEPHERDSVILLE	Bullitt.	J. F. Combs	Bullitt Co. Bk.	C. F. Troutman.
Smitland	Livingston.	J. W. Bush	See Paducah	
Somerset	Pulaski.	O. H. Waddle	First Natl. Bk.	J. A. McGee.
Springfield	Washington.	Thomas W. Simms, Jr.	First Natl. Bk.	A. C. McElroy.
Stanford	Lincoln.	J. B. Paxton	First Natl. Bk.	J. J. McRoberts.
Stanton	Powell.	John D. Atkinson	See Winchester	
Taylorsville	Spencer.	L. B. Brown	Bk. of Taylorsville	H. H. Mathis.
TOMPKINSVILLE	Monroe.	M. T. Flippin	Dep. Bk. of Monroe Co.	J. H. Richardson.
Vanceburgh	Lewis.	Thomas & Pugh	Deposit Bk.	Thomas S. Clark.
Versailles	Woodford.	E. M. Wallace	Bk. of J. Amsden & Co.	J. P. Amsden.
Warsaw	Gallatin.	D. E. Castleman	Warsaw Dep. Bk.	J. E. Mountjoy.
West Liberty	Morgan.	S. J. Sayler	See Grayson	
Whitesburgh	Letcher.	J. P. Mares	See Pikeville	
Wickliffe	Ballard.	White & White	See Bardwell	
WILLIAMSBURGH	Whitley.	R. D. Hill	Bk. of Williamsburgh	John W. Siler.
WILLIAMSTOWN	Grant.	A. G. Dejarnette	Grant Co. Dep. Bk.	C. C. Nespitt.
Winchester	Clark.	Beckner & Jouett	Clark Co. National Bk.	B. F. Curtis.

DIGEST OF KENTUCKY COMMERCIAL LAWS.

Assignments.—Voluntary assignments for the benefit of all creditors are governed by common law rules, the State having no statute regulating the same. Disposing of property by an insolvent debtor for the purpose of preference or defrauding creditors, operates under statute as an assignment for the benefit of all creditors.

Attachments.—Grounds of attachment: Non-residence of the defendant or foreign corporation; or has been absent from the State four months; or has departed this State with intent to defraud creditors; or has left the county of his residence to avoid service of summons, or conceals himself to avoid service of summons; or is about to remove, or has removed his property, or a material part thereof, out of this State, not leaving enough to satisfy plaintiff's claim; or has sold or disposed of his property with intent to defraud, hinder or delay creditors; or is about to sell, convey, or otherwise dispose of his property with such intent.

Bank Laws.—State banks are only chartered by the Legislature. There is no supervision of banks by the State authorities, but such banks are required to make and publish semi-annually, on the first of January and July, a statement of their condition, verified under oath, and a copy of this statement must also be filed with the State Auditor. Minors and married women may make deposits in their own names, and draw checks on the same as if of full age or unmarried.

KENTUCKY—Continued.

Exemptions.—Homestead not to exceed in value $1,000, is exempt to the head of the family when occupied by the family, and can be conveyed by joint deed of husband or wife.

Interest.—Legal rate is 6 per cent. All usurious contracts are void to the extent of the usury. Usury paid to assignee of the lender may be recovered of the lender. Usury paid may be recovered.

Legal Holidays.—Sunday, January 1, February 22, July 4, December 25, Public Fast and Thanksgiving, Decoration Day and Labor Day.

Limitation of Actions.—On judgments, notes and bonds, fifteen years; contracts not in writing, five years; for personal injuries, by railroads and other companies, seduction, slander, etc., one year. For the recovery of real estate the action is barred ordinarily in fifteen years from the accruing of the action.

Married Women.—Can bind her general real estate for her husband's debt only by mortgage, executed by herself; and husband cannot bind her general estate by note or otherwise, except by a lease for a term not exceeding three years, may be empowered by a Court of Equity to trade as a *femme sole*.

Notarial Fees.—Protest $1.25 and twenty-five cents for each endorser.

Notes and Bills of Exchange.—All bills of exchange are negotiable, but notes are only made so when "payable and negotiable at a bank." Non-negotiable instruments are assignable so as to vest a right of action in the assignee, but any defense good against the payee and arising before notice of the assignment is good against the assignee. Indorsers of non-negotiable notes can only be held after suit and return of "no property" against the maker commenced and prosecuted with due diligence. Three days of grace are allowed by custom. Paper maturing on a holiday becomes due the day preceding. Protest should be made upon the last day of grace. It is essential to a recovery against indorsers on foreign bills of negotiable notes placed in their rank, but an inland bill is not required by law to be protested, nor is a certificate of a notary of such protest evidence of itself of dishonor.

Stay of Executions.—An execution may be replevied for three months at any time before sale by defendant giving good security.

Transfer of Corporation Stocks.—Transferable on the books of the corporation.

LOUISIANA.

County Seat.	County.	Name of Atty.	Name of Bank.	Cashier.
Abbeville	Vermillion.	W. W. Edwards.	Bk. of Abbeville	L. O. Droussard.
Alexandria	Rapides.	White & Thornton	Rapides Bk.	Charles Owen.
Amite City	Tangipahoa.	Wm. B. Kemp	At Hammond, Bk. of Hammond	Arthur Tong.
Arcadia	Bienville.	J. E. Reynolds	Bk. of North Louisiana	S. W. Smith, Jr.
Bastrop	Morehouse.	Bussey & Naft	Bastrop State Bk.	Alex. B. Markx.
Baton Rouge	EBatonRouge	Kernan & Laycock	Bk. of Baton Rouge	Joseph Gebelin.
Bayou Sara	W. Feliciana.	S. McLawrason	Bk. of West Feliciana	E. J. Buck.
Benton	Bossier.		See Shreveport	
Cameron	Cameron.	Alexandre Dupuis	See Lake Charles	
Clinton	E. Feliciana.	W. F. Kernen	See Bayou Sara	
Colfax	Grant.	W. C. Roberts	See Alexandria	
Columbia	Caldwell.	S. H. Gilbert	See Monroe	
Convent	St. James.	Sims & Poche	See Donaldsonville	
Conshatta	Red River.	J. C. Eagan	See Minden	
Covington	St.Tammany.	F. F. Guyot	See New Orleans	
Crowley	Acadia.	P. J. Chappin	Crowley State Bk.	W. E. Ellis.
DONALDSONVILLE	Ascension.	Paul Leche	Bk. of Donaldsonville	W. D. Park.
Edgard	St.J.Baptiste.		See New Orleans	
Farmersville	Union.	Dawkins & Dawkins	See Ruston	
Floyd	West Carroll.	R. J. Loudon	See Bastrop	
Franklin	St. Mary's.	P. H. Mentz	First Natl. Bk.	H. S. Palfrey.
Franklinton	Washington.		At Hammond, Bk. of Hammond	Arthur Tong.
Greensburg	St. Helena.	Wright & Lea	See Bayou Sara	
Gretna	Jefferson.	A. E. Billings	See New Orleans	
Hahnville	St. Charles.	Charles Baquie	See New Orleans	
HARRISONBURGH	Catahoula.	D. N. Thompson	See Alexandria	
Homer	Claiborne.	J. W. Holbert	Homer Natl. Bk.	C. O. Ferguson.
Homna	Terre Bonne.	Winchester & Bryant	Bk. of Homna	Joseph H.Pullem.
Lafayette	Lafayette.	C. Deballion	Peoples State Bk.	Crow Girard.
Lake Charles	Calcasieu.	D. B. Gorham	First Natl. Bk.	A. L. Williams.
LAKE PROVIDENCE	E. Carroll.	Ransdell & Ransdell	See Bastrop	
Leesville	Vernon.	D. Searborough	See Alexandria	
Mansfield	De Soto.	E. W. Sutherlin	Bk. of Mansfield	Oscar M. Nileon.
Many	Sabine.	Ponder & Sorrelle	See Natchitoches	
Marksville	Avoyelles.	J. M. Edwards	See Alexandria	
Minden	Webster.	L. K. Watkins	Bk. of Minden	Robert H. Miller.
Monroe	Ouachita.	Stubbs & Russell	Ouachita Natl. Bk.	J. J. Jordan.
Napoleonville	Assumption.	Pugh, Pugh & Markx	See Thibodeaux	
Natchitoches	Natchitoches.	John M. Tucker	Exchange Bk.	J. C. Trichel, Jr.
New Iberia	Iberia.	Foster & Drousard	New Iberia Natl. Bk.	P. L. Renoudet.
New Orleans	Orleans.	Branch K. Miller	Whitney Natl. Bk.	J. M. Pagaud, Jr.
New Roades	Point Coupee.	Yaist & Clabone	See Bayou Sara	
Opelousas	St. Landry.	Kenneth Balillo	St. Landry State Bk.	J. T. Skipper.
Plaquemine	Iberville.	Alex. Herbert	Bk. of Plaquemine	J. M. McClure.
POINTE A LA HACHE	Plaquemines.		See New Orleans	
Port Allen	WBatonRouge	J. E. Le Blane, Jr.	See Baton Rouge	

LOUISIANA—Continued.

County Seat. County.	Name of Atty.	Name of Bank.	Cashier.
Port Vincent..Livingston.	See Baton Rouge		
Rayville........Richland.	Wells & Wells	See Bastrop	
Ruston..........Lincoln.	E. M. Graham	Ruston State Bk.	E. H. Maifield.
Shreveport....Caddo.	Wise & Herndon	Commercial Natl. Bk.	J. H. Ross.
St. Bernard....St. Bernard.	See New Orleans		
St. Joseph......Tensas.	Clinton & Ganett	See Port Gibson, Miss.	
ST. MARTINVILLE..St. Martin.	R. Martin	Bk. of St. Martinville	A. Bienvenu.
Tallulah........Madison.	W. M. Murphy	See Vicksburg, Miss.	
Thibodeaux...La Fourche.	T. A. Bodeaux	Bk. of Thibodeaux	C. P. Shaver.
Vernon..........Jackson.	N. M. Smith	See Rouston	
Vidalia..........Concordia.	York & Young	See Natches, Miss.	
Winnfield......Winn.	S. M. Brian	See Alexandria	
WINNSBOROUGH...Franklin.	C. L. Berry	See Bastrop	

DIGEST OF LOUISIANA COMMERCIAL LAWS.

Assignments.—An insolvent debtor may make surrender of property to creditors, or an involuntary surrender may be forced by any creditor who shall issue an execution which is returned unsatisfied.

Attachments.—Attachment issued whenever the debtor resides out of the State; has, or is about permanently to leave it, conceals himself in order to avoid service of citation; when he has mortgaged, assigned or disposed of, or is about to mortgage, assign or dispose of his property, rights or credits, or some part thereof, with intent to defraud his creditors, or give an undue preference to some of them; when he has converted, or is about to convert, his property into money or evidences of debt, with intent to place his property beyond the reach of his creditors. Whenever the debtor is about to remove his property out of the State before the debt becomes due, non-resident creditors are entitled to the writ to enforce their claims same as resident creditors.

Bank Laws.—Banking corporations must be organized under the general free banking laws. The number of persons organizing must exceed five. No special acts of incorporation can be passed. There are no laws requiring savings banks to invest in any particular class of bonds. There are seven banks in the City of New Orleans still doing business under State charters. Charters are granted for a period not exceeding ninety-nine years. Notes for circulation, secured by public bonds deposited with State Auditor, may be issued. Banks must make and publish quarterly statements. Stockholders are liable for the par value of stock only. Savings, safe deposit and trust banks may be organized without power to issue bank notes.

Exemptions.—To head of family, real estate, if owned and occupied as a residence, together with certain furniture, stock, implements, provisions, etc., the property not to exceed $2,000, and no exemption if wife has separate property worth over $2,000.

LOUISIANA—Continued.

Interest.—Legal rate is 5 per cent., but 8 per cent. may be agreed upon. If higher than 8 per cent. be charged, such charge forfeits entire interest. If paid it may be sued for and recovered within twelve months. But a higher rate may be recovered if included in the principal of the note.

Legal Holidays.—Sunday, January 1, January 8, February 22, Mardi-Gras, July 4, November 25 (Labor Day), December 25, Good Friday, Thanksgiving Day, designated by the President and every Saturday from noon until midnight, March 4, in New Orleans, November 1.

Limitation of Actions.—Open accounts are prescribed in three years; closed acknowledged accounts in ten years; notes in five.

Married Women.—In the absence of ante-nuptial contract, all property acquired in the marriage belongs to the "Community of gains," and all debts contracted during the same period must be discharged by the "community." The husband is the manager of the "community," and binds it by his contracts.

Notarial Fees.—Protest $2.50 to $3.50.

Notes and Bills of Exchange.—Whenever a promissory note is endorsed for the benefit of the maker thereof, if caused by the maker to be discounted in any bank in operation within the State, or if the maker obtain any money in consideration of said note from any person, the indorser shall be bound to the holders of the note as if it had been discounted or negotiated for his own use or benefit. Bills and notes, or other obligations for the payment of money, to be evidence of a debt, must express the whole sum in writing. Bills and notes are entitled to three days' grace, except bills at sight or order for money on demand, which are allowed no grace. Paper falling due on holiday is payable the business day following.

Stay of Executions.—May be applied for at any time.

Transfer of Corporation Stocks.—By endorsement and transfer on the books of the corporation.

THE LEGAL AND FINANCIAL FIGHTS OF AMERICA. 63

MAINE.

County Seat.	County.	Name of Atty.	Name of Bank.	Cashier.
Alfred...........York.		S. M. Came	See Portland	
Auburn.........Androscoggin		Tascus Atwood	First Natl. Bk.	H. C. Day.
Augusta........Kennebec.		Lendall Titcomb	First Natl. Bk.	C. S. Hichborn.
Bangor.........Penobscot.		John R. Mason	Merchants Natl. Bk.	Albert P. Baker.
Bath...........Sagadahoc.		George E. Hughes	First Natl. Bk.	W. D. Mussenden
Belfast........Waldo.		R. F. Dunton	Belfast Natl. Bk.	C. W. Wescott.
Dover..........Piscataquis.		Henry Hudson	Kineo Natl. Bk.	C. B. Kittredge.
Ellsworth......Hancock.		J. A. Peters, Jr.	First Natl. Bk.	H. W. Cushman.
Farmington....Franklin.		S. Clifford Belcher	First Natl. Bk.	J. H. Thompson.
Houlton........Aroostook.		F. A. Powers	Farmers Natl. Bk.	Geo. A. Gorham.
Machias.......Washington.		P. B. Danworth	Machias Bk.	George F. Cary.
Paris..........Oxford.		H. C. Davis	See Auburn.	
Portland......Cumberland.		B. D. & H. M. Verrill	Portland Natl. Bk.	Chas. G. Allen.
Rockland......Knox.		W. H. Fogler	Rockland Natl. Bk.	G. Howe Wiggin.
Skowhegan....Somerset.		Walton & Walton	First Natl. Bk.	Geo. N. Page.
Wiscasset......Lincoln.		Henry Ingalls	First Natl. Bk.	F. W. Sewall.

DIGEST OF MAINE COMMERCIAL LAWS.

Assignments.—No statute provision relating to common law assignments. Any debtor may apply by petition to the judge for the county within which he resides, setting forth his inability to pay his debts, and his willingness to assign all his estate and effects not exempt by law from attachment and seizure upon execution, for the benefit of his creditors.

Attachments.—Attachments of real or personal property of defendant may be made upon direction of the plaintiff. No bond or other formality required.

Bank Laws—Discount and savings banks created only by special charter; subject to examination by the Bank Examiner, who may, at any time, call for statements, and make examination; may institute proceedings to wind up; makes an annual report to the Governor and council. Capital stock of discount banks must be paid, one-half in six months and one-half in twelve months from the date of charter; they cannot go into operation until one-half the stock has been paid in; cannot circulate bills in excess of 50 per cent. of their capital stock without $1.00 in specie for every $3 of such excess; nor, at any time, more than capital stock paid in and specie on hand; must keep 5 per cent. of the capital stock in specie reserve; must not owe more than twice the amount of the capital stock, aside from deposits. Directors incurring illegal debts or illegally impairing capital are liable therefor. Stockholders are liable for an additional sum equal to the amount of stock. Officers are president, directors, and cashier. Report to examiners when required.

Exemptions.—Homestead $500, where duly registered; usual wearing apparel; furniture $50, bedding, pictures, etc., library, $150, stoves, fuel, and lumber; provisions and seed grain; sewing machine; certain working animals; a team not exceeding $300 in value, and a boat of two tons burden; and domestic fowls worth $50.

MAINE—CONTINUED.

Interest.—Legal rate is 6 per cent. where not stated in writing; any rate legal if agreed to by the parties in writing. No usury law.

Legal Holidays.—Sunday, public fast on Thanksgiving, May 30, July 4, February 22, Christmas, January 1, two days are allowed. If July 4, May 30, February 22, Christmas, January 1, is Monday, and it is the third day of grace, or is Saturday, and the following Sunday is the third day of grace, four days are allowed. Labor Day.

Limitation of Actions.—Actions on judgments of courts of record of the United States or of the State, and justice courts in this State, twenty years. Replevin, and other actions on the case, actions of debt on contract or liability not under seal, except judgments as aforesaid, within two years. Witnessed notes and all other personal actions, twenty years.

Married Women.—A married woman, of whatever age, may own in her own right personal property acquired by descent, gift or purchase, and manage, sell, convey and devise it by will without the assent or joinder of her husband, and real estate likewise, unless her husband, directly or indirectly, conveyed it to her, or paid for it, or it came to her by gift, or devise from his relatives, in which cases the husband must join; although if it was conveyed to her as security or in payment of a *bona fide* debt, due from her husband, he need not be joined. The property conveyed by a husband to his wife, without a valuable consideration, may be taken as the husband's property to pay his debts contracted before the transfer. So also may such property of the wife as was paid for under similar circumstances, from the husband's estate.

Notarial Fees.—Protest, $1.50.

Notes and Bills of Exchange.—Negotiable paper presumed to be taken in payment of debt or liability for which it is given. On notes payable at fixed place on demand at or after a time certain, no recovery unless demand proved thereof before suit; usual demand and notice to charge indorsers; notarial protest proves it; but one indorsing note at inception before payee does is a maker. Waiver of demand and notice, acceptance of bill, draft, or order must be in writing and signed. Recovery from indorser without suing maker. Rate of damages on protested bills of $100 or more, payable in this country, 1 to 9 per cent., according to place. Three days of grace on bills, notes, drafts, and orders on time or sight, and not on demand. Paper maturing on a holiday is considered due and payable the day preceding.

Stay of Executions.—Granted on review and writ of error on filing bond and against absent defendants.

Transfer of Corporation Stocks.—No transfer of stock is valid, except between the parties to it, until it is entered on the books of the corporation in such a manner as to exhibit names and residence of the parties, the number of shares and the date of transfer.

THE LEGAL AND FINANCIAL LIGHTS OF AMERICA.

MARYLAND.

County Seat.	County.	Name of Atty.	Name of Bank.	Cashier.
Annapolis	Anne Arundel	F. H. Stockett	Farmers Natl. Bk.	G. A. Culver.
Baltimore	Baltimore.	D. Meridith Reese	American Natl. Bk.	Simon P. Schott.
Bel Air	Harford.	J. L. G. Lee	Harford Natl. Bk.	W. W. Finney.
Cambridge	Dorchester.	John R. Pattison	Dorchester Natl. Bk.	T. H. Medford.
Centerville	Queen Anne.	T. J. & B. P. Keating	Centerville Natl. Bk.	J. F. Rolph.
Chestertown	Kent.	Richard D. Hynson	Chestertown Natl. Bk.	Harry Rickey.
Cumberland	Allegbany.	Benjamin A. Richmond	Second Natl. Bk.	Daniel Annan.
Denton	Caroline.	Russun & Lewis	Denton Natl. Bk.	T. C. West.
Easton	Talbot.	Wm. R. Martin	Easton Natl. Bk.	R. Thomas.
Elkton	Cecil.	L. M. Haines	Natl. Bk. of Elkton	Chas. B. Finley.
Ellicott City	Howard.	John G. Rogers	Patapsco Natl. Bk.	John F. McMullen
Frederick	Frederick.	Chas. W. Ross	Citizens Natl. Bk.	W.G. Zimmerman
Hagerstown	Washington.	Frank W. Mish	Hagerstown Bk.	E. W. Mealey.
Leonardtown	St. Mary.	Robert C. Combs	See Cambridge	
Oakland	Garrett.	G. S. Hamill	Garrett Co. Bk.	S. T. Jones.
Port Tobacco	Charles.	Adrian Posey	See Washington, D. C.	
Princess Anne	Somerset.	Miles & Stanford	Savings Bk. of Somerset Co.	W.J. Brittingham
Prince Fredericktown	Calvert.	John B. Gray	See Cambri 'ge	
Rockville	Montgomery.	H. W. Talbott	Montgomery Co. Natl. Bk.	R. H. Stokes.
Salisbury	Wicomico.	James E. Elligood	Salisbury Natl. Bk.	John H. White.
Snow Hill	W'rcester.	Clayton J. Purnell	First Natl. Bk.	I. T. Matthews.
Towson	Baltimore.	Z. Howard Isaac	Towson Natl. Bk.	W. C. Craumer.
UPPER MARLBORO	Pr. George.	F. Snowden Hill	See Washington, D. C.	
Westminster	Carroll.	Clabaugh & Roberts	Union Natl. Bk.	J. W. Hering.

DIGEST OF MARYLAND COMMERCIAL LAWS.

Assignments.—Assignments may be made by deed, but should not ordain any preference, and should convey whole estate and provide for disposition of same.

Attachments.—Attachments may be issued on judgment in twelve years from date of same by way of execution, and are liens from time of service. They are also issued where the defendant is a non-resident, or where he absconds.

Bank Laws.—The paid-up capital stock in the city of Baltimore must not be less than $300,000 in shares of $100 each, with privilege of increasing the number of shares to $20,000. Outside of the city of Baltimore the paid-up capital stock must be $50,000 in shares of $100 each, with privilege of increasing to $5,000. Any five or more persons, citizens of the United States, and a majority of them citizens of this State, may form a corporation for banking under the provisions set forth in the code, but shall not be qualified to do business until a majority of the directors shall have certified to the Treasurer and Comptroller of the State, that the required capital has been fully paid in the "lawful money" of the United States, and a certificate of such organization shall have been transmitted to the Clerk of the

MARYLAND—Continued.

Court of Appeals, and by him filed among the records of his office. The number of directors may not be more than seven, nor less than five. None but a citizen of this State and a stockholder, may be director or president. No one may be a director of more than one bank in this State at the same time. Semi-annual statements of the condition of State institutions must be made to the State Treasurer, and be published. Stockholders' liability extends to amount of their stock.

Exemptions.—There is no homestead law. Usual wearing apparel and $100 worth of personal property are exempt.

Interest.—Legal rate 6 per cent. Usury forfeits excess, with interest thereon.

Legal Holidays.—Sunday, Christmas, January 1, Good Friday, July 4, February 22, Thanksgiving, or General or Congressional Election Days, May 30, Labor Day, and every Saturday after 12 o'clock.

Limitation of Actions.—On open accounts, simple contracts, assumpsit, replevin, rent in arrears, or trespass suit, must be brought within three years ; on specialty, bond or judgment, in twelve years. Limitations do not run in case of debtor.

Married Women.—All property belonging to a woman at the time of marriage, or that she may acquire thereafter, by purchase, gift, grant, devise, bequest, descent, or otherwise, is exempt from the husband's debts, but the husband has no right to transfer property to the wife to the prejudice of the right of subsisting creditors. The wife's property is liable for her personal debts.

Notarial Fees.—Protest $1.05 and costs.

Notes and Bills of Exchange.—The maker of a promissory note or the acceptor of a bill of exchange will be held liable to an innocent holder, who takes the same before maturity for value and in good faith, even though the note was made and the bill accepted without consideration. Three days' grace are allowed except on sight or demand drafts. A protest duly made by a notary public of a note or bill is a *prima facie* evidence of the facts pertaining thereto and as stated therein. Damages recoverable, in addition to principal, interest and costs on protested bills : if drawn on any other State or Territory, 6 per cent.; foreign country, 15 per cent. Paper maturing on a holiday becomes due on the secular day next succeeding.

Stay of Executions.—In Justice Courts for six months, when amount is under $30; if over $30, one year. In Court of Records, six months on any amount.

Transfer of Corporation Stocks.—The stock of a corporation is deemed personal property and may be transferred as provided by the by-laws.

THE LEGAL AND FINANCIAL LIGHTS OF AMERICA. 67

MASSACHUSETTS.

County Seat.	County.	Name of Atty.	Name of Bank.	Cashier.
Barnstable	Barnstable.	Hiram P. Harriman	At Hyannis, First Natl. Bk.	G. E. Tillson.
Boston	Suffolk.	John Haskell Butler	Natl. Bk. of the Republic	Henry D. Forbes.
Dedham	Norfolk.	D. G. Hill	Dedham Natl. Bk.	E. A. Brooks.
Edgarton	Dukes.	B. T. Hillman	Martha's Vineyard Natl. Bk.	John E. White.
Greenfield	Franklin.	John A. Aiken	Franklin Co. Natl. Bk.	H. O. Edgerton.
Lowell	Middlesex.	George F. Richardson	Traders Natl. Bk.	Wm. F. Hills.
Nantucket	Nantucket.	Allen Coffin	Pacific Natl. Bk.	Albert G. Brock.
New Bedford	Bristol.	Stetson & Stetson	Merchant's Natl. Bk.	H. C. W. Mosher.
Newburyport	Essex.	N. N. Jones	First Natl. Bk.	W. F. Houston.
Northampton	Hampshire.	Wm. G. Bassett	Hampshire Co. Natl. Bk.	F. A. Macomber.
Pittsfield	Berkshire.	Crosby & Noxon	Third Natl. Bk.	R. B. Bardwell.
Plymouth	Plymouth.	Charles S. Davis	Old Colony Natl. Bk.	James B. Brown.
Springfield	Hampton.	T. M. Brown	Pynchon Natl. Bk.	George R. Bond.
Worcester	Worcester.	W. W. Rice	Citizens Natl. Bk.	George A. Smith.

PRINCIPAL CITIES (NOT COUNTY SEATS) IN MASSACHUSETTS.

Fall River	Bristol.	Lincoln & Hood	Pocasset Natl. Bk.	E. E. Hathaway.
Fitchburg	Worcester.	Charles E. Ware	Wachusett Natl. Bk.	W. G. Corey.
Holyoke	Hampton.	E. W. Chapin	Holyoke Natl. Bk.	W. G. Twing.
Lawrence	Essex.	Sweeney & Dow	Arlington Natl. Bk.	F. L. Leighton.
Salem	Essex.	Henry P. Moulton	Merchants Natl. Bk.	H. M. Batchelder.

DIGEST OF MASSACHUSETTS COMMERCIAL LAWS.

Assignments.—The insolvent law has no jurisdiction over debts contracted outside of the State, unless the same are proved in the insolvency proceeding. An assignment to trustee to divide property among creditors cannot be avoided by attaching creditors, but only by assignee in insolvency. Any person owing one hundred dollars or more may obtain relief; and any creditor may apply within ninety days after commission of act of insolvency for seizure and distribution of estate.

Attachments.—All real estate, goods and chattels liable to be taken on execution may be attached upon the original writ and held to satisfy the judgment which may be obtained; but no attachment shall be made on a writ returnable before a trial justice, municipal, district or police court, unless the debt or damage demanded exceed twenty dollars. No preliminary bond is required. Perishable property, or that sold after it is attached and the proceeds held subject to the attachment, railroad cars and engines and steamboats in regular use cannot be attached within forty-eight hours previous to their time of departure, unless the officers have made a demand for other property in order to attach it, and such demand has been refused or compliance therewith neglected. Attachment may be made while the suit is pending by special order of Court. Attachment may be dissolved by defendant's giving a bond, with sufficient sureties, either to pay the judgment that may be recovered, or to pay the value of the property

MASSACHUSETTS—Continued.

Bank Laws.—Ten or more persons and their successors may form a corporation for the purpose of carrying on the business of banking. The General Court may, by special act, annul or dissolve any such corporation; but its dissolution shall not impair any remedy against the same for liability previously incurred. The capital stock of each bank shall not be less than $100,000 nor more than $1,000,000. The stock shall be paid in gold or silver money, one-half before the bank goes into operation, and the remainder within one year thereafter. Before commencing business the president and directors shall make a certificate specifying the corporate name, which shall be different from any previously organized in the Commonwealth; the location of said bank, the amount and number of shares of its capital stock; name, and residence and number of shares of each stockholder, and the time when it is to go into operation; a copy of which certificate shall be filed with the Secretary of the Commonwealth. Every bank doing business in Boston, except in the suburban districts which form a part of Boston, shall on every Monday morning transmit to the Secretary of the Commonwealth a statement under oath of the president or cashier of the amount of capital stock, assets and liabilities of the bank, including amount in Boston clearing house, which statement shall be based upon the condition of the bank on the day of the week next preceding said Monday. Monthly reports are required from every bank in the State not included in those above mentioned, to be made to the Secretary of the Commonwealth.

Exemptions.—A householder can create estate of homestead to the value of $800, and no more, in land and buildings owned or rightly possessed by lease or otherwise, and occupied by him as a residence. Necessary wearing apparel of family, certain specified articles of household furniture, and $300 worth in addition thereto; library $50, tools and implements $100, boats and fishing tackle, etc. $100; one cow, six sheep, one hog, and two tons of hay; sewing machine, pew in church, etc.

Interest.—Legal rate, 6 per cent., which is allowed on judgments. There are no usury laws, and any rate may be reserved or contracted for in writing, and rate reserved in note is payable after maturity of note as before.

Legal Holidays.—Sunday, Fast Day, Thanksgiving, Christmas, January 1, February 22, July 4, May 30 (Memorial Day), First Monday in September, April 19.

Limitation of Actions.—Contracts or liabilities, express or implied, and not under seal, six years; real actions, those upon an attested note and personal actions on contracts not limited, twenty years.

Married Women.—All property, either real or personal, of a married woman, whether acquired before or after marriage in any way, is her separate estate, and may be used, collected and invested in her own name, and shall not be subject to the interference or control of her husband, or liable for his debts. A married woman, doing business on her separate account, must file a certificate in the Clerk's office in the city or town where she does business, setting forth the name of her husband, the nature of her business, and the place where it is to be done, otherwise her property will be liable for her husband's debts. The husband may file such certificate, and if no such certificate is filed by either, the husband is liable upon all contracts made in such business.

Notarial Fees.—Protest $1.50, under $500; $2 on $500 and over.

Notes and Bills of Exchange.—Three days of grace are allowed on all notes and drafts. Paper maturing on a holiday becomes due on the secular day next suc-

MASSACHUSETTS—Continued.

ceeding. The drawee of a bill or draft requiring acceptance has till 2 o'clock P. M. on the next business day after presentment to decide whether he will accept. Orders and drafts for money payable within this State, in which no time of payment is expressed, shall be deemed to be payable on demand. All persons becoming parties to promissory notes payable on time by a signature in blank on the back thereof, shall be entitled to notice of the non-payment thereof the same as indorsers. Checks drawn on a bank may be paid notwithstanding the death of drawer, if presented within ten days after date, and a saving bank order if presented within ten days after date. To charge indorsers of a promissory note payable on demand, a demand made after the expiration of sixty days from the date thereof, without grace, or at any time within that term is necessary to fix the liability of the indorser, and shall be deemed to be made within a reasonable time. No presentment of such note to the promissor and demand of payment will charge the indorser, unless made on or before the last day of said term of sixty days.

Transfer of Corporation Stocks.—Delivery of certificate to a *bona fide* purchaser or pledgee for value, with a written transfer of the same, or a written power of attorney to transfer same, passes title as against all parties, but does not affect the right of the corporation to treat the record holder in fact, until the transfer is recorded upon the books of the company. If stock is transferred as collateral security, it must so appear on the face of the certificate of stock issued to the pledgee, and the name of the pledgor should be stated therein, who alone will be responsible as a stockholder.

70   THE LEGAL AND FINANCIAL LIGHTS OF AMERICA.

MICHIGAN.

County Seat.	County.	Name of Atty.	Name of Bank.	Cashier.
Adrian	Lenawee.	Watts, Bean & Smith	Adrian State Savings Bk.	B. E. Tobias.
Allegan	Allegan.	H. H. Pope	First Natl. Bk.	F. L. Chichester.
Alpena	Alpena.	Joseph H. Cobb	Alpena Natl. Bk.	Jno. C. Comfort.
Ann Arbor	Washtenaw.	Harriman & Thompson	Farmers & Mechanics Bk.	Fred. H. Beleer.
Au Train	Alger.	H. B. Freeman	See Marquette	
Bad Axe	Huron.	W. T. Pope	Bk. of Frank W. Hubbard & Co.	Jno. Ryan.
Baldwin	Lake.	H. W. Newkirk	See Ludington	
Bay City	Bay.	C. L. Collins	Bay City Bk.	Geo. H. Young.
Bellaire	Antrim.	M. W. Newkirk	Bk. of Bellaire	F. E. Turrell.
Benzonia	Benzie.	Geo. G. Covell	Exchange Bk.	G. M. Sprout.
Bessemer	Gogebic.	Howell & Cooper	First Natl. Bk.	Wm. I. Prince.
Big Rapids	Mecosta.	M. Brown	Mecosta Co. Savings Bk.	C.W.Cunningham
Boyne	Charlevoix.	J. M. Harris	Boyne River Bk.	J. F. Fairchild.
Cadillac	Wexford.	Sawyer & Bishop.	Bk. of D. B. Blodgett & Co.	
Caro	Tuscola.	T. W. Atwood	Tuscola Co. Bk.	Jno. F. Seeley.
Cassopolis	Cass.	Howell & Carr	First Natl. Bk.	C. A. Ritter.
Centreville	St. Joseph.	Alfred	First State Bk.	Frank Wolf.
Charlotte	Eaton.	J. M. C. Smith	First Natl. Bk.	W. P. Lacey.
Cheboygan	Cheboygan.	George E. Frost	First Natl. Bk.	A. W. Ramsey.
Coldwater	Branch.	H. H. Barlow	Southern Michigan Natl. Bk.	A. S. Upson.
Corunna	Shiawassee.	Jno. J. McCurdy	First Natl. Bk.	W.A.Rosenkranz.
Crystal Falls	Iron.	Moriarty & Abbott	Iron Co. Bk.	J. J. F. Corcocan.
Detroit	Wayne.	Bowen, Douglas & Whiting. Tarsney & Wicker	First Natl. Bk.	Jno. T. Shaw.
Eagle River	Keweenaw.	Edwin R. Smith	At Calumet, First Natl. Bk.	W. B. Anderson.
Escanaba	Delta.	Mead & Jennings	First Natl. Bk.	R. Lyman.
Flint	Genesee.	Durand & Carton	First Natl. Bk.	C. S. Brown.
Gaylord	Otsego.	Marshall & Townsend	Gaylord State Savings Bk.	Sanford W. Buck.
Gladwin	Gladwin.	Swift & Wilmot	Bk. of M. C. Scrafford & Co.	
Grand Haven	Ottawa.	George A. Fair	Natl. Bk. of Grand Haven.	George Stickney.
Grand Rapids	Kent.	Earle & Hyde	Fourth Natl. Bk.	W. H. Anderson.
Grayling	Crawford.	Geo. L. Alexander	Grayling Exchange Bk.	Staley & French.
HARBOR SPRINGS	Emmet.	Chalmers Curtis	Harbor Springs Bk.	Curtis & Curtis.
Harrison	Clare.		Bk. of L. Saviers & Co.	F. Weathearhead.
Harrisville	Alcona.	O. H. Smith	See Tawas City	
Hart	Oceana.	T. S. Gurney	Citizens Exchange Bk.	A. S. White.
Hastings	Barry.	J. A. Sweezey	Hastings City Bk.	D. W. Reynolds.
Hersey	Osceola.	C. M. Beardsley	At Evart, First State Savings Bk.	Wm. Rogers.
Hillman	Montmorency.	J. B. Beverly	See Gaylord	
Hillsdale	Hillsdale.	F. A. Lyons	First Natl. Bk.	C. F. Stewart.
Houghton	Houghton.	T. L. Chadbourne	Natl. Bk. of Houghton	James B. Sturgis.
Howell	Livingston.	W. P. Van Winkle	First State & Sav. Bk.	H. J. Winchell.
Ionia	Ionia.	V. H. Smith	First Natl. Bk.	Frank A.Sessions.
IRON MOUNTAIN	Dickinson.	Cook & Pelham	First Natl. Bk.	M. A. Northrop.
Ithaca	Gratiot.	George P. Stone	First Natl. Bk.	M. F. Chafey.
Jackson	Jackson.	F. C. Badgley	Union Bk.	Charles C. Ames.
Kalamazoo	Kalamazoo.	Osborn, Mills & Master	City Natl. Bk.	E. C. Dayton.
Kalkaska	Kalkaska.	Wm. D. Totten	Kalkaska City Bk.	J. C. Gray.

THE LEGAL AND FINANCIAL LIGHTS OF AMERICA. 71

MICHIGAN—Continued.

County Seat.	County.	Name of Atty.	Name of Bank.	Cashier.
Lake City	Missaukee.	F. O. Gaffney	Missaukee Co. Bk.	James Cavanagh.
L'Anse	Baraga.	P. R. McKernan	See Houghton	
Lapeer	Lapeer.	Geer & Williams	First Natl. Bk.	C. G. White.
Leland	Leelanaw.	Alex. McKercher	See Traverse City	
Ludington	Mason.	D. W. Reardon	First Natl. Bk.	W. L. Hammond.
Manistee	Manistee.	McAlvay & Grant	First Natl. Bk.	G. A. Dunham.
Manistique	Schoolcraft.	C. W. Dunton	Manistique Bk.	H. W. Clarke.
Marquette	Marquette.	Ball & Ball	First Natl. Bk.	F. J. Jennison.
BATTLE CREEK	Calhoun	C. W. HARVEY		
Menominee	Menominee.	Sawyer, Waite & Waite	First Natl. Bk.	G. A. Blesch.
Midland	Midland.	George B. Sanford	State Bk. of Midland	F. E. Barbour.
Mio	Oscoda.	John J. McCarthy	See Grayling	
Monroe	Monroe.	P. R. Gilday	First Natl. Bk.	George L. Little.
Mt. Clemens	Macomb.	Crocker & Knight	Mt. Clemens Savings Bk.	G. A. Skinner.
Mt. Pleasant	Isabella.	Free Estee	First Natl. Bk.	D. Scott Partridge.
Muskegon	Muskegon.	Bunker & Carpenter	Hackley Natl. Bk.	George A. Abbott
Newaygo	Newaygo.	George Luton	Bk. of Weber & Hatch	M. F. Hatch.
Newberry	Luce.	See Sault St. Marie	Newberry Sav. Bk.	S. N. Dutcher.
Omer	Arenac.	L. McHugh	At Standish, Arenac Co. Bk.	Robert Hall.
Ontonagon	Ontonagon.	W. W. Wendell	Ontonagon Bk.	C. Meilleur.
Paw Paw	Van Buren.	Heckert & Chandler	First Natl. Bk.	E. F. Parker.
Pontiac	Oakland.	James A. Jacokes	First Commercial Bk.	B. S. Tregent.
Port Huron	St. Clair.	Frank Whipple	Commercial Bk.	John W. Porter.
Rogers City	Presque Isle.	Wm. E. Rice	Presque Isle Co. Bk.	C. H. Osgood.
Roscommon	Roscommon.	Chas. L. DeWaele	Exchange Bk.	J. H. Sly.
Saginaw	Saginaw.	Humphrey & Grant	Bk. of Saginaw	D. W. Briggs.
SanillacCentre	Sanillac.	E. C. Babcock	Sandusky Bk.	James McCaren.
St. Ignace	Mackinac.	H. Hoffman	First Natl. Bk.	E. H. Hotchkiss.
St. James	Maniton.	J. J. Brown	See St. Ignace.	
St. Johns	Clinton.	Lyon & Dooling	State Bk. of St. Johns	J. W. Fitzgerald.
St. Joseph	Berrien.	W. R. Lyon	Union Bk. Co	O. Jordan.
SaultSte.Marie	Chippewa.	George A. Cady	First Natl. Bk.	Edward H. Mead.
Stanton	Montcalm.	F. A. Miller	Bk. of H. R. Wagar	James C. Percival
Tawas City	Iosco.	G. L. Cornville	Bk. of A. H. Phinney & Co.	
Traverse City	Gr'd Traverse	Patchin & Loranger	Traverse City State Bk.	J. T. Hannah.
West Branch	Ogemaw.	F. R. Snodgrass	Commercial Bk.	T. W. Ballantine.

DIGEST OF MICHIGAN COMMERCIAL LAWS.

Assignments.—Assignment for benefit of creditors must be of all the assignor's property not exempt from execution, and must be without preference.

Attachments.—Attachments may issue where the debtor has absconded or is about to abscond from the State, or is concealed therein, to the injury of his creditors; where he has assigned, disposed of, or concealed any of his property, or is about to do so, with intent to defraud his creditors; where he has removed, or is about to re-

MICHIGAN—Continued.

move any of his property out of the State with intent to defraud his creditors; where he has fraudulently contracted the debt; where he is not a resident of this State, and has not resided therein for three months before the commencement of suit, or where the defendant is a foreign corporation.

Bank Laws.—Not less than five persons may establish banks and savings associations. The minimum amount of capital stock must not be less than $100,000; except in town of 1,500 and less the minimum is $15,000, and in towns not exceeding 5,000, the minimum is $25,000, and in towns not exceeding 25,000, it is $50,000. The articles of association shall specify: The name of the bank, which shall not be similar to that of any other bank; the county and city or village of its location; whether a commercial or savings bank, or both; the amount of its capital, which must be divided into shares of $100 each; the names and places of residence of the stockholders and the number of shares held by each; the period for which the bank is organized not to exceed thirty years. Fifty per cent. of the capital stock must be paid in before the bank can begin business, and the remainder in monthly install- ments of 10 per cent. each. Bank are to be examined once in each year by the Commissioner of the State Banking Department and report made to State Treasurer.

Exemptions.—A home of one lot in any town or city, or not more than forty acres of land outside, not exceeding $1,500 in value, owned and occupied by a resident of the State, is exempt from execution; apparel, books to the value of $150; family pic- tures, two cows, five swine, with provisions and fuel for six months; tools, team of horses, wagon necessary to carry on trade, business, profession, not exceeding in value $250; to each householder goods, furniture, etc., not exceeding in value $250.

Interest.—Legal rate is 6 per cent. Parties may contract in writing for 8 per cent. The penalty for usury is a forfeiture of all interest. Usurious interest, voluntarily paid, cannot be recovered.

Legal Holidays.—Sunday, January 1, February 22, May 30, July 4, December 25 Thanksgiving, Labor Day, First Monday of September. Every Saturday from twelve o'clock noon until twelve o'clock at night, and any day appointed by the Governor or President for fasting and thanksgiving shall, for the payment of notes "be treated and considered as the first day of the week, commonly called Sunday." When these holidays fall on Sunday, then the following Monday is considered as a holiday.

Limitation of Actions.—On actions and notes and other simple contracts, six years; on sealed instruments and judgments, ten years. Revivor, part payment or prom- ise in writing to pay.

Married Women.—May make contracts in regard to their real and personal property, and encumbered, sell or otherwise dispose of it the same as if unmarried. The homestead cannot be conveyed without the wife's signature to the conveyance, and she also retains the common law right of dower in her husband's lands.

Notarial Fees.—Protest, fifty cents; each notice, twenty-five cents and postage.

Notes and Bills of Exchange.—On all bills of exchange and negotiable notes and acceptances payable within this State, three days of grace are allowed, and it is not necessary to protest the same for non-acceptance; but such bills of exchange and checks should be presented within a reasonable time for payees to hold drawers or indorsers. Paper falling due on holidays is payable the next business day suc- ceeding. In all other cases demand, protest for non-payment and the sending

MICHIGAN—Continued.

notices of protest to the indorser at his reputed place of business or residence, are necessary to bind the indorser. Parties, other than payees to paper, being such before or at its inception, are held as joint makers, and not entitled to notice of non-payment. Damages on domestic bills when protested, three to ten per cent.; on foreign bills, five per cent.

Stay of Executions.—In Justice Courts, under fifty dollars, four months; over fifty dollars, six months.

Transfer of Corporation Stocks.—Shares of stock may be transferred by the indorsement and delivery of the certificates; but such transfer shall not be valid, except between the parties thereto, until the same shall have been so entered upon the books of the corporation as to show the names of the parties by and to whom transferred, the number and designation of the shares, and the date of transfer.

MINNESOTA.

County Seat.	County.	Name of Atty.	Name of Bank.	Cashier.
Ada	Norman.	W. W. Calkins	Bk. of Ada	S. Perterson.
Aitkin	Aitkin.	A. Y. Merrill	See Brainerd	
Albert Lea	Freeborn.	W. E. Todd	Albert Lea Natl. Bk.	C. B. Kellar.
Alexandria	Douglas.	Jeinkins & Treat	First Natl. Bk.	G. B. Ward.
Anoka	Anoka.	A. F. Giddings	Anoka Natl. Bk.	L. J. Greenwald.
Austin	Mower.	Kingsley	First Natl. Bk.	N. P. Banfield.
Beaver Bay	Lake.	John Divan	Bk. of Sellwood, Burke & Co.	D. A. Burke.
Beaver Falls	Renville.	S. R. Miller	Farmers Bk.	Hans Gronnerud.
Benson	Swift.	F. M. Thornton	Swift Co. Bk.	H. W. Stone.
BLUE EARTH CITY	Faribault.	Quinn & Putnam	Farmers & Merchants Bk.	Alex. Anderson.
Brainerd	Crow Wing.	C. E. Chipperfield	First Natl. Bk.	J. D. La Bar.
Breckenridge	Wilken.	E. G. Valentine	First Natl. Bk.	Howard Dykman.
BROWN'S VALLEY	Traverse.	A. S. Crossfield	Browns Valley State Bk.	O. Gunderson.
Buffalo	Wright.	John T. Alley	Bk. of C. E. Oakley & Co.	
Caledonia	Houston.	E. H. Smalley	Bk. of Caledonia	A. D. Sprague.
Cambridge	Isanti.	H. F. Barker	Isanti Co. Bk.	II. Engberg.
Carlton	Carlton.	H. H. Hawkins	Carlton Co. Bk.	Asa Paine.
Centre City	Chisago.	J. D. Markham	At Rush City, Bk. of Rush City	John C. Carlson.
Chaska	Carver.	W. C. Odell	Carver Co. Bk.	V. J. Greiner.
Crookston	Polk.	A. A. Miller	Scandia American Bk.	J. W. Wheeler.
Detroit City	Baker.	J. H. Irish	First Natl. Bk.	W. J. Bettingen.
Duluth	St. Louis.	Wilson & Wray	Security Bk. of Duluth	W. P. Lardner.
Elbow Lake	Grant.	A. O. Ofsthun	Bk. of Elbow Lake	H. Sampson.
Elk River	Sherburne.	Chas. S. Wheaton	Bk. of Elk River	Henry Castle.
Fairmont	Martin.	Ward, Dunn & Ward	Martin Co. Bk.	A. C. Frey.
Faribault	Rice.	H. S. Gibson	First Natl. Bk.	C. M. Whitney.
Fergus Falls	Otter Tail.	Parsons & Brown	Fergus Falls Natl. Bk.	F. J. Evans.
Glencoe	McLeod.	F. R. Allen	Bk. of Glencoe	L. W. Gilbert.
Glenwood	Pope.	E. M. Webster	Bk. of Glenwood	P. Piterson.
Grand Rapids	Ithasca.	C. L. Pratt	First Natl. Bk.	A. P. White.
Grand Marais	Cook.	A. J. Thomas	See Ely, Bk. of Ely	W. T. James.
Granite Falls	Yellow Medicine.	McLarty & Volstead	Granite Falls Bk.	J. G. Dodsworth.
Hallock	Kittson.	E. C. Yetter	Kittson Co. Bk.	W. H. Douglas.
Hastings	Dakota.	E. A. Whitford	First Natl. Bk.	John Heinen.
Henderson	Sibley.	W. H. Leeman	Sibley County Bk.	E. L. Welch.
Jackson	Jackson.	L. J. Knox	State Bk. of Jackson	A. B. Cheadle.
Lac qui parle	Lac qui parle.	Frank Palmer	At Madison, Farmers State Bk.	P. E. Jacobson.
Lake Benton	Lincoln.	Jno. McKenzie	First Natl. Bk.	John S. Tucker.
Leech Lake	Cass.	See Park Rapids.		
LE SUEUR CENTRE	Le Sueur.	Caldwell & Parker	First State Bk.	H. F. Wels.
Litchfield	Meeker.	Peterson & Foster	Bk. of Litchfield	F. F. McClure.
Little Falls	Morrison.	C. A. Lindbergh	First Natl. Bk.	A. R. Davidson.
Long Prairie	Todd.	J. D. Van Dyke	Bk. of Long Prairie	R. H. Harkens.
Luverne	Rock.	W. N. Davidson	First Natl. Bk.	A. D. La Due.
Mankato	Blue Earth.	Thomas Hughes	Natl. Citizens Bk.	W. G. Hoerr.
Mantorville	Dodge.	George A. Norton	Security Bk.	L. M. Blauch.
Marshall	Lyon.	V. B. Seward	First Natl. Bk.	M. W. Hardin.

THE LEGAL AND FINANCIAL LIGHTS OF AMERICA. 75

MINNESOTA—Continued.

County Seat.	County.	Name of Atty.	Name of Bank.	Cashier.
Minneapolis	Hennepin.	George D. Emery	Security Bk. of Minnesota	Perry Harrison.
Montevido	Chippewa.	Lyndon A. Smith	Citizens State Bk.	M. E. Titus.
Moorhead	Clay.	George E. Perley	First Natl. Bk.	Lew. A. Huntoon.
Mora	Kanabec.	J. C. Pope	Kanabec Co. Bk.	Geo. H. Newbert.
Morris	Stevens.	S. A. Flaherty	First Natl. Bk.	L. O. Hollister.
New Ulm	Brown.	Lind & Hagberg	Citizens Bk.	W. F. Selter.
Ortonville	Big Stone.	F. L. Cliff	Bk. of Ortonville	E. J. Miller.
Owatonna	Steele.	Wheelock & Sperry	First Natl. Bk.	George R. Kinyon
Park Rapids	Hubbard.	F. A. Vanderpoel	Shell Prairie Bk.	Wm. M. Taber.
Pine City	Pine.	L. H. McCusick	At Rush City, Bk. of Rush City	John C. Carlson.
Pipe Stone	Pipe Stone.	Evans & Evans	First Natl. Bk.	W. C. Briggs.
Preston	Fillmore.	Wells & Hopp	Fillmore Co. Bk.	M. R. Todd.
Princeton	Mille Lacs.	J. A. Ross	Citizens State Bk.	G. A. Eaton.
Red Lake	Beltrami.	Bennett & Street	At Fosston, Bk. of Fosston	Lewis Lobn.
Red Wing	Goodhue.	Albert Johnson	Goodhue Co. Bk.	F. Busch.
REDWOOD FALLS	Redwood.	H. D. Baldwin	Redwood Co. Bk.	H. A. Baldwin.
Rochester	Olmstead.	B. W. Eaton	Union Natl. Bk.	T. H. Titus.
St. Cloud	Stearns.	Geo. H. Reynolds	First Natl. Bk.	J. G. Smith.
St. James	Watonwan.	J. W. Seager	First Natl. Bk.	Frank O'Meara.
St. Paul	Ramsey.	Davis, Kellogg & Severance.	Bk. of Minnesota	Wm. Dawson, Jr.
St. Peter	Nicollet.	A. A. Stone	First Natl. Bk.	E. S. Pettijohn.
Sauk Rapids	Benton.	M. C. Kelsey	See St. Cloud	
Shakopee	Scott.	Southworth & Collier	First Natl. Bank	John Thiem.
Slayton	Murray.	H. C. Gross	State Bk. of Slayton	C. E. Dinehart.
Stillwater	Washington.	Clapp & Macartney	First Natl. Bk.	R. H. Bronson.
Wabasha	Wabasha.	Mullen & Bowditch	First Natl. Bk.	L. Whitmore.
Wadena	Wadena.	A. G. Broker	First Natl. Bk.	C. W. Baumbach.
Warren	Marshall.	S. Cooke	State Bk. of Warren	A. Melgaard.
Waseca	Waseca.	James E. Child	Citizens State Bk.	S. Swenson.
Willmar	Kandiyohi.	G. E. Quale	Bk. of Willmar	F. G. Handy.
Windom	Cottonwood.	J. G. Redding	Bk. of Windom	J. N. McGregor.
Winona	Winona.	Brown & Abbott	Second Natl. Bk.	W. H. Garlock.
Worthington	Nobles.	George W. Wilson	Bk. of Worthington	George O. Moore

DIGEST OF MINNESOTA COMMERCIAL LAWS.

Assignments.—An assignment may be made of all assignor's property, and must be without preference.

Attachments.—Attachment issues when the defendant's debt was fraudulently contracted ; or when the defendant is a foreign corporation, or a non-resident of the State ; or has departed therefrom, as deponent believes, with intent to defraud his creditors, or to avoid the service of a summons, or keeps himself concealed with like intent; or has disposed, or is about to dispose of his property, with intent to defraud creditors.

MINNESOTA—Continued.

Bank Laws.—Banks may be organized by the execution and recording of a certificate containing the name, place of business, amount of capital stock, names and places of residence of shareholders, and the period for which the organization is made. The capital stock must amount to at least $10,000 in towns of population not exceeding 1,000; $15.000 in towns not exceeding 1,500; $20,000 in towns not exceeding 2,000; $25,000 in towns of more than 2,000 population. Such association has the usual powers of banks. It may issue circulating notes, to be secured by the assignment and deposit with the State Auditor of like amount of the public stock of a State of the United States, or the stock securities of the United States. Private banks are prohibited from doing business under an artificial or corporate name. Banks are required to make at least four detailed reports in each year, to the State Auditor, and oftener, if required by him, the reports to be published in a newspaper at the direction of the State Auditor. The public examiner is required to examine the books, accounts, and securities of all banks in the State at least once in each year and report such examination to the Governor, and the governor is to publish the report.

Exemptions.—A homestead, consisting of land not exceeding eighty acres and the dwelling house thereon, and its appurtenances, to be selected by the owner thereof, and not included in the platted portion of any incorporated town, city or village, or, instead thereof, at the owner's option, a quantity of land not exceeding in amount one lot if within the platted portion of any incorporated town, city or village having over 5,000 inhabitants, or one-half acre if within the platted portion of any incorporated town, city or village having less than 5,000 inhabitants, and the dwelling house thereon and its appurtenances, owned and occupied by any resident of this State, is not liable for debts of owner.

Interest.—Seven per cent. is the legal rate. Parties may agree to pay as high as ten per cent. per annum. All usurious contracts are void, and Court will decree cancellation. Where usurious interest has actually been paid the entire interest may be recovered in a civil action, half to go to party bringing action and half to public schools, with all interest.

Legal Holidays.—Sunday, Thanksgiving, Good Friday, Christmas, January 1, February 22, May 30, July 4, General Election Day, Labor Day.

Limitation of Actions.—Actions for recovery of real estate, within fifteen years; on judgments, within ten years; upon any contract, obligation, or upon a liability created by statute, or to enforce a trust or compel an accounting, within six years.

Married Women.—All property, real or personal, belonging to a woman at the time of marriage continues her separate estate. She is responsible for her torts, her property is liable for her debts, is capable of making, and is bound by her contracts the same as if she were a *femme sole*. Husband is only liable for necessaries furnished after marriage. Neither husband or wife can be agent for the other in regard to the conveyance of real estate of either. In relation to all other subjects, either may be the agent of the other. A married woman may sue or be sued in her own name without joining her husband.

Notarial Fees.—Protest $1.50, each notice fifty cents.

Notes and Bills of Exchange.—On all bills of exchange payable at sight, or at a future day certain, and all negotiable promissory notes, orders and drafts payable at a future day certain, within this State, in which there is no express stipulation to

MINNESOTA—Continued.

the contrary, grace is allowed of three days. Paper falling due on a holiday is payable the preceding business day. Notice of protest must be given immediately after. Protest is made by mailing the same to each party protested against at his reputed place of residence. The notary certifies to the giving of the notice upon the instrument of notice, and records the latter in his register, which is *prima facie* evidence. Damages, five per cent. on domestic and ten per cent. on foreign paper protested. Notes obtained by fraudulent representation without negligence on part of maker void.

Transfer of Corporation Stocks.—As between parties endorsed on back of stock. As against corporations it is entered on the books of the corporation.

MISSISSIPPI.

County Seat.	County.	Name of Atty.	Name of Bank.	Cashier.
Aberdeen	Monroe.	George C. Paine	First Natl. Bk.	C. R. Sykes.
Ashland	Benton.	McDonald & McDonald	See Holly Springs	
Augusta	Perry.	J. S. Bradford	See Ellisville	
Bay St. Louis	Hancock.	E. J. Bowers	See Scranton	
Belen	Quitman.	F. M. Hamblet	At Jonestown, Bk. of G. B. Moseley	
Boonville	Prentiss.	B. A. P. Selman	At Corinth, Fishomigo Savgs. Bk.	J. W. Taylor.
Brandon	Rankin.	J. R. Enochs	See Jackson	
Brookhaven	Lincoln.	Cassedy & Cassedy	Commercial Bk.	F. F. Becker.
Canton	Madison.	W. H. Powell	Mississippi State Bk.	B. L. Roberts.
Carrollton	Carroll.	T. H. Somerville	Bk. of Carrollton	C. J. Nelson.
Carthage	Leake.	D. E. Sullivan	See Canton	
Charleston	Tallabatchie.	Bailey & Bailey	See Grenada	
Chester	Choctaw.	J. W. Pinson	See Starkville	
Coffeeville	Yalobusha.	R. H. Golladay	At Water Valley, Bk. of Water Valley	G. D. Able.
Columbia	Marion.	T. S. Ford	See Magnolia	
Columbus	Lowndes.	E. T. Sykes	Columbus Ins. & Bkg. Co.	W. H. Lee.
Corinth	Alcorn.	J. M. Boone	Tishomingo Savgs. Institution	J. W. Taylor.
Decatur	Newton.	Thomas Keith	See Meridian	
De Kalb	Kemper.	T. P. Bell	See Meridian	
Ellisville	Jones.	N. C. Hill	Bk. of Ellisville	W. S. Pettis.
Fayette	Jefferson.	Torrey & Torrey	See Natches	
Forest	Scott.	S. H. Kirkland	See Jackson	
Friars Point	Coahomo.	D. A. Scott	Bk. of Friar's Point	J. C. Johnston.
Fulton	Itawamaba.	A. N. Cayse	See Tupelo	
Greenville	Washington.	Yerger & Percy	Merchants & Planters Bk.	S. C. Lane.
Greenwood	Le Flore.	A. M. C. Kimbrough	Bk. of Greenwood	E. R. McShane.
Grenada	Grenada.	Wm. C. McLean	Grenada Bk.	J. T. Thomas.
Hazlehurst	Copiah.	R. N. Miller	Merchants & Planters Bk.	Isaac N. Ellis.
Hernando	De Soto.	McKenzie & Holmes	Hernando Bk.	E. W. Smith.
Holly Springs	Marshall.	R. T. Fant	Bk. of Holly Springs.	II. C. Fort.
Houston	Chickasaw.	E. A. Moseley	At Okolona, Jno. Trice Bkg. Co.	J. S. Bramlitt.
Indianolo	Sunflower.	A. G. Paxton	See Greenville	
Iuka	Tishomingo.	W. B. Ellis	Bk. of Iuka	J. A. E. Pyle.
Jackson	Hinds.	Calhoon & Green	Capital State Bk.	E. M. Parker.
Kosciusko	Attala.	Dodd & Armstead	Merchants & Farmers Bk.	Jno. M. Fletcher.
Leakesville	Greene.	W. H. McIntosh	See Mobile, Alabama	
Lexington	Holmes.	Wm. P. Tackett	Bk. of Holmes Co.	W. L. Young.
Liberty	Amite.	Theodore McKnight	See Magnolia	
Louisville	Winston.	See Kosciusko	See Macon	
Macon	Noxubee.	Ames & Drake	Merchants & Farmers Bk.	R. W. Jones, Jr.
Magnolia	Pike.	J. H. Price	Peoples Bk.	J. E. Wolfe.
Mayers	Issaquena.		See Vicksburg	
Meadville	Franklin.	C. E. Williams	See Natchez	
Meridian	Lauderdale.	Cochran & Bozeman	Meridian Natl. Bk.	E. B. McRaven.
MISSISSIPPI CITY	Harrison.	R. Seal	At Biloxi, Bk. of Biloxi	C. E. Theobald.
Monticello	Lawrence.	A. W. Cooper	See Brookhaven	
Natchez	Adams.	Reed & Brandon	First Natchez Bk.	R. L. Wood.

THE LEGAL AND FINANCIAL LIGHTS OF AMERICA. 79

MISSISSIPPI—Continued.

New Albany...Union.	L. R. Kennedy	See Pontotoc	
Oxford ....Lafayette.	W. V. Sullivan	Bk. of Oxford	B. Price.
Paulding ......Jasper.	B. W. Sharborough	See Meridian	
Philadelphia..Neshoba.	A. M. Boyd	See Meridian	
Pittsborough .Calhoun.	J. L. Lyon	See Granada	
Pontotoc.......Pontotoc.	C. B. Mitchell	Bk. of Pontotoc	M. B. Pitts.
Poplarville....Pearl River.	See Ellisville	See Ellisville	
Port Gibson...Claiborne.	J. McC. Martin	Port Gibson Bk.	J. W. Person.
Quitman ....Clarke.	J. E. Terral	See Meridian	
Raleigh........Smith.	W. H. Jones	See Jackson	
Ripley ....Tippah.	C. M. Thurmond	See Pontotoc	
Rolling Fork.Sharkey.	M. D. Brown	See Vicksburg	
Rosedale ......Bolivar.	Charles Scott	Bk. of Rosedale	T. F. Doris.
Sardis ....Panola.	R. H. Taylor	Bk. of Sardis	T. J. Hunter.
Scranton ......Jackson.	H. B. Everett	Scranton State Bk.	H. M. Plummer.
Senatopia .....Tate.	G. D. Shands	Tate Co. Bk.	P. A. Rush.
Starkville.....Oktibbeha.	Muldrow & Nash	Peoples Savings Bk.	A. C. Ervin.
Tunica.........Tunica.	J. T. Lowe	At Jonestown, Bk. of G. B. Moseley	
Tupelo ....Lee.	Blain & Anderson	First Natl. Bk.	F. Johnson.
Vicksburg.....Warren.	Dabney & McCabe	Merchants Natl. Bk.	W. S. Jones.
Walthall......Webster.	J. E. Clark	See Winona	
Waynesboro'..Wayne.	D. M. Taylor	See Ellisville	
West Point...Clay.	Fox & Roane	First Natl. Bk.	T. M. Moseley.
Westville......Simpson.	G. R. Gowen	See Hazlehurst	
Williamsburg.Covington.	J. O. Napier	See Ellisville	
Winona........Montgomery.	Somerville & McLean	Citizens Bk.	F. M. Purnell.
Woodville.....Wilkinson.	D. C. Bramlett	Bk. of Edward Aaron	
Yazoo City.....Yazoo.	Barnett & Thompson	Bk. of Yazoo City	S. R. Berry.

DIGEST OF MISSISSIPPI COMMERCIAL LAWS.

Assignments.—Debtor may make assignments to secure creditors, and may prefer creditors, but no benefit, direct or indirect, may be reserved to the debtor.

Attachments.—Attachment may issue where defendant is a foreign corporation or non-resident of the State ; or he has removed, or is about to remove himself or property out of the State ; or absconds or conceals himself so that he cannot be served with summons ; or contracted the debt or incurred the obligation in conducting the business of a ship, steamboat or other craft in some of the navigable waters of this State ; or has property or rights which he conceals and refuses to apply to the payment of his debts ; or is about to assign or dispose of his property ; or has, or is about to convert his property into money or evidences of debt with intent to place it beyond the reach of his creditors ; or that he fraudulently contracted the debt.

Bank Laws.—No special laws relating to banks, except that they are required to furnish, not less than four times a year, sworn statements, which are to be published. The auditor of public accounts may call for such statement at any time.

THE LEGAL AND FINANCIAL LIGHTS OF AMERICA.

MISSISSIPPI—Continued.

Exemptions.—In the country 160 acres of land not exceeding in value $2,000, is exempt to every citizen, male or female, being a householder, and having a family. In cities, the land and building owned and occupied as a residence, not to exceed in value $2,000, is exempt from levy and sale under execution or attachment.

Legal Holidays.—Sunday, Thanksgiving, Good Friday, Christmas, January 1, February 22, May 30, July 4, General Election Day.

Limitation of Actions.—Actions on open accounts and other unwritten contracts must be brought within three years; on all other contracts, six years. Action on domestic judgments, seven years. A set-off held against a claim is not barred until the principal debt is barred.

Married Women.—All property acquired before or after maraiage remains her separate estate. If she engages in trade she is bound by all contracts made in the course of trade. All such debts are binding upon and may be satisfied out of her separate estate.

Notarial Fees.—Protest, $1.50.

Notes and Bills of Exchange.—Promissory notes are not required to be protested, but demand and notice are necessary to fix liability of parties secondarily liable. Notes are not protestable; domestic and foreign bills are protestable. All notes, bills, drafts, etc., are assignable, and suit may be maintained in the name of the assignee; but defendant can make all defenses which he had against payee before notice of assignment. Foreign bills of exchange payable out of the United States protested for non-acceptance or non-payment, draw 10 per cent. damages and legal interest; bills drawn payable in the United States. protested for non-acceptance, draw damages at the rate of 5 per cent., besides legal interest. Notes, bills, etc., and sight drafts are entitled to the usual days of grace. Paper maturing on a holiday becomes payable next day preceding. Domestic bills of exchange drawn on and payable in this State for $20 or upward must be protested for non-acceptance, or, if accepted for non-payment, they are governed by the same customs and usages as foreign bills of exchange, but no damage accrues.

Stay of Executions.—In Justice Courts stay may be taken for sixty days.

Transfer of Corporation Stocks.—As provided for by the by-laws of the corporation.

THE LEGAL AND FINANCIAL LIGHTS OF AMERICA. 81

MISSOURI.

County Seat.	County.	Name of Atty.	Name of Bank.	Cashier.
Albany	Gentry.	McCullough & Perry	Gentry Co. Bk.	M. L. Millen.
Alton	Oregon.	L. P. Norman	Bk. of Alton	G. S. Woodside.
Ava	Douglass.	Adams Bros.	Bk. of Ava	J. A. G. Reynolds.
Benton	Scott.	Wm. Hunter	At Morley, Scott Co. Bk.	John Hunter.
Bethany	Harrison.	A. F. Woodruff	Harrison Co. Bk.	C. Crossan.
Bloomfield	Stoddard.	H. H. Bedford	Bk. of Dexter	A. Wilcox.
Bolivar	Polk.	J. D. Abbee	Polk Co. Bk.	W. B. Dunnegan.
Boonville	Cooper.	Draffen & Williams	Commercial Bk.	W.R.Hutchinson.
BowlingGreen	Pike.	Major & Motley	Citizens Bk.	G. Phillips.
Buffalo	Dallas.	D. M. Rush	Bk. of Buffalo	D. M. Rush.
Butler	Bates.	T. G. Smith	Farmers Bk. of Bates Co.	E. D. Kipp.
California	Moniteau.	L. F. Wood	Farmers & Traders Bk.	F. B. Lander.
Carrollton	Carroll.	John B. Hale	First Natl. Bk.	T. B. Goodson.
Carthage	Jasper.	E. O. Brown	Bk. of Carthage	J. A. Mitchell.
Cassville	Barry.	Pepper & Steele	Barry Co. Bk.	J. M. Bayless.
Centreville	Reynolds.	L. O. Nelder	See Salem	
Charleston	Mississippi.	J. J. Russell	Charleston Bk.	Scott Alexander.
Chillicothe	Livingston.	C. A. Loomis	First Natl. Bk.	Geo. Milbank, Jr.
Clinton	Henry.	J. D. Lindsay	Henry Co. Bk.	A. P. Frowein.
Columbia	Boone.	C. B. Sebastian	Boone Co. Natl. Bk.	J. O. Hockaday.
Danville	Montgomery.	James D. Barnett	At New Florence, New Florence Bk.	A. H. Kallmeyer.
Doniphan	Ripley.	J. C. Sheppard	Ripley Co. Bk.	C. C. Chandler.
Edina	Knox.	J. W. Ennis	Bk. of Edina	F. J. Wilson.
Eminence	Shannon.	L. B. Shuck	See Houston	
Farmington	St. Francois.	Carter & Webb	Bk. of Farmington	M. P. Cayce.
Fayette	Howard.	R. C. Clark	Farmers & Merchants Bk.	H. K. Gibens.
Forsyth	Taney.	Jas. R. Vaughan	Taney Co. Bk.	W. M. Wade.
FREDERICKTOWN	Madison.	E. D. Anthony	Madison Co. Bk.	N. B. Watts.
Fulton	Callaway.	J. A. Boulware	Southern Bk. of Fulton	Chas.W. Jameson
Gainesville	Ozark.	G. T. Harrison	Bk. of Gainesville	W. T. Hardin.
Galena	Stone.	T. L. Viles	Bk. of Galena	C. B. Swift.
Gallatin	Daviess.	Hamilton & Dudley	Daviess Co. Savings Association.	F. E. Clingan.
Gayoso	Pemiscott.	F. D. Roberts	At Caruthersville,Pemiscot Co.Bk.	H. C. Schnlt.
Grant City	Worth.	Jesse Benson	First Natl. Bk.	J. F. Robertson.
Greenfield	Dade.	Mann & Talbutt	R. S. Jacobs Bkg. Co.	J. L. Wetzel.
Greenville	Wayne.	Raincy & Carty	At Piedmont, Farmers & Merchants Bk.	W. C. Shields.
Harrisonville	Cass.	Burney & Burney	Bk. of Harrisonville	A. S. Deacon.
Hartville	Wright.	S. E. Pope	Wright Co. Bk.	J. H. Simmons.
Hermann	Gasconade.	August Meyer	Hermann Savings Bk.	E. F. Rittstein.
Hermitage	Hickory.	Wm. L. Pitts	Hermitage Bk.	Joe. S. Hartman.
Hillsborough	Jefferson.	Joseph J. Williams	Bk. of Hillsborough.	W. R. Donnell,Jr.
Houston	Texas.	Jno. D. Young	Bk. of Houston	T. F. Nicholas.
Huntsville	Randolph.	W. T. Austin	J. M. Hammett Bkg. Co.	W. F. Hammett.
Independence	Jackson.	Jno. G. Paxton	First Natl. Bk.	W.A. Symington.
Ironton	Iron.	Wm. R. Edgar	See Fredericktown	
Jackson	C. Girardeau.	J. W. Limbaugh	Jackson Exchange Bk.	Hugh R. Quinn.
JEFFERSON CITY	Cole.	Ewing & Hough	Exchange Bk.	W. A. Dallmeyer.

6

THE LEGAL AND FINANCIAL LIGHTS OF AMERICA.

MISSOURI—CONTINUED.

County Seat.	County.	Name of Atty.	Name of Bank.	Cashier.
Kahoka	Clark.	H. M. & Charles Hiller	Clark Co. Savings Bk.	Wm. McDermott.
Keytesville	Chariton.	Crawley & Son	Farmers Bk.	A. F. Tooley.
Kingston	Caldwell.	S. C. Rogers	Kingston Savings Bk.	J. H. Botthoff.
Kirksville	Adair.	M. D. Campbell	First International Bk.	W. T. Baird.
Lamar	Barton.	Bowling & McCluer	C. H. Brown Bkg. Co.	G. L. Crenshaw.
Lancaster	Schuyler.	Nat. M. Shelton	Schuyler Co. Bk.	Frank P. Hays.
Lebanon	Laclede.	J. P. Nixon	Laclede Co. Bk.	C. W. Rubey.
Lexington	Lafayette.	Wm. H. Chiles	Commercial Bk.	E. M. Taubman.
Liberty	Clay.	Simrall & Trimble	First Natl. Bk.	George S. Ritchey
Linn	Osage.	E. M. Carter	Bk. of Osage Co.	J. R. McCord.
Linn Creek	Camden.	H. W. Chalfant	Camden Co. Bk.	J. M. Vincent.
Linneus	Linn.	E. W. Wilcox	Farmers & Merchants Bk.	C. E. Trumbo.
Macon City	Macon.	Webb M. Ruby	First Natl. Bk.	John Scovern.
Maldin	Dunklin.	W. S. C. Walker	Dunklin Co. Bk.	W. J. Davis.
Marble Hill	Bollinger.	Geo. E. Conrad	At Lutesville, Bollinger Co. Bk.	B. F.Stevens.
Marshall	Saline,	Boyd & Murrell	Wood & Huston Bk.	J. P. Huston.
Marshfield	Webster.	James Case	State Bk.	Freeman Evans.
Maryville	Nodaway.	Gallatin Craig	First Natl. Bk.	S. H. Kemp.
Maysville	De Kalb.	Frank Costello	Maysville Bk.	Mack Jones.
Memphis	Scotland.	Smoot, Mudd & Wagner	Citizens Bk.	N. V. Leslie.
Mexico	Audrain.	J. G. Trimble	First Natl. Bk.	R. R. Arnold.
Milan	Sullivan.	Jno. P. Butler	First Natl. Bk.	J. C. McCoy.
Monticello	Lewis.	Blair & Marchand	Monticello Savings Bk.	G. W. Marchand.
Mount Vernon	Lawrence.	Henry Brumback	Farmers Bk.	Geo. A. McCanse.
Neosho	Newton.	Lyman W. White	Bk. of Neosho	W. G. Wills.
Nevada	Vernon.	O. H. Hoss	First Natl. Bk.	WellingtonBarnes
New London	Ralls.	James P. Wood	Bk. of New London.	Alex. C. James.
New Madrid	New Madrid.	J. R. Brewer	New Madrid Bkg. Co.	W. H. Garanflo.
Oregon	Holt.	T. C. Dungan	Citizens Bk.	C. J. Hunt.
Osceola	St. Clair.	J. H. Lucas	State Bk.	C.F. Weidemeyer
Ozark	Christian.	G. A. Watson	Christian Co. Bk.	John C. Rogers.
Palmyra	Marion.	H. J. Drummond	First Natl. Bk.	James W. Proctor
Paris	Monroe.	James M. Crutcher	Natl. Bk. of Paris	Wm. F. Buckner.
Perryville	Perry.	Edward Robb	Bk. of Perryville	Thos. L. Phillips.
Pineville	McDonald.	A. V. Manning	McDonald Co. Bk.	Shields&Manning
Platte City	Platte.	N. P. Anderson	Wells Bkg. Co.	H. C. Wells.
Plattsburgh	Clinton.	E. C. Hall	First Natl. Bk.	George R. Riley.
Poplar Bluff	Butler.	E. R. Lentz	Bk. of Poplar Bluff	M. C. Horton.
Potosi	Washington.	E. T. Eversole	Washington Co. Bk.	J. F. Evans.
Princeton	Mercer.	Ira B. Hyde	Bk. of Princeton	M. F. Robinson.
Richmond	Ray.	C. T. Garner & Son	Bkg. House of J. S. Hughes & Co.	Burnett Hughes.
Rockport	Atchison.	Lewis & Ramsay	Citizens Bk.	D. A. Colvin.
Rolla	Phelps.	Robert Merriweather	Natl. Bk. of Rolla	D. W. Malcolm.
St. Charles	St. Charles.	J. H. Alexander	First Natl. Bk.	Henry Augert.
STE. GENEVIEVE	Ste.Genevieve	E. A. Rozier	Bk. of Henri Rozier	
St. Joseph	Buchanan.	Hall & Woodson	Natl. Bk. of St. Joseph	Geo. C. Hull.
St. Louis	St. Louis.	Samuel N. Holliday	Natl. Bk. of Commerce	J.C.Van Blarcom.

THE LEGAL AND FINANCIAL LIGHTS OF AMERICA. 83

MISSOURI—Continued.

County Seat.	County.	Name of Atty.	Name of Bank.	Cashier.
Salem..........Dent.		L. Judson	Bk. of Salem	W. A. Young.
Savannah......Andrew.		Booker & Williams	State Bk.	W. S. Wells.
Sedalia..........Pettis.		Sangree & Lamb	Third Natl. Bk.	R. H. Moses.
Shelbyville....Shelby.		P. B. Dunn	Shelbyville Bk.	M. Dimmitt.
Springfield.....Greene.		Hefferman & Buckley	Hollands Bk.	W. B. Sandford.
Steelville.......Crawford.		J. T. Woodruff	Bk. of Steelville	Thos. R. Gibson.
Stockton........Cedar.		Ira E. Barber	Cedar Co. Bk.	W. B. Humphreys
Trenton.........Grundy.		Hugh C. Smith	Trenton Natl. Bk.	R. M. Cook.
Troy............Lincoln.		C. H. Avery	Peoples Savings Bk.	R. S. Shelton.
Tuscumbla....Miller.		E. C. Swalen	At Olean, Miller Co. Exchange Bk.	S. R. English.
Union..........Franklin.		Chas. F. Gallenkamp	Bk. of Union	A. W. Hoffman.
Unionville.....Putnam.		H. D. Marshall	Natl. Bk. of Unionville	F. H. Wentworth.
Van Buren.....Carter.		J. C. Carter	See Poplar Bluff	
Versailles......Morgan.		Blevins & Daniels	Bk. of Versailles.	W. L. Stephens.
Vienna..........Maries.		J. D. Crozier	See Rolla.	
Warrensburg..Johnson.		J. W. Sudluth	Citizens Bk.	W. B. Drummond
Warrenton....Warren.		Peers & Morsey	Bk. of Warren Co.	T. J. Fariss.
Warsaw........Benton.		H. A. Tompkins	Osage Valley Bk.	W. J. Huse.
Waynesville...Pulaski.		Joseph McGregor	At Richland, Pulaski Co. Bk.	H. M. Smith.
West Plains...Howell.		James Orchard	West Plains Bk.	M. B. Clarke.

PRINCIPAL CITY, NOT COUNTY SEAT.

| Kansas City....Jackson. | Gage, Ladd & Small | First Natl. Bk. | E. F. Swinney. |

DIGEST OF MISSOURI COMMERCIAL LAWS.

Assignments.—Every voluntary assignment must be for the benefit of all the creditors of the assignor in proportion to their respective claims.

Attachments.—Buying and selling or dealing in futures within six months next before suing out the attachment; or is in default for public money; or is a banker or banking company and receives deposits of money, knowing at the time he or it was insolvent; or has made or published a false or fraudulent statement as to the financial condition thereof. Attachments may be obtained by both resident and non-resident plaintiffs where it can be proven that the defendant is not a resident of the State; or is a corporation whose chief office or place of business is out of this State; or conceals himself so that the ordinary process of law cannot be served upon him; or has absconded or absented himself from his usual place of abode in this State, so that the ordinary process of law cannot be served upon him; or is about to remove his property or effects out of this State; or is about to remove out of this State with the intent to change his domicile; or has fraudulently conveyed or assigned his property or effects; has fraudulently concealed, removed or disposed of his property or effects: or is about fraudulently to convey or assign his

MISSOURI—Continued.

property or effects; or is about fraudulently to conceal, remove or dispose of his property or effects; or that the cause of action occurred out of this State, and the defendant has absconded or secretly removed his property or effects into this State.

Bank Laws.—Any five or more persons may associate themselves for the purpose of establishing a bank of deposit, or discount, or both, by filing articles of association. The cash capital must be not less than $10,000 nor more than $5,000,000. In cities having a population exceeding 150,000 inhabitants the capital stock shall not be less than $100,000. The entire capital must be subscribed, and one-half thereof actually paid up, before corporate existence can be acquired, and the other half within one year. No person can be a director who is not a resident of this State, nor at the same time a director in two State banks, or in a State bank, or in a National bank. There is no system of bank examination, but sworn statements of the condition of the corporation must be filed in the office of the Secretary of State whenever by him required, but not less than twice in each year. False statements, as well as the receipt or assent to the reception of deposits, with knowledge of the fact that the bank is insolvent or in failing circumstances, are punishable by a fine or imprisonment. Loans of more than 25 per cent. of its capital stock to any individual, corporation or company are forbidden. No person or company of persons may engage in the business of banking as private bankers without a paid up capital of not less than $5,000.

Exemptions.—Homestead in the country shall not include more than 160 acres of land, or exceed the total value of $1,500; in cities having a population of 40,000 or more, such homestead shall not include more than eighteen square rods of ground, or exceed the total value of $3,000; in cities having a population of 10,000, and less than 40,000, such homestead shall not include more than thirty square rods of ground, or exceed the total value of $1,500; in cities and incorporated towns and villages having a population of less than 10,000, such homestead shall not include more than five acres of ground or exceed the value of $1,500.

Interest.—Legal rate is six per cent. Parties may contract for eight per cent. Penalty for usury, forfeiture of interest at eight per cent. to the common schools and recovery by defendant of his costs. Judgments bear six per cent. per annum, unless the instrument sued on bears a different rate, not to exceed eight per cent.

Legal Holidays.—January 1, Sunday, February 22, July 4, December 25, any General or State Election Day, and any Thanksgiving Day.

Married Women.—All property of married women, whether acquired before or after marriage, is her separate estate, and cannot be taken for debt of her husband, unless for necessaries of the family. A married woman can make contracts in her own name, buy goods, give notes in settlement of purchases, binding her own separate property whether real or personal.

Notarial Fees.—Protest $1.50 and twenty-five cents for each notice.

Notes and Bills of Exchange.—The acceptance of a bill of exchange must be in writing signed by the acceptor. A promise in writing to accept a bill before it is drawn has the effect of an actual acceptance in favor of every person who on the faith thereof shall pay value for the bill. Every person on whom a bill is drawn, and to whom the same shall be delivered for acceptance, who shall destroy it or refuse within twenty-four hours to return it, shall be deemed to have accepted it.

MISSOURI—Continued.

Bills drawn or negotiated within this State and protested draw 4 per cent. damages, if drawn on any person within this State; if on any person out of this State, but within the United States, 10 per cent.; if on any person at a place without the United States, 10 per cent.; if on any person without the United States, 20 per cent. Such damages are only recoverable by the holder of a bill who shall have acquired the same for a valuable consideration. No damages are allowed if the bill be paid within twenty days after demand. Promissory notes are governed by the same rules of damages. Three days of grace are allowed on all bills or notes except those payable at sight or demand. Paper falling due on a holiday shall be considered payable on the next succeeding day.

Stay of Executions.—There is no law.

Transfer of Corporation Stocks.—Stock may be transferred in any manner provided by the by-laws of the corporation, provided the previous calls thereon have been paid. It is usually made by proper endorsement on certificate authorizing endorsee to have transfer made on books of corporation.

MONTANA.

County Seat.	County.	Name of Atty.	Name of Bank.	Cashier.
Billings	Yellowstone.	O. F. Goddard	Yellowstone Natl. Bk.	J. A. Griggs.
Boulder	Jefferson.	George D. Greene	Bk. of Boulder	F. C. Barendes.
Bozeman	Gallatin.	Hartman & Hartman	Bozeman Natl. Bk.	Peter Koch.
Butte City	Silver Bow.	Corbett & Wellcome	First Natl. Bk.	Andrew J. Davis.
Choteau	Teton.	See Great Falls		
DEER LODGE CITY	Deer Lodge.	Cole & Whiteside	Bk. of Larabie Bros. & Co.	
Dillon	Beaverhead.	H. J. Burleigh	First Natl. Bk.	Otto Klemm.
Fort Benton	Choteau.	Jno. W. Tattan	Stockmens Natl. Bk.	Chas. E. Duer.
Glasgow	Valley.	Jno. J. Kerr	Bkg. House of R. P. Lewis	John M. Lewis.
Glendive	Dawson.	T. C. Holmes	Merchants Bk.	C. W. Butler.
Great Falls	Cascade.	Leslie & Downing	First Natl. Bk.	G. T. Curtis.
Helena	Lewis&Clarke	H. S. Hepner	First Natl. Bk.	George F. Cope.
Kalispel	Flathead.	Sanford & Grubb	Conrad Natl. Bk.	W. A. Conrad.
Lewiston	Fergus.	Von Tobel & Cheadle	Bk. of Fergus Co.	James H. Moe.
Livingston	Park.	John T. Smith	Natl. Park Bk.	J. C. Vilas.
Miles City	Custer.	Strevell & Porter	First Natl. Bk.	H. B. Wiley.
Missoula	Missoula.	F. G. Webster	First Natl. Bk.	J. M. Keith.
Phillipsburg	Granite.	W. E. Moore	Merchants & Miners Natl. Bk.	C. H. Eshbaugh.
Stevensville	Pravalli.	See Missoula		
Virginia City	Madison.	W. A. Clark	Bk. of Hall & Bennett	
White Sulphur Springs	Meagher.	Smith & Gormley	First Natl. Bk.	James T. Wood.
Crow Indian Reservation		See Billings		

DIGEST OF MONTANA COMMERCIAL LAWS.

Assignments.—There is no assignment or insolvency law, except that upon an assignment of property, all wage-workers are privileged for work performed 60 days prior to the assignment.

Attachments.—Attachments are allowed without any allegation of fraud in the affidavit therefor, if account or debt is due ; if not, then upon an allegation of fraudulent transfer, bond is required.

Bank Laws.—Three or more persons may form a bank of discount and deposit with a paid-up capital of not less than $20,000. A certificate, under oath, of the president and cashier must be made to the effect that all the capital has been paid in, which certificate is filed with the State Auditor, and in the office of the Clerk and Recorder of the county where the bank is to be located. This certificate must specify the name of the bank, the county and town where located, the amount of the capital, the number of shares (which must be of the par value of $100 each), the names and residences of the stockholders, the number of shares held by each, and the time when the association shall begin and terminate. One copy of this certificate must be filed with the Secretary of State, and one with the Clerk and Recorder of the county where the bank is to be situated. Every director must be

THE LEGAL AND FINANCIAL LIGHTS OF AMERICA.

MONTANA—Continued.

a citizen of the United States, and at least three-fourths of them must be citizens of the State, and each must own at least ten shares of stock. Each must take an oath that he will diligently and honestly administer the bank's affairs. No bank can hold any real estate, except such as may be necessary for the transaction of its business and such as shall be mortgaged or conveyed to it as security for debts previously owing and such as it may purchase at judicial sales. The chief officer shall, on the first Monday of January and July, make a statement to the State Auditor of the bank's affairs. Officers and stockholders are individually liable for all debts equally and ratably, to the extent of their stock.

Exemptions.—Homestead of 160 acres if not in town, or one lot if in town and buildings thereon, all worth no more than $2,500, is exempt.

Interest.—Interest is allowed at rate of 10 per cent., but by special contract 12 per cent. may be provided for. There is no usury law.

Legal Holidays.—Sunday, January 1, February 22, May 30, July 4, September 1, December 25, public fast and Thanksgiving, General Election Day.

Limitation of Actions.—Limitation of actions on claims evidenced by a written instrument must be commenced within eight years; if not a written instrument, five years from the time of the accrual of the action; if upon an open and running account, five years from date of last item thereof.

Notarial Fees.—Protest $1.50 and fifty cents for each notice.

Notes and Bills of Exchange.— Notes and bills of exchange are negotiable obligations collected by and in the name of the holder and owner thereof. The holder may sue all the parties or any of them at his option. Grace is not allowed on notes and bills of exchange. Paper maturing on a legal holiday shall be considered as due and payable the day preceding. The protest of a notary public, under his hand and seal, is *prima facie* evidence of the facts contained therein. After demand of payment and refusal by the maker, drawer or acceptor of any commercial paper the notary public making such a demand may inform the indorser or any party to be charged if in the same town or township, by notice deposited in the nearest post-office to the party to be charged on the day of the demand, and no other notice shall be necessary to charge said party.

Transfer of Corporation Stocks.—A transfer of stock is good only between the parties thereto until transferred on the company's books.

NEBRASKA.

County Seat.	County.	Name of Atty.	Name of Bank.	Cashier.
Ainsworth	Brown.	P. D. McAndrew	Exchange Bk.	J. M. Kingery.
Albion	Boone.	J. A. Price	Albion Natl. Bk.	W. Baker.
Alma	Harlan.	D. S. Hardin	First Natl. Bk.	C. W. Griffin.
Auburn	Nemaha.	Jno. S. Stull	Carson Natl. Bk.	E. M. Boyd.
Aurora	Hamilton.	Howard M. Kellogg	First Natl. Bk.	J. F. Honseman.
Bartlett	Wheeler.	R. L. Staple	See Burwell	
Bassett	Rock.	J. J. Carlin	State Bk. of Bassett	J. A. Hillburg.
Beatrice	Gage.	Griggs, Rinaker & Bibb	Beatrice Natl. Bk.	D. W. Cook.
Beaver City	Furnace.	McClure & Anderson	First Natl. Bk.	C. E. V. Smith.
Benkleman	Dundy.	J. W. James	Bk. of Benkleman	Oscar Calliham.
Big Springs	Denel.	E. D. Hamilton	State Bk. of Big Springs	R. J. Vinton.
Blair	Washington.	Walton & Mummert	Bkg. House of A. Castetter	F. M. Castetter.
Bloomington	Franklin.	A. H. Byrum	Franklin Co. Bk.	Chas. K. Hart.
Brewster	Blaine.	E. R. Riggs	International State Bk.	P. C. Erickson.
Broken Bow	Custer.	Sullivan & Gutterson	Farmers Bk.	J. A. Harris.
Burwell	Garfield.	Guy Laverty	First Bk. of Burwell.	A. I. Cram.
Butte	Boyd.	Geo. F. Knapp	Farmers & Merchants Bk.	H. W. Andrews.
Central City	Merrick.	W. T. Thompson	Farmers State Bk.	W. C. Kerr.
Chadron	Dawes.	Albert W. Crites	Chadron Bkg. Co.	A. P. Sloan.
Clay Centre	Clay.	J. L. Epperson & Sons	State Bk. of Clay Centre	W. J. Gardiner.
Columbus	Platte.	Albert & Reeder	First Natl. Bk.	O. T. Roen.
Dakota	Dakota.	Joy & Beck	Bk. of Dakota City	M. O. Ayres.
David City	Butler.	S. H. Steele	Central Nebraska Natl. Bk.	Geo. R. Colton.
Elwood	Gosper.	A. M. White	State Bk. of Elwood	E. Shallenberger.
Fairbury	Jefferson.	W. P. Freeman	Herbine Bk. of Fairbury	H. F. Hole.
Falls City	Richardson.	C. Gillespie	Richardson Co. Bk.	G. W. Holland.
Fremont	Dodge.	Munger & Courtwright	Fremont Natl. Bk.	Julius Beckman.
Fullerton	Nance.	W. F. Critchfield	Citizens State Bk.	F. M. La Grange.
Gandy	Logan.	J. E. Morrison	State Bk. of Gandy	E. R. Smith.
Geneva	Fillmore.	Charles H. Sloan	Geneva Natl. Bk.	M. R. Chettick.
Gering	Scotts Bluff.	M. J. Huffman	Bk. of Gering.	Peter McFarlane.
Grand Island	Hall.	Geo. H. Thummel	First Natl. Bk.	C. F. Bentley.
Grant	Perkins.	B. F. Hastings	At Madrid, Bk. of Madrid.	G. W. Snider.
Harrisburg	Banner.	Ed. A. Mann	Banner Co. Bk.	C. J. Carlisle.
Harrison	Sioux.	A. T. Clark	Commercial Bk.	D. H. Griswold.
Hartington	Cedar.	J. C. Robinson	Hartington State Bk.	A. M. Merrill.
Hastings	Adams.	Tibbets, Morey & Ferris	First Natl. Bk.	G. H. Pratt.
Hayes Centre	Hayes.	R. C. Orr	State Bk. of Hayes Centre	J. L. Blood.
Hebron	Thayer.	M. H. Weiss	First Natl. Bk.	J. H. Lynch.
Hemingford	Box Butte.	Tuttle & Tate	Box Butte Bk.	C. A. Burlew.
Holdrege	Phelps.	Rhea Bros.	First Natl. Bk.	E. J. Titus.
Hyannis	Grant.	See Hemingford	See Thedford	
Imperial	Chase.	C. W. Meeker	Farmers & Merchants Bk.	O.P.Shallenberger
Indianola	Red Willow.	J. S. Phillips	State Bk.	Michael Morris.
Kearney	Buffalo.	Dryden & Main	City Natl. Bk.	J. S. Adair.
Kimball	Kimball.	J. W. Davis	Bk. of Kimball	L. W. Bickel.
Lexington	Dawson.	C. W. McNamara	First Natl. Bk.	H. V. Temple.

THE LEGAL AND FINANCIAL LIGHTS OF AMERICA. 89

NEBRASKA—Continued.

County Seat.	County.	Name of Atty.	Name of Bank.	Cashier.
Lincoln	Lancaster.	Sawyer, Snell & Frost	First Natl. Bk.	F. M. Cook.
Loup City	Sherman.	Long & Mathew	Farmers State Bk.	Wm. Shaedla
Madison	Madison.	Moyer Bros.	First Natl. Bk.	M. C. Garrett.
McPherson	McPherson.	See Gandy		
Minden	Kearney.	J. L. McPheely	Minden Exchange Bk.	Kingsley Bros.
Mullen	Hooker.	See Thedford		
Nebraska City	Otoc.	John C. Watson	Merchants Natl. Bk.	H. N. Shewell.
Neligh	Antelope.	N. D. Jackson	First Natl. Bk.	C. R. Allder.
Nelson	Nucols.	Searle & Coleman	First Natl. Bk.	S. A. Lapp.
Niobrara	Knox.	E. A. Houston	Niobrara Valley Bk.	S. Draper.
North Platte	Lincoln.	French & Baldwin	First Natl. Bk.	A. McNamara.
Ogallala	Keith.	Muldoon & Phelps	Bk. of Ogallala.	F. G. Hoxie.
Omaha	Douglas.	Lake & Hamilton	First Natl. Bk.	F. H. Davis.
O'Neill	Holt.	M. F. Harrington	State Bk. of O'Neill	John McHugh.
Ord	Valley.	Clements Bros.	First Natl. Bk.	E. N. Mitchell.
Osceola	Polk.	E. L. King	Osceola Bk.	O. E. Mickey.
Papillion	Sarpy.	James Hassett	Bk. of E. W. Clarke	J. D. Clarke.
Pawnee City	Pawnee.	Story & Story	First Natl. Bk.	John C. David.
Pender	Thurston.	R. G. Strong	First Natl. Bk.	E. A. Wiltse.
Pierce	Pierce.	W. W. Quivey	First Natl. Bk.	Woods Cones.
Plattsmouth	Cass.	Beeson & Root	Bk. of Cass Co.	J. M. Patterson.
Ponca	Dixon.	J. J. McCarthy	Bk. of Dixon Co.	H. C. Howe.
Red Cloud	Webster.	Case & McNitt	State Bk. of Red Cloud	W. T. Auld.
Rushville	Sheridan.	W. W. Wood	Citizens Bk.	M.P.Musser & Co.
St. Paul	Howard.	T. T. Bell	St. Paul Natl. Bk.	A. U. Dann.
Schuyler	Colfax.	Geo. H. Thomas	First Natl. Bk.	Morris Palmer.
Scotia	Greeley.	H. S. Sprecher	Peoples Bk.	W. E. Hannon.
Seward	Seward.	Anderson & Terwilliger	State Bk. of Nebraska.	C. W. Barkley.
Sidney	Cheyenne.	James L. McIntosh	American Bk.	George E. Taylor.
Springview	Keya Paha.	J. B. Farnsworth	Keya Paha Co. Bk.	F. H. Jones.
Stanton	Stanton.	John A. Ehrhardt	First Natl. Bk.	Wm. Gerecke.
Stockville	Frontier.	L. H. Cheney	Farmers & Merchants State Bk.	H. H. Griffith.
Taylor	Loup.	A. S. Moon	Taylor State Bk.	A. S. Moon.
Tecumseh	Johnson.	S. P. Davidson	Chamberlain Bkg. House.	C.M.Chamberlain
Tekamah	Burt.	I. O. Hopewell	First Natl. Bk.	Ed. Latta.
Thedford	Thomas.	Jno. H. Evans	Thedford Bk.	J. M. McMillan.
Trenton	Hitchcock.	Button & Button	Trenton State Bk.	A. O. Robinson.
Valentine	Cherry.	F. M. Walcott	Cherry Co. Bk.	Chas. Sparks.
Wahoo	Saunders.	Good & Good	First Natl. Bk.	Peter Anderson.
Wayne	Wayne.	A. A. Walsh	Citizens Bk.	D. C. Main.
West Point	Cuming.	J. C. Crawford	National Bk.	J. W. Shearer.
Wilber	Saline.	Hastings & McGintie	State Bk. of Wilber.	F. F. Gay.
York	York.	Gilbert Bros.	First Natl. Bk.	E. J. Whitman.

NEBRASKA—Continued.
DIGEST OF NEBRASKA COMMERCIAL LAWS.

Assignments.—An assignment must include all property of assignor and no preferences are allowed.

Attachments.—Attachments may issue where the defendant is a non-resident or foreign corporation ; has absconded with the intent to defraud creditors ; has left the county of his residence to avoid service of summons; so conceals himself that summons cannot be served upon him ; is about to move his property out of the jurisdiction of the court with the intention to defraud his creditors ; is about to convert his property into money for the purpose of placing it beyond their reach ; has property or rights in action which he conceals ; has assigned, removed or disposed of, or is about to dispose of his property with fraudulent intent ; fraudulently contracted the debt.

Bank Laws.—Any number of persons may form a corporation for banking purposes. They must adopt and record in office of the County Clerk of the county where the business is to be transacted, their articles of association. Notice must be published in a newspaper in the proposed place of business, giving the name of the bank, its place of business, capital, time and condition of payment of the capital, the beginning and termination of corporate existence, the maximum liability that may be incurred, and the names of the officers. The liabilities of the bank must not exceed two-thirds of the capital stock, except in cases of banks of deposit only. All banks must publish quarterly statements of their assets and liabilities, and stockholders are liable to the creditors of the bank in an amount equal to the par value of the stock held by them in addition to the cost of said stock. The cash capital of banks must be as follows: In villages of 1,000 population, $5,000 and upwards; those of 1,500 population, $10,000 and upwards; those of 3,000, $20,000 and upwards; those of 5,000 population, $30,000 and upwards, and those of 10,000 population, $50,000 and upwards. Reports must be made by the bank officers not less than three times per year, to the State Board, consisting of the State Auditor, State Treasurer and Attorney-General, showing the bank's condition.

Exemptions.—There is exempt from judicial sale to every family a homestead, not exceeding in value $2,000, consisting of a dwelling house in which claimant resides and its appurtenances and lands on which the same is situated, not exceeding 160 acres, or if within an incorporated city or village a quantity of contiguous lands not exceeding two lots.

Interest.—Legal rate is 7 per cent., but by agreement may be 10 per cent. The penalty for taking a greater rate of interest than 10 per cent. is loss of all interest and costs of an action.

Legal Holidays.—Sunday, January 1, February 22, April 22, May 30, July 4, September 1, December 25, public fast and Thanksgiving, Labor Day.

Limitation of Actions.—Upon a contract not in writing, expressed or implied, four years. Upon a specialty or an agreement, contract or promise in writing, or foreign judgment, five years. For the recovery of the title or possession of land, tenements or hereditaments, including also mortgages, ten years.

Married Women.—All property of married women, whether acquired before or after marriage, except gifts of the husband, are her sole and separate estate, and are not liable for the husband's debts. She may buy, sell, and trade on her own account, and her separate estate is liable for her debts so contracted.

NEBRASKA—Continued.

Notarial Fees.—Protest $1, copy fifty cents, each notice twenty-five cents and postage.

Notes and Bills of Exchange.—Notes and bills of exchange are entitled to three days' grace. When holiday occurs on Monday, notes, etc., falling due on that day are payable the day thereafter; all other business, contracts, etc., remain unaffected by holidays. Foreign bills of exchange, notes, and drafts must be protested, and protest fees can be recovered. Where all the parties are within this State, no protest is necessary, and fees, therefore, cannot be recovered, but prompt notice must be given. Damages on domestic bills, 6 per cent., and on foreign bills, 12 per cent.

Transfer of Corporation Stocks.—No statute or decision on this point. Question now pending in Supreme Court.

NEVADA.

County Seat.	County.	Name of Atty.	Name of Bank.	Cashier.
Austin	Lander.	W. D. Jones	State Bk. of Nevada	G. A. Land.
Belmont	Nye.	J. P. Lamb	See Austin	
Carson City	Ormsby.	T. Coffin	Bullion & Exchange Bk.	T. R. Hofer.
Dayton	Lyon.	John Lathrop	See Virginia City	
Elko	Elko.	E. S. Farington	Henderson Bkg. Co.	John Henderson.
Eureka	Eureka.	Theodore Wren	Eureka Co. Bk.	John Torre.
Hamilton	White Pine.	See Eureka		
Hawthorne	Esmeralda.	Benjamin Curler	See Carson City	
Genoa	Douglass.	D. W. Virgin	See Carson City	
Pioche	Lincoln.	T. J. Osborne	J. Eiseman (Broker)	
Reno	Washoe.	T. V. Julien	First Natl. Bk.	Chas. T. Bender.
Stillwater	Churchill.	L. Allen	See Virginia City	
Virginia City	Storey.	W. E. F. Deal	Bk. of California.	A. I. Bloch (Agt.).
Winnemucca	Humboldt.	M. J. Bonnifield	First Natl. Bk.	Geo. S. Nixon.

DIGEST OF NEVADA COMMERCIAL LAWS.

Assignments.—Every insolvent debtor may be discharged from his debts upon executing an assignment of all his property, real, personal or mixed, for the benefit of all his creditors, and upon compliance with the general provisions of the Insolvent Act.

Attachments.—Attachment may issue in an action upon a contract for the direct payment of money made or by the terms thereof payable in this State, which is not secured by mortgage, lien or pledge upon real or personal property situated or being in this State, and if so secured when such security has been rendered nugatory by the act of the defendant; in an action against a defendant not residing in this State; in an action by a resident of this State for the recovery of the value of property, where such property has been conveyed by a defendant without the consent of the owner where the defendant has absconded, or is about to abscond, with the intent to defraud his creditors; where a defendant conceals himself so that service of summons cannot be made upon him; where a defendant is about to remove his property, or any part thereof beyond the jurisdiction of the court, with the intent to defraud his creditors; where a defendant is about to convert his property into money with the intent to place it beyond the reach of his creditors; where a defendant has assigned, removed, disposed of, or is about to dispose of his property, or any part thereof, with intent to defraud his creditors; where a defendant has fraudulently or criminally contracted the debt or incurred the obligation for which suit has been commenced.

Bank Laws.—Three or more persons may form a banking company upon signing and acknowledging a certificate, stating the corporate name of the proposed bank, the amount of its capital, the time for which it is to exist, the number of shares into which the capital is to be divided, the number and names of the persons who are to act as trustees for the first six months, and the name of the place where the business is to be transacted, and filing and recording this certificate in the office of the Clerk of the county within which the principal place of business of the bank is to be

NEVADA—Continued.

located, and having a certified copy thereof filed in the office of the Secretary of State. There is no provision for official visitation; nor are banks required to make report of their condition.

Exemptions.—A homestead not exceeding $5,000 to be selected by the husband and wife, or either of them, or other head of the family, is exempt from forced sale on execution, or other process from the courts.

Interest.—Legal rate is 7 per cent., but parties may agree in writing, for any rate of interest whatever on any contract. Banks are allowed interest at the rate of 24 per cent. per annum when there is no contract in writing for a different rate, for all money due on instruments in writing payable to them, on overdrawn accounts with them and on any judgment recovered therefor.

Legal Holidays.—Sunday, January 1, February 22, July 4, December 25, and Thanksgiving Day.

Limitation of Actions.—Upon a contract, obligation or liability, founded upon an instrument in writing, except when a disability prevents the institution of an action, within six years. An action on an open account for goods, wares and merchandise, sold and delivered; for any article charged in a store account; upon a contract, obligation or liability, not founded upon an instrument in writing within four years.

Married Women.—All property of the wife owned by her before marriage, or acquired afterwards by gift, bequest, devise or descent, is her sole estate. All property obtained since marriage is common property; the husband has absolute control of common property. The wife may buy, sell or trade, and give notes in payment of purchases, and her separate property is liable for the same.

Notarial Fees.—Protest $1.50 and seventy-five cents for each notice.

Notes and Bills of Exchange.—Commercial paper includes promises to pay to order or bearer, without condition, for a sum certain, and at a time certain. No requirement respecting place of payment, but, if place of payment is named, demand should be made before protest at place named. Protest and notice will hold the indorser, and the general statute of limitation, six years, and on open account, four years, is the limitation of the right of action. Fifteen per cent. damages are allowed on domestic, and twenty per cent. on foreign bills protested. Three days of grace are allowed on notes and bills of exchange, but not on sight drafts. Paper maturing on a holiday is due and payable on the preceding day.

Stay of Executions.—Discretionary with the courts.

Transfer of Corporation Stocks.—By endorsement and delivery of the stock.

NEW HAMPSHIRE.

County Seat.	County.	Name of Atty.	Name of Bank.	Cashier.
Colebrook	Coos.	T. F. Johnson	Colebrook Natl. Bk.	H. F. Bailey.
Concord	Merrimac.	Sargent & Hollis	First Natl. Bk.	Chas. G. Remick.
Dover	Strafford.	R. G. Pike	Strafford Natl. Bk.	C. S. Cartland.
Exeter	Rockingham.	Eastman, Young & O'Neil	Exeter Bkg. Co.	C. E. Byington.
Keene	Cheshire.	Batchelder & Faulkner	Keene Natl. Bk.	W. L. Mason.
Laconia	Belknap.	Jewett & Plummer	Laconia Natl. Bk.	O. W. Tibbetts.
Nashua	Hillsborough.	C. J. Hamblett	Indian Head Natl. Bk.	Ira F. Harris.
Newport	Sullivan.	A. S. Wait	Citizens Natl. Bk.	P. A. Johnson.
Ossipee	Carroll.	Frank Weeks	At Wolfeboro, Wolfeboro Loan & Bkg. Co.	C. F. Piper.
Plymouth	Grafton.	Burleigh & Adams	Pemigewasset Natl. Bk.	R. E. Smythe.

PRINCIPAL CITIES, NOT COUNTY SEATS.

Lancaster	Coos.	Drew, Jordan & Buckley	Lancaster Natl. Bk.	F. D. Hutchins.
Manchester	Hillsborough.	David Cross	Manchester Natl. Bk.	W. B. Stearns.
Portsmouth	Rockingham.	J. S. H. Frink	New Hampshire Natl. Bk.	W. C. Walton.

DIGEST OF NEW HAMPSHIRE COMMERCIAL LAWS.

Assignments.—Assignment must include all the debtor's property, except what is exempt from attachment, for the equal benefits of all his creditors.

Attachments.—In most actions, any property which may be taken upon execution, may be attached and holden as security for the judgment the plaintiff may recover. The property of the defendant in the hands of a third person, and debts due the defendant, may be attached by trustee process, service being made upon the defendant and trustee as in other cases. Property attached is holden for thirty days from the rendition of judgment, and the levy of the execution must be commenced within that time. No valid attachment can be made to secure claims not due at the commencement of the action. Attaching creditors acquire a lien in the order of their attachments, and do not share in the attached property, *pro rata*.

Bank Laws.—State banks are chartered by the Legislature only, and capital must be fully paid up in actual cash before business is begun. Each stockholder is liable only for the par value of his stock. Statement of condition to be made once in three months to the Secretary of State. Three Bank Commissioners appointed by the Governor examine all banks once, at least every year, and report their conditions to the Governor.

Exemptions.—The wife, widow and children of every person who is the owner of a homestead, or any interest therein, are entitled to so much thereof as does not exceed in value $500. If the wife owns a homestead at her decease, the life estate of the surviving husband, not exceeding the value of $500, is exempt to him. A homestead of the value of $500 is also exempt to an unmarried person owning the same.

THE LEGAL AND FINANCIAL LIGHTS OF AMERICA.

NEW HAMPSHIRE—Continued.

Interest.—Legal rate is six per cent. per annum, unless a lower rate is stipulated. The penalty for usury is forfeiture of all the interest.

Legal Holidays.—Sunday, Thanksgiving, Fast Day, Christmas, July 4, February 22, May 30, or any day on which a general election is held for members of the Legislature, first Monday of September (Labor Day).

Limitation of Actions.—Actions for the recovery of real estate, upon notes secured by mortgage and upon judgments (whether domestic or foreign), recognizances and contracts under seal must be brought within twenty years. Actions for trespass to the person and defamatory words must be brought within two years, and all other personal actions within six years after the cause of action accrues. A debt is revived by any new promise, verbal or written.

Married Women.—By an act of the Legislature, passed June 2d, 1876, a married woman may make contracts, sue and be sued in all matters in law and equity, in the same manner as if she was *femme sole*; provided, however, that all laws then in force, as to contracts and conveyances between husband and wife, and as to the rights of the husband, in her property and estate, shall not be affected thereby; and provided, also, that no contract or conveyance by a married woman as surety or guarantor for her husband, nor any undertaking by her for him or in his behalf, shall be binding to her.

Notarial Fees.—Protest 50 cents and twenty-five cents for each notice.

Notes and Bills of Exchange.—Demand notes must be protested within sixty days from the date of their endorsement to hold endorsers. All negotiable paper, save that payable on demand, is entitled to three days of grace, and all such paper maturing on a holiday is payable the preceding business day. Notaries public are the proper protesting officers. Notice of the non-payment or the non-acceptance upon residents by mail is sufficient.

Stay of Executions.—By special order of court only.

Transfer of Corporation Stocks.—The delivery of a stock certificate to a *bona fide* purchaser or pledgee, with a written transfer of same, is sufficient to to transfer the title against all persons but the corporation.

NEW JERSEY.

County Seat.	County.	Name of Atty.	Name of Bank.	Cashier.
Belvidere	Warren.	L. D. Taylor	Belvidere Natl. Bk.	A. B. Kelsey.
Bridgeton	Cumberland.	James R. Hoagland	Cumberland Natl. Bk.	F. M. Riley.
Camden	Camden.	Howard M. Cooper	Natl. State Bk.	W. F. Rose.
Cape May	Cape May.	J. S. Leaming	New Jersey Tr. & Safe Dep. Co.	H. C. Thompson.
Elizabeth	Union.	P. H. Gilhooly	First Natl. Bk.	E. L. Tilton.
Flemington	Hunterdon.	H. S. Fluck	Flemington Natl. Bk.	N. D. Stiger.
Freehold	Monmouth.	F. Parker	First Natl. Bk.	J.W.S. Campbell.
Hackensack	Bergen.	Johnson & Ackerson	Hackensack Bk.	H. D. Terhune.
Jersey City	Hudson.	Babbit & Lawrence	First Natl. Bk.	G. W. Conklin.
May's Landing	Atlantic.	J. E. P. Abbott	At Atlantic City, Atlantic City Natl. Bk.	F. P. Quigley.
Morristown	Morris.	Stephen H. Little	First Natl. Bk.	J. H. Van Doren.
Mount Holly	Burlington.	Franklin B. Lewis	Farmers Natl. Bk.	J. B. Davis.
Newark	Essex.	George W. Hubbel	Essel Co. Natl. Bk.	F. B. Adams.
NEW BRUNSWICK	Middlesex.	Woodbridge, Strong & Sons.	Natl. Bk. of New Jersey	H. G. Parker.
Newton	Sussex.	L. Van Blarcom	Merchants Natl. Bk.	John C. Howell.
Paterson	Passaic.	G. A. Hobart	First Natl. Bk.	W. G. Scott.
Salem	Salem.	M. P. Grey	Salem Natl. Bkg. Co.	H. M. Rumsey.
Somerville	Somerset.	James J. Bergen	First Natl. Bk.	Wm. H. Taylor.
Tom's River	Ocean.	T. W. Middleton	First Natl. Bk.	Wm. A. Low.
Trenton	Mercer.	Lowthorp & Oliphant	First Natl. Bk.	Chas. Whitehead.
Woodbury	Gloucester.	John S. Jessup	First Natl. Bk.	John F. Graham.

DIGEST OF NEW JERSEY COMMERCIAL LAWS.

Assignments.—Assignments by debtors for the benefit of creditors must be without preference, and all others are void.

Attachments.—A creditor may attach the property of a non-resident or absconding debtor by making oath to the fact, and to the amount of his claim. Attachments are for the benefit of all applying creditors. Debts not due may be proved under any attachment issued and receive their *pro rata* dividend.

Bank Laws.—Any number of persons, not less than seven citizens of the State, may associate to establish a bank or a banking company, but the aggregate amount of the capital stock of any such association shall not be less than $50,000. The persons so associating shall, under their hands and seals, make a certificate, by the terms of which such association shall be bound, which shall specify the name assumed to distinguish such association; the place where the business is to be carried on; the amount of the capital stock, and the number of shares; the names and places of residence of the shareholders, and the number of shares held by each of them, and the period at which such association shall commence and terminate, which shall not be for a longer term than twenty years. This certificate shall be proved or acknowledged in the same manner as deeds, and recorded in the office of the Secretary of

NEW JERSEY—Continued.

State and in the Clerk's Office of the county where the office of such association shall be established; but it shall not be lawful for any association to locate their office in any other than one of the county towns, or incorporated cities, boroughs or towns, except by permission of the Commissioner of Banking and Insurance, to whom all matters relating to banks are committed, and in whom lies the right of examination. The Legislature may dissolve any company created by virtue of this act. The Chancellor may order an examination on application of creditors or stockholders. Banks usually publish a statement, and make annual reports to the State Treasurer.

Exemptions.—House and lot to the value of $1,000. The conveyance should show that the property is to be held as a homestead, or a notice to that effect should be recorded in the clerk's office and published for six weeks in one or more newspapers of the county.

Interest.—Legal rate is 6 per cent., and the penalty of usury is loss of all interest and costs if suit be necessary to recover.

Legal Holidays.—Sunday, January 1, February 22, May 30, July 4, First Monday of September (Labor Day), Thanksgiving Day, December 25, any General Election Day, every Saturday from noon until midnight, and every Thanksgiving or Fast Day recommended by the Governor or President.

Limitation of Actions.—Contracts not under seal, six years ; real actions and judgments, twenty years ; notes secured by mortgages and contracts under seal, sixteen years.

Married Women.—The real and personal property of the wife at marriage, and such as she acquires thereafter by gift, grant, descent, devise or bequest. and all revenue therefrom, are her separate estate. Since January 1, 1875, the wife has a right to bind herself by contract in the same manner and to the same extent, as though she was unmarried, and her sole estate is responsible for said contracts. She cannot become an accommodation endorser, guarantor or surety. She may buy, sell and trade in her own name.

Notarial Fees.—Protest $1 30 under $100 ; $1.50 over $100.

Notes and Bills of Exchange.—Inland bills of exchange are, in general, subject to the laws of foreign bills ; they must be protested. Sight bills or drafts have no days of grace. The action required to hold indorser is the same as under the general mercantile law. Paper due on a legal holiday is payable the day after, and notice of non-payment may be given within twenty-four hours after. If the legal holiday should fall upon a Sunday or Monday, bills are payable on Tuesday, and notice may be given on Wednesday.

Stay of Executions.—In Justice Courts, stay for one month on fifteen dollars and under ; fifteen dollars to sixty dollars, three months; over sixty dollars, six months.

Transfer of Corporation Stocks.—Transferable on the books of the company in such manner as the by-laws may provide.

NEW MEXICO.

County Seat.	County.	Name of Atty.	Name of Bank.	Cashier.
Albuquerque..Bernalilio.		Johnston & Finical	First Natl. Bk.	A. A. Keene.
Aztec............San Juan.		Childers & Dobson	San Juan Co. Bk.	RobertC.Prewett.
Clayton..........Union.		George McCormick	At Raton, First Natl. Bk.	C. N. Blackwell.
Eddy.............Eddy.		W. A. Hawkins	First Natl. Bk.	C. E. Conway.
Hillsborough.Sierra.		A. B. Elliott	Sierra Co. Bk.	Wm. H. Bucher.
Las Cruces......Donna Ana.		S. B. Newcomb	George D. Bowman & Son	H. D. Bowman.
Las Vegas......San Miquel.		A. A. Jones	San Miquel Natl. Bk.	D. T. Hoskins.
Lincoln..........Lincoln.		George B. Barber	At White Oaks, Exchange Bk.	Frank J. Sager.
Los Lumas.....Valencia.		See Albuquerque		
Mora.............Mora.		A. L. Branch	See Taos	
PUERTO DE LUMA..Guadaloupe.		See Las Vegas		
Roswell.........Chaves.		G. A. Richardson	Bk. of Roswell	E. A. Cahoon.
Santa Fe........Santa Fe.		Thomas B. Catron	First Natl. Bk.	John H. Vaughn.
Silver City......Grant.		T. F. Conway	Silver City Natl. Bk.	J. W. Carter.
Socorro..........Socorro.		James G. Fitch	New Mexico Natl. Bk.	E. E. Nold.
Springer........Colfax.		G. W. Abbott	Andrew Morton & Co.	A. Morton.
Taos.............Taos.		Santiago Valdez	Taos Co. Bk.	C. Santistevan.
TIERRA AMARILLA.Rio Arriba.		F. P. Chancy	See Taos	

DIGEST OF NEW MEXICO COMMERCIAL LAWS.

Assignments.—An insolvent debtor may make a voluntary assignment for the benefit of his creditors. No preferences allowed.

Attachments.—Attachments issue when the debtor is not a resident of the Territory of New Mexico; when the debtor has concealed himself or absconded or absented himself from his usual place of abode in this Territory, so that the ordinary process of law cannot be passed upon him; when the debtor is about to remove his property or effects out of this Territory, or has fraudulently concealed or disposed of his property or effects; when the debtor is about to fraudulently convey or assign, conceal or dispose of his property and effects; when the debt was contracted outside of this Territory, and the debtor has absconded or secretly removed his property or effects into the Territory; when the defendant is a corporation whose principal office or place of business is out of the Territory, unless such corporation shall have a designated agent in the Territory, upon whom service of process may be made in suits against the corporation.

Bank Laws.—Any number of persons, not less than three, may be chartered as a bank. The capital shall not be less than $30,000, one-half of which must be paid in before beginning business, and the remainder within one year. Statements are required to be sent twice a year to the Territorial Treasurer, showing the condition of the bank, on the first Monday of January and July, and these statements are required to be published for three consecutive weeks in a newspaper of the county where the bank is located. The officers and stockholders of every bank are individually liable for all debts contracted during the time that they were such officers or stockholders ratably to the extent of their respective shares.

NEW MEXICO—Continued.

Exemptions.—Husband and wife, widow or widower, living with an unmarried daughter, or unmarried minor son, may hold exempt a family homestead not exceeding $1,000 in value. Any resident of this territory who is the head of a family and not the owner of a homestead may hold exempt real or personal property, to be selected by such person, not exceeding $500 in value, in addition to the amount of chattel property otherwise by law exempted.

Interest.—Legal rate is six per cent. Parties may contract in writing for twelve per cent. Usury is punished by fine and forfeiture of double amount of interest paid.

Legal Holidays.—Sunday, January 1, July 4, December 25, and all days for fasting or thanksgiving.

Limitation of Actions.—Within six years: upon any bond, promissory note, bill of exchange or other contract in writing, or of any judgment of a court not of record. Within four years: upon accounts and unwritten contracts, injuries to property or the conversion thereof, and for relief upon the ground of fraud, and all other actions not otherwise provided for.

Notarial Fees.—Protest, $2.00, and twenty-five cents for each notice.

Notes and Bills of Exchange.—In absence of any designated place of payment the common law prevails. Three days of grace are allowed on promissory notes. Any promissory note, due and payable on any holiday, shall be construed to fall due and become payable on the next business day thereafter.

Transfer of Corporation Stocks.—Transferable only on the books of the company.

100   THE LEGAL AND FINANCIAL LIGHTS OF AMERICA.

NEW YORK.

County Seat.	County.	Name of Atty.	Name of Bank.	Cashier.
Albany	Albany.	Harris & Rudd	Natl. Commercial Bk.	E. A. Groesbeck.
Albion	Orleans.	Thomas A. Kirby	Orleans Co. Natl. Bk.	J. W. Cornell.
Auburn	Cayuga.	Rich & Alkem	Cayuga Co. Natl. Bk.	F. G. Jones.
Ballston Spa	Saratoga.	J. W. Verbeck	Ballston Spa Natl. Bk.	Thomas Kerley.
Batavia	Genesee.	Tarbox & Sherwood	Bk. of Batavia.	H. T. Miller.
Belmont	Allegany.	V. A. Willard	State Bk. of Belmont	W. J. Richardson.
BINGHAMTON	Broome.	George Whitney	First Natl. Bk.	John Manier.
Brooklyn	Kings.	C. & T. Perry	Manufacturers Natl. Bk.	T. C. Disbrow.
Buffalo	Erie.	Clinton & Clark	Marine Bk. of Buffalo.	J. H. Lascelles.
Canandaiga	Ontario.	J. H. Metcalf	Canandaiga Natl. Bk.	H. T. Parmele.
Canton	St. Lawrence.	John C. Keeler	First Natl. Bk.	W. N. Beard.
Carmel	Putnam.	George E. Anderson	Putnam Co. Natl. Bk.	H. Ryder.
Catskill	Greene.	Jennings & Chase	Tanners Natl. Bk.	Wm. Palmatier.
Cooperstown	Otsego.	George Brooks	Second Natl. Bk.	George M. Jarvis.
Corning	Steuben.	A. S. Kendall	First Natl. Bk.	D. S. Drake.
Cortland	Cortland.	B. A. Benedict	First Natl. Bk.	E. Alley.
Delhi	Delaware.	Wagner & Fisher	Delaware Natl. Bk.	W. G. Edgerton.
ELIZABETHTOWN	Essex.	Richard L. Hand	At Port Henry, First Natl. Bk.	F. S. Atwell.
Elmira	Chemung.	Chas. R. Pratt	Second Natl. Bk.	D. M. Pratt.
Fonda	Montgomery.	Daniel Yost	Natl. Mohawk River Bk.	J. L. Hess.
Geneseo	Livingston.	Strong & Doty	Genesee Valley Natl. Bk.	T. F. Olmsted.
Goshen	Orange.	Nanny & Mead	Natl. Bk. of Orange Co.	C. J. Everett.
Herkimer	Herkimer.	Charles Bell	First Natl. Bk.	A. W. Haslehurst.
Hudson	Columbia.	Isaac N. Collier	Natl. Hudson River Bk.	Wm. Postwick.
Ithaca	Tompkins.	S. D. Halliday	First Natl. Bk.	Henry B. Lord.
Jamaica	Queens.	Henry A. Montfort	Bk. of Jamaica.	Wm. L. Wood.
Johnstown	Fulton.	A. J. Nellis	Peoples Bk.	Edward Wells.
Kingston	Ulster.	Bernard & Van Wagoner	Kingston Natl. Bk.	C. Hume.
Lake George	Warren.	E. Hunt	At Warrensburgh, Emerson & Co.	J. A. Emerson.
Lake Pleasant	Hamilton.	Vacant	At Dolgeville, Potter & Marsden	
Little Valley	Cattaraugus.	E. A. Nash	Crissey & Crissey	
Lockport	Niagara.	Ellsworth, Potter & Stoors.	Natl. Exchange Bk.	Wm. E. McComb.
Lowville	Lewis.	Merrill, Ryel & Merrill	First Natl. Bk.	Edward H. Bush.
Lyons	Wayne.	D. S. Chamberlain	Lyons Natl. Bk.	G. T. Kennedy.
Malone	Franklin.	Cantwell & Cantwell	Peoples Natl. Bk.	H. T. French.
Mayville	Chautauqua.	W. H. Tennant	State Bk. of Mayville	C. R. Cipperly.
Monticello	Sullivan.	T. F. Bush	Natl. Union Bk.	Edwin H. Strong.
Morrisville	Madison.	Smith & Smith	First Natl. Bk.	B. Tompkins.
New City	Rockland.	Irving Bros. at Haverstraw.	Peoples Bk.	H. C. Ver-Valen.
New York	New York.	Hastings & Gleason	First National Bk.	E. Scofield.

NEW YORK—Continued.

County Seat.	County.	Name of Atty.	Name of Bank.	Cashier.
Norwich	Chenango.	Albert F. Gladding	Chenango Natl. Bk.	Geo. T. Dunham.
Oswego	Oswego.	S. M. Coon	First Natl. Bk.	J. D. W. Case.
Owego	Tioga.	Clarke & Tuthill	First Natl. Bk.	W. S. Truman.
Penn Yan	Yates.	Briggs & Kimball	Baldwin's Bk.	F. S. Plaisted.
Plattsburgh	Clinton.	S. L. Wheeler	Merchants Natl. Bk.	J. M. Wever.
Poughkeepsie.	Dutchess.	Peter Hulme	Farmers & Manufacturers Natl.Bk.	G. H. Sherman.
Richmond	Richmond.	N. J. Wreth	At Stapleton, Bk. of Staten Island.	Otto Ahlmann.
Riverhead	Suffolk.	Timothy M. Griffing	Suffolk Co. Natl. Bk.	Henry P. Terry.
Rochester	Monroe.	Cogswell & Cogswell	Traders Natl. Bk.	C. H. Palmer.
Salem	Washington.	S. W. Russell	First Natl. Bk.	C. A. Beattie.
Schenectady	Schenectady.	A. P. Strong	Mohawk Natl. Bk.	J. G. L. Ackerman
Schoharie	Schoharie.	Krum & Grant	Schoharie Co. Bk.	R. A. Dewey.
Syracuse	Onondaga.	Wilson & Forbes	First Natl. Bk.	G. B. Leonard.
Troy	Rensselaer.	Frank W. Thomas	Manufacturers Natl. Bk.	S. O. Gleason.
Utica	Oneida.	Chas. G. Irish	First Natl. Bk.	John A. Goodale.
Warsaw	Wyoming.	M. E. & E. N. Bartlett	Wyoming Co. Natl. Bk.	F. J. Humphrey.
Waterloo	Seneca	F. L. Manning	First Natl. Bk.	P. M. Kendig.
Watertown	Jefferson.	A. H. Sawyer	Jefferson Co. Natl. Bk.	S. T. Wolworth.
Watkins	Schuyler.	C. N. Woodward	Farmers & Merchants Bk.	Wm. Roberts.
White Plains	Westchester.	Wilson Brown, Jr.	Central Bk.	H. E. Foster.

DIGEST OF NEW YORK COMMERCIAL LAWS.

Assignments.—Voluntary general assignments, for the benefit of creditors, may be made. Preferences are allowed.

Attachments.—An attachment will be granted when it is proven that the defendant is either a foreign corporation or not a resident of the State ; or if a natural person and a resident of the State, that he has departed therefrom with intent to defraud his creditors, or to avoid the service of a summons, or keeps himself concealed with like intent ; or if the defendant is a natural person or a domestic corporation, that he or it has removed, or is about to remove property from the State, with intent to defraud his or its creditors ; or has assigned, disposed of, or secreted, or is about to assign, dispose of or secrete his property with like intent.

Bank Laws.—Banks may be chartered under general laws of the State. In places of 6,000 inhabitants or less the minimum capital must be $25,000 ; in places of 30,000 inhabitants or less the minimum capital must be $50,000 ; and in places with upwards of 30,000 inhabitants the minimum capital must be at least $100,000. A deposit is required to be made with banking department to secure the bank's circulating notes, and $1,000 must also be so deposited as a guarantee of compliance with the banking laws, which the Superintendent of the Banking Department is author-

NEW YORK—Continued.

ized to apply to the extent required in payment of any penalty incurred by the bank or any assessment imposed upon it. Stockholders in banks of issue are liable to the amount of their respective shares for its debts. Holders of the bank's notes in case of insolvency are entitled to a preference over all other creditors. On the first day of February, May, August and November reports are required to be made to the Superintendent of the Banking Department, which report is required to be published in the newspapers of the place where the bank is located. The Superintendent has visitorial powers, and is required to make an annual report to the Legislature of the performance of his duties.

Exemptions.—A lot of land with one or more buildings thereon, not exceeding in value $1,000, owned and occupied as a residence by a householder having a family, when recorded is exempt.

Interest.—Legal rate is 6 per cent. Penalty for usury is forfeiture of principal and interest except a State bank forfeits double the amount of interest. Usurious interest may be recovered if action is brought therefor within one year. Usury is also a misdemeanor.

Legal Holidays.—Sunday, January 1, February 22, May 30, July 4, First Monday of September (Labor Day), December 25, any general election day. Every Saturday, from 12 o'clock at noon until 12 o'clock at midnight, which is designated a half holiday, and any day appointed or recommended by the Governor or President as a day of thanksgiving or fasting and prayer, or other religious observance shall, for all purposes whatever as regards the presenting for payment or acceptance, and of the protesting and giving notice of the dishonor of bills of exchange, bank checks and promissory notes made after the passage of this act, be treated and considered as the first day of the week, commonly called Sunday, and as a public holiday or half holiday.

Limitation of Actions.—Within twenty years, actions for the recovery of real property or judgment of a court of record, or upon a sealed instrument, or for dower. Within six years, an action upon a contract, express or implied, except a judgment or sealed instrument ; an action to recover upon liability created by statute, except a penalty or forfeiture ; an action to procure a judgment other than for a sum of money on the ground of fraud.

Married Women.—In an action or special proceeding, a married woman appears, prosecutes, or defends a loan or joined with other parties, as if she was single. She may carry on any business in her own name, and the earnings shall be her separate property.

Notarial Fees.—Protest 75 cents and ten cents for each notice.

Notes and Bills of Exchange.—Foreign bills of exchange, drafts, checks, and promissory notes payable to bearer, the maker or his order, or the order of any third party, are negotiable. Bills of exchange, or drafts drawn payable at sight at any place within the State, are made due at presentation, without grace. Checks, bills of exchange, or drafts, drawn on banks or bankers, and which are payable on a specified day, or in any number of days after the date of sight thereof, are payable without grace, and it is not necessary to protest the same for non-acceptance. All bills, checks, notes, etc., falling due on a holiday are deemed payable the business day succeeding. If not paid when due they may be protested, and the certificate of protest is *prima facie* evidence of presentation and non-payment. To charge indorser, notice of non-payment must at once be given to him.

NEW YORK—Continued.

Stay of Executions.—No stay except by order of court.

Transfer of Corporation Stocks.—An assignment in writing is the common method of transfer, generally coupled with a blank power of attorney, signed by the owner and acknowledged, which on presentation to the corporation it is transferred on their stock books, by assignment.

NORTH CAROLINA.

County Seat.	County.	Name of Atty.	Name of Bank.	Cashier.
Albemarle	Stanley.	Pemberton & Jerome	See Salisbury.	
Ashborough	Randolph.	J. A. Blair	At High Point, Commercial Natl. Bk.	W. G. Bradshaw.
Asheville	Buncombe.	S. H. Reed	Natl. Bk. of Ashville	Wm. J. Cocke.
Bakersville	Mitchell.	J. T. Greene	See Lenoir	
Bayboro	Pamlico.	W. T. Caho	At Aurora, J. B. Bonner	
Beaufort	Carteret.	C. B. Felton	See New Berne	
Boone	Watauga.	W. B. Councill	See Lenoir	
Brevard	Transylvania.	W. A. Gash	See Hendersonville	
Bryson City	Swain.	Fry & Nenby	See Waynesville	
Burgaw	Pender.	Bruce William	See Wilmington	
Burnsville	Yancey.	Wm. Moore	See Morganton	
Camden	Camden.	G. G. Luke	See Elizabeth City	
Carthage	Moore.	W. C. Douglass	See Rockingham	
Charlotte	Mecklenburg	Walker & Cansler	Commercial Natl. Bk.	D. H. Anderson.
Clinton	Sampson.	J. L. Stewart	See Fayetteville	
Columbia	Tyrrell.	Mark Majett	See Edenton	
Columbus	Polk.	See Hendersonville		
Concord	Cabarrus.	Montgomery & Crowell	Concord Natl. Bk.	D. B. Coltrane.
Currituck	Currituck.	G. G. Luke	See Elizabeth City	
Dallas	Gaston.	R. W. Santifer	At Gastonia, First Natl. Bk.	E. S. Pegram.
Danbury	Stokes.	W. W. King	At Reidsville, Bk. of Reidsville	C. N. Evans.
Dobson	Surry.	Folger & Folger	At Mt. Airy, First Natl. Bk.	M. L. Fawcette.
Durham	Durham.	Fuller & Fuller	Fidelity Bk.	John F. Wily.
Edenton	Chowon.	Pruden & Vann	Bk. of Edenton	John M. Martin.
Elizabeth City	Pasquotank.	J. H. Sawer	First Natl. Bk.	Wm. T. Old.
ELIZABETHTOWN	Bladen.	R. H. Lyon	See Wilmington	
Fayetteville	Cumberland.	C. W. Bradford	Bk. of Fayetteville	John C. Haigh.
Franklin	Macon.	Jones & Daniels	See Waynesville	
Gatesville	Gates.	L. L. Smith	See Elizabeth City	
Goldsborough	Wayne.	W. C. Munroe	Bk. of Wayne	W. E. Borden.
Graham	Alamance.	E. S. Parker	See Greensborough	
Greensboro'	Gulfford.	Levi M. Scott	Natl. Bk. of Greensborough	A. H. Alderman.
Greenville	Pitt.	W. H. Long	Tyson & Rawls.	
Halifax	Halifax.	J. M. Grizzard	At Scotland Neck, Scotland Neck Bk.	F. B. Shields.
Hayesville	Clay.	M. R. Kimsey	See Waynesville	
Henderson	Vance.	A. C. Zollicoffer	Citizens Bk.	W. A. Hunt.
HENDERSONVILLE	Henderson.	W. A. Smith	State Bk. of Commerce	J. A. Maddrey.
Hertford	Perquimans.	J. H. Blount	See Elizabeth City	
Hillsborough	Orange.	John W. Graham	See Rocksborough	
Jackson	Northampton	Peebles & Harris	At Weldon, Bk. of Weldon	W. R. Smith.
Jacksonville	Onslow.	R. W. Nixon	See New Berne	
Jefferson	Ashe.	E. S. Blackburn	See Winston	
Kenansville	Duplin.	A. D. Ward	See Wilmington	
Kinston	Lenoir.	A. J. Loftin	S. H. Loftin	R. C. Strong.
Lenoir	Caldwell.	Edward Jones	Bk. of Lenoir	G. F. Harper.
Lexington	Davidson.	Robbins & Roper	Bk. of Lexington	G. W. Montcastle.
Lillington	Harnett.	Oscar J. Spears	See Smithfield	

THE LEGAL AND FINANCIAL LIGHTS OF AMERICA. 105

NORTH CAROLINA—Continued.

County Seat.	County.	Name of Atty.	Name of Bank.	Cashier.
Lincolnton	....Lincoln.	David Robinson	See Shelby	
Louisburg	......Franklin.	C. M. Cooke	Farmers & Merchants Bk.	J. S. Barrow.
Lumberton	.....Robeson.	E. K. Procter, Jr.	See Fayetteville	
Manteo	..........Dare.	See Edenton		
Marion	.........McDowell.	J. L. C. Bird	See Asheville	
Marshall	.......Madison.	J. C. Pritchard	See Asheville	
Mocksville	.....Davie.	T. B. Bailey	See Winston	
Monroe	.........Union.	Adams & Redwin	Peoples Bk. of Monroe	W. H. Fitzgerald.
Morganton	.....Burke.	S. C. W. Tate	Piedmont Bk.	S. T. Pearson.
Murphy	.........Cherokee.	Leatherwood & Bell	See Waynesville	
Nashville	.......Nash.	Taylor & Worthington	See Louisburg	
New Berne	.....Craven.	O. H. Gulon	Natl. Bk. of New Berne	G. H. Roberts.
Newton	.........Catawba.	L. L. Witherspoon	Catawba Co. Bk.	W. C. Kenyon.
Oxford	..........Granville.	B. S. Royster	Bk. of Granville	J. B. Roller.
Pittsboro'	......Chatham.	F. B. Wornock	See Greensborough	
Plymouth	......Washington.	Charles Latham	See Edenton	
Raleigh	.........Wake.	R. H. Battle	Citizens Natl. Bk.	H. E. Litchford.
Robbinville	...Graham.	W. B. Ferguson	See Waynesville	
Rockingham	..Richmond.	Cole & McNeil	Bk. of Pee Dee	W. L. Parsons.
ROCKSBOROUGH	...Person.	Merritt & Bryant	Peoples Bk.	J. S. Bradsher.
RUTHERFORDTON	..Rutherford.	J. H. Justice	Carpenter & Morrow	D. F. Morrow.
Salisbury	.......Rowan.	L. H. Clement	Davis & Wiley	O. D. Davis.
Shelby	...........Cleveland.	Webb & Webb	H. D. Lee & Co.	
Smithfield	......Johnston.	Pou & Pou	W. M. Sanders	
Snow Hill	.....Greene.	George M. Lindsey	See Goldsborough	
Southport	......Brunswick.	See Wilmington		
Sparta	...........Alleghany.	H. K. Boyer	At Mount Airy, First Natl. Bk.	M. L. Fawcette.
Statesville	......Iredell.	Robbins & Long	First Natl. Bk.	George H. Brown
Swan Quarter.	Hyde.	John H. Small	See Washington	
Tarboro	.........Edgecombe.	Henry Johnston	Pamlico Ins. & Bkg. Co.	Job Copp.
Taylorsville	...Alexander.	R. Z. Linney	See Statesville	
Trenton	........Jones.	P. M. Pearsall	See New Berne	
Troy	.............Montgomery.	Douglas, Shaw & Scales	See Concord	
WADESBOROUGH	..Anson.	J. A. Lockhart	First Natl. Bk.	J. D. Leak.
Warrenton	....Warren.	H. A. Boyd	Gardner & Jeffress	J. M. Gardner.
Washington	...Beaufort.	W. B. Rodman	Bk. of Washington	Thos. J. Latham.
Waynesville	...Haywood.	Moody & Leach	Bk. of Waynesville	T. C. Skinner.
Webster	........Jackson.	J. J. Hooker	See Waynesville	
Wentworth	....Rockingham.	Reid & Reid	At Leaksville, Bk. of Leaksville.	A. E. Millner.
Whiteville	.....Columbus.	Lewis & Burkhard	See Wilmington	
Wilkesboro'	...Wilkes.	Hackett & Hackett	See Statesville	
Williamston	..Martin.	Wheeler Martin	See Tarboro	
Wilmington	...New Hanover	Junius Davis	Atlantic Natl. Bk.	W. J. Toomer.
Wilson	..........Wilson.	H. J. Connor	Branch & Co.	J. C. Hales.
Windsor	........Bertie.	F. D. Winston	Gillam & Lyon	
Winston	........Forsyth.	Eugene E. Gray	Wachovia Natl. Bk.	James A. Gray.
Winton	.........Hertford.	George V. Cooper	At Weldon, Bk. of Weldon	W. R. Smith.
Yadkinville	....Yadkin.	R. C. Puryear	See Winston	
Yanceyville	....Caswell.	A. E. Henderson	At Milton, Merchants & Planters Bk.	W. W. Lucke.

NORTH CAROLINA—Continued.

DIGEST OF NORTH CAROLINA COMMERCIAL LAWS.

Assignments.—Any person has the right to make an assignment of his property for the benefit of his creditors, and to prefer any number of creditors to the exclusion of others.

Attachments.—Attachment may be granted for breach of contract, express or implied ; wrongful conversion of personal property; any other injury to real or personal property, in consequence of negligence, fraud or wrongful act. That the defendant is either a foreign corporation, a non-resident of the State, or if he is a natural person and a resident of the State, that he has departed therefrom, with intent to defraud his creditors, or to avoid service of summons, or keeps himself concealed therein with like intent, or if the defendant is a natural person, or a domestic corporation, that he has removed, or is about to remove property from the State with intent to defraud his or its creditors ; or has assigned, disposed or secreted, or is about to assign, dispose of or secrete property with a like intent.

Bank Laws.—Banking corporations can be organized only by special act of the Legislature. The personal liability of stockholders depends upon the terms of the charter. There is no statute regulating the transfer of bank stock or providing how a stockholder shall put an end to his liability. All joint-stock companies organized under the laws of the State, for the purpose of conducting a banking business, whether savings or general, and all private banks and bankers that solicit or receive deposits, are required to make to the State Treasurer statements of their financial condition at such times as national banks are required to make statements to the Comptroller of the Currency. Statements are to be published as in case of national banks, and shall be made in accordance with the form to be prescribed by the State Treasurer ; one copy of the statement is to be filed with the State Treasurer and another in the office of the bank, banking institution, or banker.

Exemptions.—Every resident of this State is entitled to real estate of the value of $1,000 and personal property of the value of $500 as a homestead and personal property exemption, which property shall be exempt from sale and execution. The homestead remains exempt from sale under execution to the widow and infant children, until the youngest child becomes 21 years of age.

Interest.—Legal rate is 6 per cent. Usury works a forfeiture of the entire interest and in case a greater rate has been paid, the person paying the same, or his legal representative, may recover back in an action of debt, twice the amount of the interest so paid.

Legal Holidays.—Sunday, January 1, January 19, February 22, May 10, May 20, July 4, December 25, Thanksgiving, General Lee's Birthday.

Litimation of Actions.—Actions upon any contract, obligation or liability, or for trespass upon real property, or for taking, detaining, converting or injuring any personal property shall be commenced within three years.

Married Women.—Own and control their estates as before marriage, but cannot convey without their husbands join. By filing certificate with written consent of husband, a married woman may engage in any business.

Notarial Fees.—Protest $1.00 and twenty-five cents for each notice.

Notes and Bills of Exchange.—All bills and notes bear interest from maturity, unless otherwise stipulated. An indorser of a note is deemed a surety, and no de-

NORTH CAROLINA—Continued.

mand on the maker is necessary before commencing suit against surety or endorser; but this does not apply to bills of exchange. Grace is allowed on all drafts except those payable on demand. Where a bill is drawn or indorsed in this State upon any person or corporation in any other of the United States or any of the Territories, and is protested it, shall bear damages, viz., three per cent. on the principal sum. A bill or note may be protested by a notary public, justice of the peace or clerk of a court of record. Bills of exchange and promissory notes are negotiable; and all notes and bonds with more than one obligor are by statute joint and several. To charge indorser of bill of exchange, notice of non-payment must be given him. Paper falling due on a holiday is due the day before.

Stay of Executions.—On giving security the judgment debtor may stay executions as follows : On less than $25, one month ; $25 to $50, three months ; $50 to $100, four months ; above $100, six months ; but such judgment draws interest. Supplementary proceedings to enforce execution allowed.

Transfer of Corporation Stocks.—No provision directing how stock shall be transferred.

NORTH DAKOTA.

County Seat.	County.	Name of Atty.	Name of Bank.	Cashier.
Ashley	McIntosh.	See Ellendale	Wishek, Lilly & Co.	
Bismark	Burleigh.	J. F. Philbrick	Bismark Bk.	P. E. Byrne.
Bottineau	Bottineau.	A. G. Burr	Bottineau Co. Bk.	V. B. Noble.
Caledonia	Traill.	J. S. Anderson	State Bk. of Caledonia	J. P. Clark.
Cando	Towner.	N. C. Meacham	Towner Co. Bk.	C. J. Lord.
Carrington	Foster.	B. Barton	Carrington State Bk.	P. W. Farnham.
Cooperstown	Griggs.	David Bartlett *	First Bk. of Cooperstown	M. W. Buck.
Devils Lake	Ramsay.	M. H. Brennon	First Natl. Bk.	J. A. Stewart.
Dickinson	Stark.	R. H. Johnson	First Natl. Bk.	R. H. Johnson.
Ellendale	Dickey.	A. T. Cole	Citizens State Bk.	B. R. Crabtree.
Fargo	Cass.	Newman, Spalding & Phelps	First Natl. Bk.	S. S. Lyon.
Fort Buford	Alfred.		See Dickinson	
Grafton	Walsh.	Phelps & Phelps	First Natl. Bk.	J. L. Cashel.
Grand Forks	Grand Forks.	Burke Corbet	Second Natl. Bk.	D. S. Doyon.
Grand Rapids	Lamoure.	G. B. Crum	At Edgeley, State Bk. of Edgeley	J. T. Butler.
Jamestown	Stutsman.	E. W. Camp	James River Natl. Bk.	R. A. Shattuck.
Lakota	Nelson.	F. A. Kelley	Peoples State Bk.	H. G. Merritt.
Langdon	Cavalier.	W. F. Kessler	Citizens State Bk.	W. A. Laidlaw.
Lisbon	Ransom.	P. H. Rourke	First Natl. Bk.	H. K. Adams.
Mandan	Morton.	E. C. Rice	First Natl. Bk.	C. L. Timmerman
Medicine Pole	Bowman.	Vacant	See Dickinson	
Medora	Billings.	See Dickinson		
Milnor	Sargent.	E. W. Thorp	Bk. of Sargent Co.	F. W. Vail.
MINNEWAUKON	Benson.	E. S. Rolfe	Benson Co. State Bk.	O. T. Hegge.
Minot	Ward.	C. E. Gregory	First Natl. Bk.	S. L. Page.
Napoleon	Logan.	See Steele		
New England City	Hettinger.	See Dickinson		
NEW ROCKFORD	Eddy.	C. J. Maddux	Bk. of New Rockford.	J. H. Hohl.
Oakdale	Dunn.	See Dickinson		
Pembina	Pembina.	W. J. Kneeshaw	First Natl. Bk.	George W. Ryan.
Rugby	Pierce.	See Towner		
St. Johns	Rolette.	John Burke	See Cando.	
Sauger	Oliver.	See Bismark		
Sherbrooke	Steele.	At Hope	Steele Co. Bk.	J. D. Brown.
Stanton	Mercer.	H. C. Loy	See Bismark	
Steele	Kidder.	J. W. Walker	State Bk. of Steele.	A. G. Clark.
Sykeston	Wells.	See Carrington		
Towner	McHenry.	L. M. Torson	Towner Merchants Bk.	John Lohn.
Valley City	Barnes.	Winter & Winter	First Natl. Bk.	George Kanouse.
Wahpeton	Richland.	McCumber & Bogart	Peoples Bk.	W. D. Henry.
Washburn	McLean.	See Bismark		
Williamsport	Emmons.	H. A. Armstrong	See Bismark	
Williston	Williams.	See Minot		
Organizing	Boreman.			
"	McKenzie.			
"	Wallace.			

THE LEGAL AND FINANCIAL LIGHTS OF AMERICA. 109

NORTH DAKOTA—Continued.
DIGEST OF NORTH DAKOTA COMMERCIAL LAWS.

Assignments.—An assignment may be made. It is void if it prefers creditors.

Attachments.—Attachment may issue against a foreign corporation; or against a defendant who is not a resident of this State, or against a defendant who has absconded or concealed himself ; or whenever the defendant is about to remove any of his or its property from the State ; or has assigned, disposed of, or secreted, or is about to assign, dispose of or secrete any of his or its property, with intent to defraud his creditors, or is about to remove from the county where he resides, with the intention of permanently changing his place of residence, upon failing or neglecting to give security for the debts after its being demanded.

Bank Laws.—Three or more persons, one third of whom shall be residents of the State, may form a banking association, who shall make an organization certificate, which must be acknowledged and recorded in the office of the Register of Deeds in the county where such bank may be established, and such certificate also recorded in the office of the Secretary of State. It is made a misdemeanor to carry on a bank without forming such association. The capital is graded according to the population of the town or city. At least four reports shall be made each year to the public examiner and published, and the examiner is empowered to call for special reports at any time. Penalty of $200 for not making same.

Exemptions.—A homestead not exceeding in value $5,000 to be selected and appraised as provided by statute, is exempt from judgment lien and execution of forced sale.

Limitation of Actions.—An action upon a judgment or decree of any court in the United States, or of any State or Territory within the United States, and upon a sealed instrument, within twenty years. Actions upon a contract. obligation or liability, express or implied ; actions upon a liability created by statute other than a penalty or forfeiture ; for trespass on real property, within six years ; an action for slander, libel, assault, battery or false imprisonment ; actions upon the statute for a forfeiture or penalty to the people of this State, within two years.

Married Women.—No law.

Notarial Fees.—Protest $1.50, recording 50 cents, seal 25 cents, notices 25 cents.

Notes and Bills of Exchange.—Bills of exchange, promissory notes, bank notes, checks, bonds and certificates of deposits are negotiable instruments. When no place of payment is specified, they are payable at the residence or place of business or wherever maker may be found. Bill or note maturing on a holiday becomes due on next business day. Three days of grace allowed on foreign or inland bills of exchange or drafts payable at sight, or promissory notes, bills of exchange, and drafts on the face of which time is given or specified, and on notes due on demand, after demand is made.

Transfer of Corporation Stocks.—Are transferred by endorsement and delivery ; but such transfer is only valid between the parties until entered on the books of corporation.

OHIO.

County Seat. County.	Name of Atty.	Name of Bank.	Cashier.
Akron..........Summitt.	Kohler & Musser	First Natl. Bk.	F. H. Adams.
Ashland........Ashland.	F. C. Semple	First Natl. Bk.	Jos. Patterson.
Athens..........Athens.	Wood & Wood	Bk. of Athens	C. W. Harris.
Batavia.........Clermont.	Hulick & Bishop	First Natl. Bk.	J. F. Dial.
Bellefontaine..Logan.	West & West	Peoples Natl. Bk.	R. B. Keller.
BOWLING GREEN..Wood.	Parker & Moore	First Natl. Bk.	D. B. Beers.
Bryan,..........Williams.	T. Emery	Farmers Natl. Bk.	E. Lattanner.
Bucyrus........Crawford.	F. S. Monnett	First Natl. Bk.	J. C. Gormly.
Cadiz...........Harrison.	Milton Taggart	Harrison Natl. Bk.	John M. Sharon.
Caldwell.......Noble.	D. S. Spriggs	Noble Co. Natl. Bk.	G. W. Taylor.
Cambridge.....Guernsey.	Jno. S. Black	Old Natl. Bk.	A. R. Murray.
Canton..........Stark.	Miller & Pomerene	Farmers Bk.	Fred. M. Fast.
Carrolton......Carroll.	McCoy & Eckley	J. P. Cummings Bk. Co.	T. J. Saltsman.
Celina.........Mercer.	Tonvelle & Kenney	Commercial Bk.	J. Milligan.
Chardon........Geauga.	J. E. Stephenson	First Natl. Bk.	S. S. Smith.
Chillicothe....Ross.	Albert Douglas, Jr.	First Natl. Bk.	E. R. McKee.
Cincinnati.....Hamilton.	Stephens, Lincoln & Smith	First Natl. Bk.	W. S. Rowe.
Circleville....Pickaway.	Smith & Morris	Second Natl. Bk.	E. E. Winship.
Cleveland......Cuyahoga.	Webster, Angell & McKisson	Euclid Ave. Natl. Bk.	E. G. Tillotson.
Columbus......Franklin.	Frank E. Davis	Deshler Natl. Bk.	Charles J. Hardy.
Coshocton.....Coshocton.	E. W. James	Commercial Bkg. Co.	H. H. Herbig.
Dayton.........Montgomery.	Gunckel, Rowe & Shuey	City Natl. Bk.	W. B. Gebhart.
Defiance.......Defiance.	S. T. Sutphen	First Natl. Bk.	Elbert E. Carter.
Delaware.......Delaware.	C. H. McElroy	Deposit Bkg. Co.	H. A. Welch.
Eaton..........Preble.	Fisher & Vaughan	Preble Co. Natl. Bk.	J. W. Acton.
Elyria.........Lorain.	G. D. Holliday	Savings Deposit Bkg. Co.	A. L. Garford.
Findlay........Hancock.	A. & F. P. Blackford	First Natl. Bk.	George P. Jones.
Fremont........Sandusky.	Garver & Garver	First Natl. Bk.	Anson H. Miller.
Gallipolis.....Gallia.	S. A. Nash	First Natl. Bk.	W. G. Wheaton.
Georgetown....Brown.	Rufus L. Fite	First Natl. Bk.	W. S. Whiteman.
Greenville.....Darke.	Anderson & Bowman	Farmers Natl. Bk.	J. M. Ladsdowne.
Hamilton.......Butler.	Belden & Fitton	First Natl. Bk.	S. D. Fitton.
Hillsborough..Highland.	Steele & Hoogsett	First Natl. Bk.	John Hullett.
Ironton........Lawrence.	T. N. Ross	Citizens Natl. Bk.	Chas. Lintner.
Jackson........Jackson.	John Harper	Iron Bk.	J. C. Hurd.
Jefferson......Ashtabula.	A. C. White	First Natl. Bk.	D. S. Crosby.
Kenton.........Hardin.	Crane & Johnson	First Natl. Bk.	H. W. Gramlich.
Lancaster......Fairfield.	George E. Hardin	Lancaster Bk.	G. W. Beck.
Lebanon........Warren.	J. A. Runyan	Lebanon Natl. Bk.	J. M. Oglesby.
Lima...........Allen.	Cable & Parmenter	First Natl. Bk.	C. D. Crites.
Logan..........Hocking.	S. H. Bright	First Bk. of Logan.	Chas. E. Bowen.
London.........Madison.	S. W. Durflinger	Madison Natl. Bk.	Wyatt Minshall.
McArthur......Vinton.	James W. Darby	At Wellston, First Natl. Bk.	J. H. Sellers.
McCONNELSVILLE.Morgan.	Corner & Fonts	Citizens Bk.	C. L. Alderman.
Mansfield......Richland.	H. P. Davis	Citizens Natl. Bk.	S. A. Jennings.

OHIO—Continued.

County Seat.	County.	Name of Atty.	Name of Bank.	Cashier.
Marietta	Washington.	Nye & Follett	City Natl. Bk.	E. M. Booth.
Marion	Marion.	Geo. D. Copeland	Farmers & Mechanics Bk.	H. B. Hane.
Marysville	Union.	Porter & Porter	Bk. of Marysville.	W. C. Fullington.
Medina	Medina.	J. Andrew	Old Phoenix Natl. Bk.	B. Hendrickson.
Millersburgh	Holmes.	Maxwell & Sharp	Commercial Bk.	B. C. Sill.
Mt. Gilead	Morrow.	L. K. Powell	Morrow Co. Natl. Bk.	Samuel P. Gage.
Mt. Vernon	Knox.	C. F. Colville	First Natl. Bk.	F. D. Sturges.
Napoleon	Henry.	M. Donnelly	Meekison's Bk.	W. H. Brownell.
Newark	Licking.	Carl Norpell	First Natl. Bk.	F. S. Wright.
NEW LEXINGTON	Perry.	L. A. Tussing	Perry Co. Bk. Co.	S. Chappelear.
New Lisbon	Columbiana.	R. W. Tayler	At Leetonia, First Natl. Bk.	John Leavitt.
New Philadelphia	Tuscaravas.	Jno. S. Graham	Citizens Natl. Bk.	B. P. Scott.
Norwalk	Huron.	C. L. Kennan	Huron Co. Bkg. Co.	Oitt Curties.
Ottawa	Putnam.	Handy & Ogan	A. V. Rice & Co.	N. E. Matthews.
Painsville	Lake.	Harley Barnes	Painsville Natl. Bk.	C. H. Frank.
Paulding	Paulding.	K. E. Shuster	Paulding Deposit Bk.	E. P. Copeland.
Pomeroy	Meigs.	Merrick & Lochary	Pomeroy Natl. Bk.	John McQuigg.
Port Clinton	Ottawa.	S. P. Alexander	German American Bk.	B. W. Wilson.
Portsmouth	Scioto.	Bannon & Bannon	Portsmouth Natl. Bk.	C. B. Taylor.
Ravenna	Portage.	W. J. Beckley	Second Natl. Bk.	W. H. Beebe.
St. Clairsville	Belmont.	A. W. Kennon	First Natl. Bk.	J. R. Mitchell.
Sandusky	Erie.	Phinney & Merrill	Third Natl. Exchange Bk.	F. P. Zollinger.
Sidney	Shelby.	S. J. Hatfield	Citizens Bk.	Wm. A. Graham.
Springfield	Clarke.	John C. Bassetl, Jr.	Lagonda Natl. Bk.	D. P. Jefferies.
Steubenville	Jefferson.	James F. Dalon	Natl. Exchange Bk.	T. A. Hammond.
Tiffin	Seneca.	J. H. Ridgely	Commercial Bk.	John B. Runyan.
Toledo	Lucas.	Swayne, Swayne & Hayes	Second Natl. Bk.	C. F. Adams.
Troy	Miami.	H. H. Williams	Troy Natl. Bk.	Noah Yount.
UPPER SANDUSKY	Wyandot.	Jno. D. Sears	First Natl. Bk.	Charles F. Plumb.
Urbana	Champaign.	Frank Chance	Citizens Natl. Bk.	W. W. Wilson.
Van Wert	Van Wert.	C. V. Hoke	First Natl. Bk.	John Van Liew.
Wapakoneta	Auglaize.	Layton & Steuve	First Natl. Bk.	Chas. F. Herbst.
Warren	Trumbull.	Washington Hyde	Second Natl. Bk.	C. A. Harrington.
WASHINGTON C. H.	Fayette.	A. R. Creamer	Commercial Bk.	A. S. Ballard.
Wauseon	Fulton.	Files & Fuller	Peoples Bk.	Chas. W. Struble.
Waverly	Pike.	Chas. M. Caldwell	Hayes, Jones & Co.	W. F. Taylor.
West Union	Adams.	Henry Scott	Adams Co. Bk.	H. W. Dickinson.
Wilmington	Clinton.	Mills & Clevenger	Clinton Co. Natl. Bk.	J. W. Denver, Jr.
Woodsfield	Monroe.	J. P. Spriggs & Son	Monroe Bk.	W. C. Mooney.
Wooster	Wayne.	Yocum & Taggart	Wayne Co. Natl. Bk.	C. S. Frost.
Xenia	Greene.	F. N. Shaffer	Xenia Natl. Bk.	A. S. Frazer.
Youngstown	Mahoning.	Thos. W. Sanderson	Second Natl. Bk.	Henry M. Garlick
Zanesville	Muskingum.	Howard E. Buker	First Natl. Bk.	G. H. Stewart

OHIO—Continued.

DIGEST OF OHIO COMMERCIAL LAWS.

Assignments.—An insolvent debtor may make an assignment in trust for the benefit of creditors. An assignment made with intent to prefer one or more creditors inures to the benefit of all creditors.

Attachments.—Attachment may be had when the defendant is a non-resident or a foreign corporation: or has absconded or concealed himself; or is about to remove, convert, or assign, or has concealed his property, with intent to defraud creditors; or where the debt is fraudulently contracted.

Bank Laws.—No law can be passed authorizing the establishment of banks until the same be submitted to the people at a general election and approved by them, and no such law has been adopted since this prohibition has been inserted in the constitution of the State. The Supreme Court has held, however, that building and loan associations, organized under the Act of 1868, and savings and loan associations, organized under the Act of 1873, may be formed, and numbers of these are doing a banking business. There are no banks of issue in the State. All banks are required to make a report to the State Auditor twice a year, showing the condition of their affairs on the first Monday of April and October. This report must be published in the newspaper. No visitorial powers, however, are granted to the State Auditor.

Exemptions.—Husband and wife living together, widow or widower living with an unmarried daughter or unmarried minor son, may hold exempt from sale on judgment or order a family homestead not exceeding $1,000 value; the wife may make demand if the husband refuse, but neither can make such demand if the other has a homestead. Where the homestead is sold for the payment of liens thereon, after payment of such liens, the owner may claim $500 out of the balance of the proceeds of the sale, if any, in lieu of a homestead.

Interest.—Legal rate is 6 per cent. but parties may contract in writing for 8 per cent. If a contract be made for a higher rate than 8 per cent. the contract as to interest is void, and the recovery is limited to the principal sum and 6 per cent.

Legal Holidays.—Sunday, January 1, February 22, May 30, July 4, First Monday in September, December 25 and Thanksgiving.

Limitation of Actions.—Upon contracts not in writing, express or implied, six years; specialty or any agreement in writing, fifteen years; real action, twenty-one years. an action may be taken out of the statute by part payment, acknowledgment, or promise in writing.

Married Women.—Have sole control of, and separate property in all real and personal property acquired before or after marriage, together with the rents, incomes and profits thereof. Such property cannot be taken for the debts of her husband, unless he has reduced the personal property to possession with her assent. They may contract in their own name for labor or materials in repairing or improving their real estate, and may lease for three years. If a husband deserts his family or from any cause becomes incapacitated or neglects to provide for them, the wife may contract for and collect in her own name her and her minor children's earnings, and may obtain an order vesting her with the right of a *femme sole* as to ac_quiring property. A wife has dower in all her husband's real estate held during coverture. She may engage in business as owner or partner, and may sue and be sued alone on account of such business, and her property is liable on the judgment

OHIO—Continued.

rendered against her in such suit. Married women cannot prosecute or defend by next friend, but her husband must be joined with her, unless action contains her separate property or her separate business, or is upon her written obligation, or brought to set aside a deed or will, or between her and her husband. When they are sued together she may defend, for her own right, and if he neglects to defend his she may defend for him. Mortgages are executed in like manner with deeds. Those presented first for record must have the preference. Are not valid against innocent subsequent mortgage or purchase, unless recorded; when paid, must be cancelled of record.

Notarial Fees.—Protest $1 and costs.

Notes and Bills of Exchange.—Bonds, notes and bills payable at a day certain after date, or after sight when made payable to order or bearer are negotiable by indorsement thereon, and vest the title thereof in indorsee. They need not be payable at a bank, or any particular place, to be negotiable. Three days of grace are allowed in the time of payment. Bill or note maturing on a holiday becomes due the preceding day.

Stay of Executions.—On judgments by Justices of the Peace only.

Transfer of Corporation Stocks.—Endorsement on back of stock effects an equitable transfer only.

OKLAHOMA.

County Seat.	County.	Name of Atty.	Name of Bank.	Cashier.
Alva	M.	Ellis & Shelley	Alva State Bk.	W. S. Fallis.
Arapahoe	G.	See El Reno		
Beaver	Beaver.	See Woodward		
Birds Point	L.	Dailey & Weston at Pond Creek.	Bk. of Pond Creek	J. W. Berryman.
Chandler	Lincoln.	L. E. Payne	Lincoln Co. Bk.	O. B. Kee.
Cheyenne	Roger Mills.	See El Reno	Wachita Valley Bk.	J. W. McMurtry.
Cloud Chief	Washita.	See El Reno		
El Reno	Canadian.	Blake & Blake	Stock Exchange Bk.	M. Eichhoff.
Enid	O.	W. O. Cromwell	Bk. of Enid	W. T. Dugan.
Fort Still	Kiowa & Comanche.	At Marlow, Ind. Ter.	Bk. of Marlow	H. L. Jarboe, Jr.
Guthrie	Logan.	S. L. Overstreet	Capitol Natl. Bk.	G. E. Billingsley.
Ioland	Day.	See Woodward		
Kaw Agency	Kansas.	William Rouse at New Kirk.	Bk. of Santa Fe	C. A. Eastman.
Kingfisher	Kingfisher.	D. K. Cunningham	Bk. of Kingfisher	J. M. Spelce.
Mangum	Greer.	See El Reno	S. C. Van Leer	
Norman	Cleveland.	C. L. Botsford	Farmers & Merchants Bk.	E. F. Taylor.
OKLAHOMA CITY	Oklahoma.	Hayes & Jenkens	First Natl. Bk.	J. P. Boyle.
Pawhuska	Osages.	See Pawnee		
Pawnee	Q.	Hill, Fitzpatrick & McGuire.	Bk. of Pawnee.	C. E. Vandervoort
Perry	P.	C. H. Wynn	Bk of Perry	F. W. Farrar.
Ponca City	K.	D. J. Donahoe	Bk. of Ponca City	Barnes & Dalton.
Stillwater	Payne.	J. S. Workman	Farmers & Merchants Bk.	F. J. Wikoff.
Taloga	D.	See Kingfisher		
Tecumseh	Pottawatomie	W. S. Pendleton	Bk. of Tecumseh	John W. Lewis.
Watonga	Blaine.	See Kingfisher		
Wilbur	I.	See El Reno		
Woodward	N.	Houston & Roy	Exchange Bk.	John M. Pugh.

DIGEST OF OKLAHOMA COMMERCIAL LAWS.

Assignments.—Voluntary assignments, without preference, for the benefit of creditors may be made by debtors of all their property (but they may except property exempted by law).

Attachments.—Attachments will be granted when the defendant or one of several defendants is a foreign corporation or non-resident of this Territory (but no attachment shall be allowed on this ground for any claim other than a debt or demand arising upon contract, judgment or decree); has absconded with intent to defraud his creditors; has left the county of his residence to avoid the service of summons; so conceals himself that summons cannot be served upon him; is about to remove his property, or a part thereof, out of the jurisdiction of the court with the intent to defraud his creditors; is about to convert his property, or a part thereof into money for the purpose of placing it beyond the reach of his creditors; has property or rights in action which he conceals; has assigned, removed or disposed of, or is about

OKLAHOMA—Continued.

to dispose of his property or part thereof, with intent to defraud his creditors; fraudulently contracted the debt or incurred the obligation for which suit is about to be or has been brought.

Bank Laws.—There is no territorial law authorizing the formation of banking corporations, but it is provided that if any officer of a bank or private banker receive or permit, or assent to the reception of money, deposits or things of value in such bank; or if such officer or banker create or assent to the creation of any indebtedness by a bank or banker after he shall have knowledge of its or his insolvency, he is individually liable for such indebtedness and is also liable to be prosecuted for larceny.

Exemptions.—Homestead of debtor, not exceeding $2,000 in value, and not exceeding 160 acres of land, if outside of incorporated city or village, or two contiguous lots if in any incorporated city or village.

Interest.—Legal rate 7 per cent. where no rate is specified. There is no usury law.

Legal Holidays.—Sunday, January 1, February 22, July 4, December 25, May 30, every day on which an election is held throughout the Territory, and every day appointed by the President of the United States or by the Governor of the Territory for a public fast, thanksgiving or holiday. Whenever a legal holiday other than Sunday falls upon Sunday, the Monday following shall be observed as such holiday. Labor Day.

Notes and Bills of Exchange.—Bills of exchange, promissory notes, bank notes, checks, bonds, and certificates of deposit, if without date, are payable immediately, and if without specified place of payment are payable where maker may be found. Three days of grace allowed on all bills of exchange, or drafts payable at sight. Paper maturing on a holiday becomes due on the next business day. Protest, presentment and notice may be waived. Waiver of protest waives presentment and notice. Reasonable care and diligence in presentment required. Damages for accrued interest, re-exchange, expenses, etc., are, if in this Territory, two per cent.; in Nebraska, Iowa, Minnesota, Wisconsin, Illinois and Missouri, two per cent.; in any other State or Territory, five per cent., and in any foreign country, ten per cent.

Transfer of Corporation Stocks.—Stocks of corporation may be transferred by endorsement and delivery of the certificates of such stock by the owner or his attorney or legal representative. Such transfer is not valid between the parties hereto until same is entered upon the books of the coporation so as to show the name of the parties by and to whom transferred, the number or designation of the shares and the date of transfer.

OREGON.

County Seat.	County.	Name of Atty.	Name of Bank.	Cashier.
Albany	Linn.	Whitney & Newport	First Natl. Bk.	E. W. Langdon.
Arlington	Gilliam.	A. A. Jayne	Arlington Natl. Bk.	F. T. Hurlburt.
Astoria	Clatsop.	Noland & Thompson	First Natl. Bk.	S. S. Gordon.
Baker City	Baker.	Butcher & Johns	First Natl. Bk.	J. T. Donnelly.
Canyon City	Grant.	See Baker City		
Corvallis	Benton.	John Burnett	First Natl. Bk.	W. T. Peet.
Dallas	Polk.	Butler & Townsend	Dallas City Bk.	C. J. Coad.
Ellensburgh	Curry.	J. Huntley	See Grant's Pass	
Empire City	Coos.	S. H. Hazard	See Roseburgh	
Enterprise	Wallowa.	Ivanhoe & Sheahan	Wallowa Natl. Bk.	W. R. Holmes.
Eugene City	Lane.	E. O. Potter	First Natl. Bk.	S. B. Eakin.
Grant's Pass	Josephine.	H. L. Benson	First Natl. Bk.	R. A. Booth.
Harney	Harney.	T. Williams	See Baker City	
Heppner	Morrow.	Brown & Hamilton	First Natl. Bk.	George Conser.
Hillsborough	Washington.	T. H. Tongue	First Natl. Bk.	J. D. Merryman.
Jacksonville	Jackson.	H. K. Hanna	Peekman & Reames	
Klamath	Klamath.	Cogswell & Halee	See Lake View	
Lake View	Lake.	C. A. Cogswell	Lake View Bk.	A. McCallen.
McMinnville	Yam Hill.	Ramsey & Fenton	First Natl. Bk.	WD.McDonald,Jr
Oregon City	Clackamas.	L. L. Porter	Commercial Bk.	F. E. Donaldeon.
Pendleton	Umatilla.	C. H. Carter	First Natl. Bk.	Sam. P. Sturgis.
Portland	Multnomah.	Durham, Platt & Platt	First Natl. Bk.	G. E. Withington.
Prineville	Crook.	M. E. Brink	First Natl. Bk.	T. M. Baldwin.
Roseburgh	Douglas.	A. M. Crawford	First Natl. Bk.	W. T. Wright.
St. Helen	Columbia.	F. A. Moore	See Portland	
Salem	Marion.	George C. Bingham	Capital Natl. Bk.	J. H. Albert.
The Dalles	Wasco.	Dufur & Menefee	The Dalles Natl. Bk.	M. A. Moody.
Tillamook	Tillamook.	Claude Thayer	C. & E. Thayer	
Toledo	Lincoln.	See Corwallis		
Union	Union.	Robert Eakin	First Natl. Bk.	Will Wright.
Vale	Malheur.	H. C. Napton	See Baker City	
Wasco	Sherman.	Bright & Murchie	Sherman Co. Bk.	V. C. Brock.

DIGEST OF OREGON COMMERCIAL LAWS.

Assignments.—No general assignment by an insolvent, or in contemplation of insolvency for the benefit of creditors, is valid unless made for the benefit of all his creditors in proportion to the amount of their respective claims.

Attachments.—A writ of attachment shall be issued when the defendant is indebted to the plaintiff upon a contract, express or implied, for the direct payment of money, and that the payment of the same has not been secured by any mortgage, lien or pledge, upon any real or personal property ; and that the sum for which the attachment is asked is an actual *bona fide* existing debt due and owing from the defendant to the plaintiff, and that the attachment is not sought nor the action prosecuted to hinder, delay or defraud any creditor of the defendant.

THE LEGAL AND FINANCIAL LIGHTS OF AMERICA.

OREGON—Continued.

Bank Laws.—There are no laws regulating banks or banking, and there are no State banks.

Exemptions.—Homestead of any family is exempt from judicial sale for the satisfaction of any liability hereafter contracted, or by judgment hereafter obtained on such debt, to the extent of 160 acres when not located in town or city (or if so located to the extent of one block), and to the extent of $1,500 in value.

Interest.—Legal rate is 8 per cent., but contracts to pay not to exceed 10 per cent., and to pay not to exceed 8 per cent., and taxes may be enforced. Usury is punishable by forfeiture of both principal and interest to the common school fund.

Legal Holidays.—Sunday, January 1, February 22, May 30, July 4, First Monday in September, December 25, public fast, Thanksgiving and every general election day. Whenever any legal holiday other than a Sunday falls upon Sunday, the Monday following shall be and be observed as such holiday, First Saturday in June.

Limitation of Actions.—On contracts not under seal, express or implied, six years; on judgments or decrees of any court and sealed instruments, ten years; recovery of real property, ten years.

Married Women.—All property of the wife's at marriage or afterwards acquired by gift, device or inheritance, is her sole property, and not subject to the debts of her husband. She may buy, sell and make contracts, and her separate estate is liable for the same.

Notarial Fees.—Protest $3.

Notes and Bills of Exchange.—All negotiable instruments are commercial paper. They are not required to be paid at any particular place unless a place of payment is specified in the instrument. No days of grace in this State. Negotiable instruments falling due on a holiday become due on the next business day. No person can be charged as an acceptor of a bill of exchange unless the acceptance be in writing, signed by himself or his lawful agent. Indorsers, if properly charged by protest, are liable as long as the maker. Damages allowed on protested bills of exchange: domestic, five per cent., foreign 10 per cent.

Stay of Executions.—Only by order of the Courts.

Transfer of Corporation Stocks.—The corporation, in case of a sale, is required to make the necessary transfer upon the books. By-laws generally regulate the manner of transfer.

PENNSYLVANIA.

County Seat.	County.	Name of Atty.	Name of Bank.	Cashier.
Allentown	Lehigh.	Robert E. Wright	Allentown Natl. Bk.	C. M. W. Keck.
Beaver	Beaver.	John M. Buchanan	First. Natl. Bk.	E. J. Allison.
Bedford	Bedford.	M. A. Points	First Natl. Bk.	E. S. Doty.
Bellefonte	Centre.	Ovris, Bower & Ovris	First Natl. Bk.	John P. Harris.
Bloomsburgh	Columbia.	Grant Herring	First Natl. Bk.	E. B. Tustin.
Brookville	Jefferson.	Means & Clark	Jefferson Co. Natl. Bk.	J. S. Carroll.
Butler	Butler.	Williams & Mitchell	Butler Co. Natl. Bk.	C. A. Bailey.
Carlisle	Cumberland.	R. M. Henderson	Farmers Bk.	Walter Stuart.
CHAMBERSBURG	Franklin.	W. U. Brewer	Valley Natl. Bk.	John R. Orr.
Clarion	Clarion.	James T. Maffett	Second Natl. Bk.	J. M. Shannon.
Clearfield	Clearfield.	Fielding & Betts	County Natl. Bk.	. H. B. Powell.
Coudersport	Potter.	Mann & Osmond	First Natl. Bk.	N. A. Pinney.
Danville	Montour.	James Scarlett	First Natl. Bk.	B. R. Gearhart.
Doylestown	Bucks.	Henry Lear	Doyleston Natl. Bk.	John J. Brock.
Easton	Northampton	Russell C. Stewart	Easton Trust Co.	John Bacon.
Ebensburgh	Cambria.	Kittell & Little	Johnston, Buck & Co.	
Emporium	Cameron.	D. W. Green	First Natl. Bk.	M. P. Whiting.
Erie	Erie.	T. A. Lamb	Second Natl. Bk.	C. F. Allis.
Franklin	Venango.	McCalmont & Osborne	First Natl. Bk.	F. W. Officer.
Gettyburgh	Adams.	Wm. McSherry, Jr.	First Natl. Bk.	F. M. Bushman.
Greensburgh	Westmoreland	W. C. Griffith	First Natl. Bk.	Jos. R. Eisaman.
Harrisburgh	Dauphin.	Wolfe & Bailey	Dauphin Deposit Bk.	W. K. Abricks.
HOLLIDAYSBURGH	Blair.	August S. Landis	First Natl. Bk.	O. W. Gardner.
Honesdale	Wayne.	P. F. Kimble	Honesdale Natl. Bk.	E. F. Torrey.
Huntington	Huntington.	W. McKnight Wiilamson	First Natl. Bk.	S. R. Shumaker.
Indiana	Indiana.	J. N. Banks	First Natl. Bk.	W. J. Mitchell.
Kittaning	Armstrong.	M. F. Leason	Natl. Bk. of Kittaning	Wm. Pollock.
Lancaster	Lancaster.	John E. Snyder	Fulton Natl. Bk.	John C. Carper.
La Porte	Sullivan.	E. M. Dunham	La Porte Bk.	J. A. Jordan.
Lebanon	Lebanon.	Grant Weidman	First Natl. Bk.	John H. Hoffer.
Lewisburgh	Union.	D. B. Miller	Union Natl. Bk.	John K. Kremer.
Lewiston	Mifflin.	Elber & Son	Mifflin Co. Natl. Bk.	David E. Robeson
Lock Haven	Clinton.	Jesse Merill	First Natl. Bk.	Moore Fredericks
McCONNELLSBURG	Fulton.	J. Nelson Sipes	Fulton Co. Bk.	David B. Nace.
Mauch Chunk	Carbon.	Loose & Craig	First Natl. Bk.	Edgar Twining.
Meadville	Crawford.	George F. Davenport	New First Natl. Bk.	Wm. Thomas.
Media	Delaware.	George E. Darlington	First Natl. Bk.	J. W. Hawley.
Mercer	Mercer.	Q. A. Gordon	Farmers & Mechanics Natl. Bk.	John I. Gordon.
Middleburg	Snyder.	T. J. Smith	First Natl. Bk.	J. N. Thompson, Jr.
Mifflintown	Juniata.	George J. Parker	First Natl. Bk.	Ezra C. Doty.
Milford	Pike.	H. I. Baker	At East Stroudsburg. East Stroudsburg Natl. Bk.	L. H. Nicholas.
Montrose	Susquehanna	M. S. Allen	First Natl. Bk.	Emos Nichols.
NEW BLOOMFIELD	Perry.	J. C. McAllister	At Duncannon, Duncannon Natl. Bk.	P. F. Duncan.
New Castle	Lawrence.	W. H. Falls	Natl. Bk. of Lawrence Co.	R. Crawford.
Norristown	Montgomery.	Chas. H. Stinson	First Natl. Bk.	George Shannon.
Philadelphia	Philadelphia.	Page, Allison & Penrose	First Natl. Bk.	M. McMichael, Jr.

PENNSYLVANIA—CONTINUED.

County Seat.	County.	Name of Atty.	Name of Bank.	Cashier.
Pittsburgh	Allegheny.	Knox & Reed	Farmers Deposit Natl. Bk.	J. W. Fleming.
Pottsville	Schuylkill.	John W. Ryon	Safe Deposit Bk.	Chas. H. Hazzard
Reading	Berks.	Chas. H. Schaeffer	Natl. Union Bk.	Edwin Boone.
Ridgway	Elk.	Ch. McCauley	Elk Co. Bk.	M. S. Kline.
Scranton	Lackawanna.	Taylor & Lewis	First Natl. Bk.	Isaac Post.
Smethport	McKean.	R. H. Rose	Henry Hamlin	S. C. Townsend.
Somerset	Somerset.	John H. Uhl	Somerset Co. Natl. Bk.	Milton J. Pritts.
Stroudsburgh	Monroe.	Stephen Holmes	Stroudsburgh Natl. Bk.	John S. Fisher.
Sunbury	Northnmberland.	S. J. Packer	First Natl. Bk.	G. W. Deppen.
Tionesta	Forest.	Samuel B. Irwin	May, Park & Co.	A. B. Kelly.
Towanda	Bradford.	R. A. Mercur	First Natl. Bk.	N. N. Betts.
TUNKHANNOCK	Wyoming.	James W. Piatt	Wyoming Natl. Bk.	John B. Fassett.
Uniontown	Fayette.	Samuel E. Ewing	First Natl. Bk.	E. S. Hackney.
Warren	Warren.	James O. Parmelee	Warren Natl. Bk.	F. E. Hertzel.
Washington	Washington.	T. Jeff. Duncan	First Natl. Bk.	C. S. Ritchie.
Waynesburgh	Greene.	Barb & Downey	Citizens Natl. Bk.	J. C. Garard.
WELLSBOROUGH	Tioga.	Elliott & Watrous	First Natl. Bk.	Henry C. Cox.
West Chester	Chester.	R. S. Waddell	Natl. Bk. of Chester Co.	I. Cary Carver.
Wilkes-Barre	Luzerne.	L. H. Bennett	Second Natl. Bk.	E. W. Mulligan.
Williamsport	Lycoming.	W. W. Hart	First Natl. Bk.	W. H. Sloan.
York	York.	Edward Chapin	City Bk.	R. H. Shindel.

PRINCIPAL CITIES, NOT COUNTY SEATS.

Allegheny	Allegheny.	James W. Collins	Second Natl. Bk.	A. S. Cameron.
Chester	Delaware.	George B. Lindsay	Delaware Co. Natl. Bk.	B. T. Hall.

DIGEST OF PENNSYLVANIA COMMERCIAL LAWS.

Assignments.—Assignments may be made for the benefit of all creditors, but there is no provision for the discharge of the debtor. Debtor cannot prefer any creditor by his deed except for wages of labor.

Attachments.—Attachments may issue when debtor is about to remove his property or conceal it with intent to defraud his creditors, or has fraudulently contracted the debt.

Bank Laws.—Any person or association of persons, not less than five, may establish bank of discount, deposit, and circulation with a capital of not less than $50,000 nor more than $1,900,000. Whenever any association desires to establish a bank, or increase the capital, a certificate to that effect must be made for at least six months in at least three newspapers, one published at the seat of government and the other

PENNSYLVANIA—Continued.

two in the city or county where such a bank is located. When a copy of this certificate containing the name, place of business, amount of capital stock, with the number of shares into which the same shall be divided is certified by the Attorney-General, it is recorded after the manner of deeds, and the Governor, upon a certified copy of such certificate being produced before him, causes letters patent to be issued. Every person or corporation to whom letters patent may be granted, is authorized to carry on business for twenty years from the date of patent. The Auditor General is required to report annually to the Legislature, within three days of the commencement of the session, a summary of the condition of every incorporated bank, with an abstract of the amount of banking capital returned by them. The capital stock of each bank is divided into shares of $50 each. It is the duty of every cashier to publish in the newspapers a statement giving the amount of assets and liabilities, circulation, deposits, gold and silver, with all evidences of debt, with the personal and real property of the bank; and semi-annual reports are required. The Auditor General is to require quarterly statements from cashiers of the condition of banks, and one of the statements shall be made in November. Stockholders are individually liable for the notes issued by the bank.

Exemptions.—There is no homestead law. Property, real or personal, to the value of $300, besides wearing apparel, is exempt.

Interest.—Legal interest 6 per cent. Illegal interest does not forfeit the debt, but no more than 6 per cent. can be recovered. Illegal interest can be recovered back if sued for in six months.

Legal Holidays.—Sunday, January 1, February 22, Good Friday, May 20, July 4, First Saturday of September, December 25, Saturday half-holiday, the first Tuesday after the first Monday in November (Election Day). When January 1, February 22, July 4, or December 25, shall occur on Sunday, the following Monday shall be a holiday.

Limitation of Actions.—Book accounts, debts, notes, and contracts, not under seal, expire by limitation in six years; contracts under seal in twenty-one years.

Married Women.—A married woman shall have the same right to acquire, hold, possess, improve, control, use or dispose of her property, real and personal, in possession or expectancy in the same manner as if she were *femme sole;* provided, however, that a married woman shall have no power to mortgage or convey her real estate unless her husband join in such mortgage or conveyance. She shall be capable of entering into and rendering herself liable upon any contract relating to any trade or business in which she may engage, or for necessaries, and for the use, enjoyment and improvement of her separate estate, and of suing and being sued, either upon such contracts, or for torts done to or committed by her, in all respects as if she were a *femme sole.* A married woman may make, execute, and deliver leases of her property, real and personal, and assignments, transfers and sales of her separate personal property, and notes, bills, drafts, bonds or obligations of any kind, and appoint attorneys to act for her, and it shall not be necessary for her husband to be made a party thereto or joined therein. A married woman may dispose of her property, real or personal, by last will and testament, in writing, signed by her, or manifested by her mark or cross made by her at the end thereof in the same manner as if she were unmarried, and hereafter a will executed by a woman before marriage shall not be deemed to be revoked by her subsequent marriage. Approved July 4, 1887.

PENNSYLVANIA—Continued.

Notarial Fees.—Protest $2.00.

Notes and Bills of Exchange.—Bills of exchange, checks, promissory notes and orders drawn or endorsed to order or bearer are negotiable. Those drawn at sight or payable on demand are without grace, and are due and payable on presentation thereof, but those not so drawn are allowed three days of grace. A clause in the bill of exchange, draft, note, etc., providing for the payment of attorney's commissions, costs, etc., destroys its negotiability. All bills of exchange, drafts, checks, promissory notes, etc., otherwise presentable for acceptance or payment on any holiday are presentable for acceptance or payment on the secular business day next succeeding.

Stay of Executions.—On contracts under $200, six months; over $200 and under $500, nine months; over $500, one year. In Justices' Courts, $20 and under, three months; $20 to $60, six months; over $60, nine months.

Transfer of Corporation Stocks.—The manner of transferring stock is regulated by the by-laws of each corporation. The certificate of stock and transfer books, or either, of any corporation shall be *prima facie* evidence of the right of the person named therein to vote thereon as the owner either personally or by proxy.

RHODE ISLAND.

County Seat.	County.	Name of Atty.	Name of Bank.	Cashier.
Bristol..........Bristol.		O. L. Bosworth	First Natl. Bk.	H. W. Church.
EAST GREENWICH.Kent.		Chas. A. Ames	Greenwich Natl. Bk.	S. M. Knowles.
Kingston.......Washington.		F. C. Olney	Natl. Landholders Bk.	M. F. Perry.
Newport....... Newport.		F. B. Peckham	Newport Natl. Bk.	Henry C. Stevens.
Providence.....Providence.		John T. Blodgett	Manufacturers Natl. Bk.	Francis E. Bates.

DIGEST OF RHODE ISLAND COMMERCIAL LAWS.

Assignments.—Assignments for equal benefit of all creditors can be made. All preferences are void.

Attachments.—An original writ, or writ of mesne process, to attach the real as well as the personal estate of a defendant may be issued whenever the plaintiff, his agent or attorney, shall make affidavit that the plaintiff has a just claim against the defendant that is due, and upon which he expects to recover in the action a sum sufficient to give jurisdiction thereof to the court to which said writ is made returnable. Attachments cannot issue upon a debt not matured.

Bank Laws.—Banks, like all business corporations under the constitution of Rhode Island, are chartered by special act presented to one Legislature, and, after public notice, granted by a succeeding Legislature. In most charters now in force is a provision making stockholders liable for all debts of the bank. The Legislature, or the Governor when the Legislature is not in session, may at any time appoint a special commission to examine one or more banks; and if three or more officers, stockholders or creditors of any bank make a written complaint, the Governor shall appoint such a commission. Banks are not required to make public statements of their condition, but must report to the State Auditor on a day between November 15th and December 15th in each year, the day to be subsequently designated by him.

Exemptions.—No homestead law. Necessary wearing apparel of debtor and his family; necessary working tools, not exceeding $200, and household furniture and family stores, not exceeding $300, are exempt from attachment and execution where the debtor is a householder.

Interest.—Legal rate is 6 per cent., but any rate agreed upon between the parties may be taken. There is no usury law.

Legal Holidays.—Sunday, July 4, Christmas and February 22 (if they fall on Sunday then the day following), May 30 (or if it falls on Sunday then the day preceding it), also election days, viz., the first Wednesday in April of each year, and Tuesday next after the first Monday in November, 1890, and every second year thereafter; Arbor Day, Labor Day (first Monday in September) and Thanksgiving Day. Bank holiday every Saturday after 12 M.

Limitation of Actions.—Accounts, six years; simple promissory notes, six years; sealed instruments and judgments, twenty years. An oral promise and partial payment revive the debt.

RHODE ISLAND—Continued.

Married Women.—All property acquired before or after marriage is so far secured to the wife, that it cannot be taken for the husband's debts. She cannot transact business as a trader. The separate estate of the wife is not liable for family expenses.

Notarial Fees.—Protest $1.50, each additional indorsement twenty-five cents.

Notes and Bills of Exchange.—All paper in which there is not a provision to the contrary is entitled to three days' grace. Indorsers of commercial paper are holden on notice from notary public in accordance with the usages of commercial law. Paper maturing on a holiday becomes payable on next business day. Damages on protested bills of exchange: domestic 5 per cent; foreign, 10 per cent.

Stay of Executions.—Only by order of the Court.

Transfer of Corporation Stocks.—As the by-laws of the corporation may prescribe.

SOUTH CAROLINA.

County Seat.	County.	Name of Atty.	Name of Bank.	Cashier.
Abbeville	Abbeville.	Parker & McGowan	Natl. Bk. of Abbeville	B. S. Barnwell.
Aiken	Aiken.	Henderson Bros.	Bk. of Aiken	W.W.Muckenfuss
Anderson	Anderson.	John K. Hood	Farmers & Merchants Bk.	J. R. Van Diver.
Barnwell	Barnwell.	Bates & Simms	Bk. of Barnwell	F. C. Butler.
Beauford	Beanford.	Wm. Elliott	Bk. of Beauford	D. S. Sams.
Bennetsville	Marlborough.	Dudley & Caston	Bk. of Marlborough	T. G. Matheson.
Camden	Kershaw.	Wm. M. Shannon	Bk. of Camden	C. H. Yates.
Charleston	Charleston.	Joseph W. Barnwell	Peoples Natl. Bk.	E. H. Sparkman.
Chester	Chester.	A. G. Brice	Exchange Bk.	T. H. White.
Chesterfield	Chesterfield.	R. T. Caston	At Cheraw, Bk. of Cheraw	F. A. Waddill.
Columbia	Richland.	F. H. Weston	Carolina Natl. Bk.	Willie Jones.
Conway	Horry.	Johnson & Quattlebaum	Bk. of Conway	D. A. Spivey.
Darlington	Darlington.	Boyd & Brown	Peoples Bk.	H. L. Charles.
Edgefield	Edgefield.	A. S. Tompkins	Farmers Bk.	A. E. Padgett.
Florence	Florence.	W. A. Brunson	Bk. of Florence	W. J. Brown.
Georgetown	Georgetown.	W. Hazard	Bk. of Georgetown	J. I. Hazard.
Greenville	Greenville.	Mooney & Earle	Natl. Bk. of Greenville	W. E. Beattie.
Hampton	Hampton.	W. S. Tillinghast	Bk. of Hampton	R. E. Cansey.
Kingstree	WilliamsburgT.	M. Gilland	Snow & Co.	D. J. McIntyre.
Lancaster	Lancaster.	Jones & Williams	Bk. of Lancaster	H. C. Thomson.
Laurens	Laurens.	N. B. Dial	Peoples Loan & Exchange Bk.	W. A. Watts.
Lexington	Lexington.	C. M. Efird	Lexington Savings Bk.	W. P Roof.
Manning	Clarendon.	Joseph F. Rhame	Bk. of Manning	Joseph Sprott, Jr.
Marion	Marion.	C. A. Woods	Merchants & Farmers Bk.	W. C. Cross.
Mt. Pleasant	Berkley.	H. R. Jenkins	See Charleston	
Newberry	Newberry.	J. F. J. Caldwell	Natl. Bk. of Newberry	T. S. Duncan.
Orangeburgh	Orangeburgh.	B. H. Moss	Bk. of Orangeburgh	J. E. Bull.
Pickens	Pickens.	J. E. Boggs	See Walhalla	
Spartanburgh	Spartanburgh	George W. Nichols	Natl. Bk. of Spartanburgh	W. E. Burnett.
Sumter	Sumter.	Lee & Moise	Simonds Natl. Bk.	L. S. Carson.
Union	Union.	Munro & Munro	Merchants & Planters Bk.	George Munro.
Walhalla	Oconee.	Verner & Gibson	J. D. Verner.	
WALTERBOROUGH	Colleton.	Howell, Murphy & Farrow	Walterborough Loan & Sav. Bk.	R. L. Fraser, Jr.
WINNSBOROUGH	Fairfield.	A. S. Douglass	Winnsborough Natl. Bk.	T. K. Elliott.
Yorkville	York.	C. E. Spencer	Loan & Savings Bk.	F. A. Gilbert.

DIGEST OF SOUTH CAROLINA COMMERCIAL LAWS.

Assignments.—Assignments for the benefit of creditors may be made. No preferences are allowed.

Attachments.—An attachment may issue against a corporation created by or under the laws of any other State or against a defendant who is not a resident of this State, or against a defendant who has absconded or concealed himself, or whenever any person or corporation is about to remove any of his or its property from this State, or has assigned, disposed of or secreted, or is about to assign, dispose of or secrete any of his or its property with intent to defraud creditors.

SOUTH CAROLINA—Continued.

Bank Laws.—The General Assembly can grant no charter for banking purposes, except on condition that the stockholders shall be liable for its debts to the amount of their respective shares and upon condition also that no director or officer shall borrow any money from the corporation. If any director or officer be convicted for violating this provision he may be punished by fine or imprisonment. No loans can be made for a longer period than twelve months. All State banks may invest their capital in the bonds of the State, or of the United States, to an amount not exceeding one-half of its capital. The notes of the bank in circulation must not exceed, for more than four consecutive weeks, three times the amount of gold and silver coin and bullion in its possession or subject to its control within the State and to it belonging, and the bank is liable to a forfeiture of $500 for every successive week during which such excess shall exist. Each bank is required to transmit on Wednesday of each week to the Comptroller-General a certified account of the gold and silver coin and bullion to it belonging, and it is liable to a forfeiture of $100 per day to the State if it neglect to transmit such report. If any officer of a bank receive any deposit or trust, or create any debt on behalf of the bank after he is cognizant of its insolvency he shall be deemed guilty of felony, and shall be liable also to the amount of such deposit trust or indebtedness to the person injured. The comptroller is required to collate the various statements in the returns made by the banks so as to present a comparative view of the several items thereof and publish the same in a newspaper.

Exemptions.—Homestead not to exceed in value $1,000 with the yearly products thereof; and every head of a family residing in this State, whether entitled to a homestead exemption in lands or not, personal property not to exceed in value the sum of $500.

Interest.—Legal rate is 7 per cent., but 8 per cent. may be contracted for in writing. The receipt of any interest greater than that thus allowed shall be attended not only with the forfeiture of all interest, but the lender shall be liable in a separate action for double the sum so usuriously received.

Legal Holidays.—Sunday, National Thanksgiving Days, and all General Election Days, the first day of January, the twenty-second day of February, the fourth day of July, the first Monday in September, the twenty-fifth day of December, and Labor Day.

Limitation of Actions.—Actions upon a judgment or decree of any court of the United States, or of any State or Territory, or upon a sealed instrument, other than sealed notes and personal bonds for payment of money only, which are not secured by mortgage, must be brought within twenty years. An action upon a contract, obligation or liability, express or implied, not under seal, and upon sealed notes or personal bonds for the payment of money only, which are not secured by mortgage, within six years.

Married Women.—The Constitution provides, " the real and personal property of a married woman, held at the time of her marriage, or which she may thereafter acquire, shall not be subject to levy or sale for the husband's debts, but shall be held as her separate property." A married woman may deal as a *femme sole* and her property is bound by her contracts.

Notarial Fees.—Protest $2 and postage.

Notes and Bills of Exchange.—Bills of exchange and promissory notes, drawn in the usual form, are recognized as commercial paper, and if drawn payable at sight

SOUTH CAROLINA—Continued.

are entitled to days of grace. Paper falling due on legal holiday to be paid the next day thereafter. No protest is needed on an inland bill for less than $100. On all bills of exchange drawn on persons resident within the United States, and without this State, and returned protested, the damages are ten per cent., and any other part of North America or in the West India Islands, twelve and one-half per cent. On all bills drawn on persons in any other part of the world the damages are fifteen per cent.

Stay of Executions.—No stay of execution unless ordered by the courts.

Transfer of Corporation Stocks.—Except as between the parties, transfer to be valid must be on books of company.

SOUTH DAKOTA.

County Seat.	County.	Name of Atty.	Name of Bank.	Cashier.
Aberdeen	Brown.	John H. Perry	Aberdeen Natl. Bk.	F. W. Brooks
Alexandria	Hanson.	F. B. Smith	Farmers Bk.	V. K. Stillwell.
Armour	Douglas.	E. S. Johnson	Armour State Bk.	Franklin Floete.
Bangor	Walworth.	W. R. Green	Walworth Co. Bk.	W. R. Green.
Britton	Marshall.	James Wells	State Bk. of J. Voak & Co.	J. J. Aplin.
Brookings	Brookings.	Hall & Cheever	First Natl. Bk.	Horace Fishback.
Canton	Lincoln.	O. S. Gifford	Lincoln Co. Bk.	O. K. Brown.
Castlewood	Hamlin.	Thomas & Hopkin	Hamlin Co. Bk.	H. H. Curtis.
Chamberlain	Brule.	Morrow & Wright	Bk. of Chamberlain	Patrick Henry.
Clark	Clark.	S. A. Keenan	First Natl. Bk.	Carl Jackson.
Custer	Custer.	Porter & Wood	Custer Co. Bk.	T. W. Delicate.
Deadwood	Lawrence.	Moody & Washabaugh	First Natl. Bk.	D. A. McPherson.
De Smet	Kingsbury.	C. S. Whiting	Kingsbury Co. Bk.	E. P. Sanford.
Elk Point	Union.	Ira P. Nichols	Citizens Bk.	F. M. Gilmore.
Faulkton	Faulk.	D. H. Latham	Security State Bk.	C. A. Morse.
Flandreau	Moody.	John Q. Adams	Flandreau State Bk.	Albert Faegre.
Gann Valley	Buffalo.	See Chamberlain		
Gary	Deuel.	J. C. Eakins	Exchange Bk.	A. L. Houghton.
Gettysburg	Potter.	A. L. Ellis	Potter Co. Bk.	J. R. Hughes.
Highmore	Hyde.	F. M. Barnes	Bk. of Highmore	Frank Drew.
Hot Springs	Fall River.	J. H. Boomer	Bk. of Hot Springs	G. C. Smith.
Howard	Miner.	Farmer & Farmer	Security Bk. of Dakota	C. L. Oleson.
Huron	Beadle.	John L. Pyle	Sioux Valley Bk.	Hubert Loonan.
Ipswich	Edmunds.	H. C. Briggs	Bk. of Ipswich	A. J. Beebe.
Leola	McPherson.	Andrew Williams	State Bk. of Leola	C. Turner.
Madison	Lake.	J. H. Williamson	First Natl. Bk.	G. L. McCallister.
Millbank	Grant.	Thomas L. Bouck	Farmers Bk.	F. B. Roberts.
Miller	Hand.	J. H. Cole	Citizens Bk.	W. H, Waters.
Minnesela	Butte.	See Deadwood		
Mitchell	Davison.	A. E. Hitchcock	First Natl. Bk.	F. E. Moses.
Mound City	Campbell.	H. J. Krueger	Campbell Co. State Bk.	A. F. Campbell.
Nashville	Harding.	See Deadwood		
Oacoma	Lyman.	See Chamberlain		
Olivet	Hutchinson.	J. M. Gray	At Parkston, Parkston State Bk.	H. E. Casteel.
Onida	Sully.	Coe I. Crawford	Sully Co. Savings Bk.	D. Q. Jordan.
Parker	Turner.	S. V. Jones	First Natl. Bk.	F. L. Clisby.
Pierre	Hughes.	Horner & Stewart	Pierre Natl. Bk.	Louis Kehr.
Plankinton	Aurora.	H. F, Fellows	Bk. of Plankinton	F. L. Stevens.
Rapid City	Pennington.	Jas. W. Fowler	First Natl. Bk.	James Halley.
Redfield	Spink.	Sterling & Morris	Bk. of Redfield	E. C. Isenhuth.
Rosebud	Meyer.	See Chamberlain		
Salem	McCook.	E. H. Wilson	Commercial State Bk.	D. Goldsmith.
Sioux Falls	Minnehaha.	Muller & Conway	Dakota Natl. Bk.	C. C. Carpenter.
Sturgis	Meade.	Wesley A. Stuart	First Natl. Bk.	J. J. Davenport.
Tyndall	BonneHommel.	D. Elliott	Security Bk.	Joseph Zitka.
Vermillion	Clay.	John L. Jolley	First Natl. Bk.	M. J. Lewis.
Watertown	Codington.	D. C. & W. R. Thomas	Citizens Natl. Bk.	W. D. Morris.

SOUTH DAKOTA—Continued.

County Seat.	County.	Name of Atty.	Name of Bank.	Cashier.
Webster	Day.	R. W. Parliman	Farmers & Merchants Bk.	Jno. Williams.
Wessington Springs	Jerauld.	E. H. Vance	Bk. of Wessington Springs	C. W. Lane.
Wheeler	Charles Mix.	D. L. P. Lamb	Security Bk.	J. F. Nichols.
Wilmot	Roberts.	F. A. Countryman	Bk. of Wilmot	L. V. Peek.
Woonsocket	Sanborn.	N. B. Reed	Citizens Bk.	Noah Keller.
Yankton	Yankton.	Gamble & Dillon	Yankton Natl. Bk.	Wm.H. Edmunds.
Not Organized.	Boreman.			
"	Choteau.			
"	Delano.			
"	Dewey.			
"	Ewing.			
"	Gregory.			
"	Jackson.			
"	Lugenbeel.			
"	Martin.			
"	Nowlin.			
"	Pratt.			
"	Presho.			
"	Pyatt.			
"	Rhinehart.			
"	Schnasse.			
"	Scobey.			
"	Shannon.			
"	Stanley.			
"	Sterling.			
"	Todd.			
"	Tripp.			
"	Wagner.			
"	Washabaugh.			
"	Washington.			
"	Ziebach.			

DIGEST OF SOUTH DAKOTA COMMERCIAL LAWS.

Assignments.—An insolvent debtor may execute an assignment of property for the satisfaction of his creditors, but such an assignment cannot contain any trust or condition by which any creditor is to receive a preference over any other creditor.

Attachments.—Attachments may issue against a corporation created by or under the laws of any other territory, state, government or country; or against a defendant who is not a resident of this State; or against a defendant who has absconded or concealed himself; or whenever any person or corporation is about to remove any of his or its property from this State; or has assigned, disposed of, secreted, or is about to assign, dispose of or secrete any of his or its property with intent to defraud creditors, the plaintiff, at the time of issuing the summons, or at any time afterwards, may have the property of such defendant or corporation attached as security for the satisfaction of such judgment as the plaintiff may recover.

SOUTH DAKOTA—Continued.

Bank Laws.—Banking corporations may be formed by three or more persons, one-third of whom must be residents of the State, signing articles of association which shall show: the name of the proposed bank; the place where the business is to be conducted; the amount of the capital and the number and value of the shares; the names and places of residence of the shareholders, and the number subscribed for by each; the time when such bank is to commence and terminate its business. This certificate must be acknowledged and filed with the Secretary of State, who then issues his certificate of authority for it to act as a corporation. Banks so organized cannot issue notes to circulate as money. At least one-half of the capital must be paid in before it can begin business. The shares shall be of the value of $100 each. Each director must own at least ten shares of stock. Stockholders are individually liable ratably for all debts of the bank to the extent of the amount of their stock in addition to the par value of the shares respectively held by them. There can be no special or limited partnership formed for banking purposes.

Exemptions.—The homestead, whether owned by husband or wife, is exempt from judicial sale, judgment, lien, and all process while it possesses the homestead character. It must embrace the house used as a home by the owner, and if the owner has two or more such houses, he may select which he will retain, as the homestead must only embrace contiguous lots limited to one acre of city property, 160 acres of farm property limited to $5,000 in value. Upon death of either the husband or wife, the survivor may continue to occupy the homestead.

Interest.—Legal rate 7 cent.; contract rate may be 12 per cent. Usury forfeits double amount of interest collected.

Legal Holidays.—Sunday, January 1, February 22, May 30, July 4, Thanksgiving, public fast, and December 25, and a general State or National Election Day, Labor Day.

Limitation of Actions.—Action must be commenced on judgments within ten years, on contracts, express or implied, six years from the time a cause of action accrued thereon; liability created by statute, six years; upon real property, six years. Replevin and conversion, six years.

Notarial Fees.—Protest $1.50, record fifty cents, each notice twenty-five cents and postage.

Notes and Bills of Exchange.—On all bills of exchange or sight drafts, whether foreign or domestic, and on all promissory notes, bills of exchange and drafts, on the face of which time is specified, and notes on demand for payment of same, three days' grace are allowed; holidays are excluded from the computation of days of grace. Acceptance must be in writing by the drawee or an acceptor for honor. Apparent maturity of a non-interest bearing sight or demand note is ten days after date, in addition to the time required for transmission; on interest bearing notes, one year after date. Bills and notes falling due on a holiday are deemed due and payable on the following day. To hold indorser, the instrument must be presented on the day of maturity, and notice of dishonor given. Damages are allowed in favor of holders for value on bills of exchange drawn or negotiated within the State and protested for non-acceptance or non-payment.

Transfer of Corporation Stocks.—Shares of stock are transferred by endorsement of the owner, his attorney or legal representative, by delivery of certificate and entry of transfer on the books of the company. In case of non-resident owner, an affidavit that the transferee was alive at date of transfer may be required.

TENNESSEE.

County Seat.	County.	Name of Atty.	Name of Bank.	Cashier.
Alamo	Crockett.	Wm. F. Poston	At Bells Depot, Bk. of Crockett	J. H. Thomas.
Altamont	Grundy.	J. K. P. Pearson	See McMinnville	
Ashland City	Cheatham.	J. J. Lenox	See Nashville	
Athens	McMinn.	W. D. Henderson	First Natl. Bk.	R. J. Fisher.
Benton	Polk.	W. R. Johnson	See Cleveland	
Blountville	Sullivan.	Thomas Curtin	At Bristol, Natl. Bk. of Bristol	John H. Caldwell.
Bolivar	Hardeman.	Wood & McNeal	Bk. of Bolivar	W. C. Dorlon.
Brownsville	Haywood.	Wm. Kinney	Haywood Co. Bk.	T. B. King.
Byrdstown	Pickett.	S. M. Turner	See Livingston	
Camden	Benton.	S. L. Peeler	Camden Bk. & Trust Co.	W. E. McRae.
Carthage	Smith.	W. V. Lee	Bk. of Carthage.	Herman Myer.
Celina	Clay.	C. Hull	See Gainesboro'.	
Centreville	Hickman.	Bates & Clagett.	First Natl. Bk.	J. B. Walker.
Charlotte	Dickson.	Morris & Leech	At Dickson, Dickson Bk. & Trust Co.	J. T. Dean.
Chattanooga	Hamilton.	J. A. Caldwell	First Natl. Bk.	J. H. Rathburn.
Clarksville	Montgomery.	Leech & Savage	Clarksville Natl. Bk.	A. Howell.
Cleveland	Bradley.	P. B. Mayfield & Son	Bk. of Charleston	T. J. Knox.
Clinton	Anderson.	J. A. Fowler	Union Bk.	R. S. Kincaid.
Columbia	Maury.	George T. Hughes	Maury Natl. Bk.	Chas. A. Parker.
Cookeville	Putnam.	T. L. Dewey	Bk. of Cookeville	R. L. Farley.
Covington	Tipton.	W. A. Owen	Farmers & Merchants Bk.	John T. Garner.
Crossville	Cumberland.	See Sparta		
Dandridge	Jefferson.	Pickle & Turner	At Mossy Creek, Mossy Creek Bk.	J. W. Goodwin.
Dayton	Rhea.	W. B. Miller	Dayton Bk. & Trust Co.	J. T. Dean.
Decatur	Meigs.	J. W. Lillard	See Dayton	
Decaturville	Decatur.	J. A. England	See Lexington	
Dover	Stewart.	W. M. Brandon	Stewart Co. Bk.	E. T. Peck.
Dresden	Weakley.	Jones & Hall	Weakley Co. Bk.	J. D. Little.
Dunlap	Sequatchie.	N. D. Hearn	See Pikeville	
Dyersburgh	Dyer.	Latta & Latta	Citizens Bk.	J. N. Parker.
Elizabethton	Carter.	John W. Tipton	Peoples Bk.	C. T. Cass.
Erin	Houston.	J. W. Rudolph	Bk. of Erin	D. W. Shofner.
Erwin	Unicoi.	R. W. H. Gilbert	Unicoi Co. Bk.	W. T. Williams.
Fayetteville	Lincoln.	Holman & Carter	Elk Natl. Bk.	W. B. Douthat.
Franklin	Williamson.	Wm. House	Natl. Bk. of Franklin	Joseph L. Parker.
Gainesboro	Jackson.	J. T. Anderson	Bk. of Gainesboro	J. A. Williams.
Gallatin	Sumner.	James W. Blackmore	First Natl. Bk.	D. F. Barry.
Greenville	Greene.	Newton Hacker	First Natl. Bk.	J. E. Hacker.
Hartsville	Trousdale.	John S. McMurray	Bk. of Hartsville	M. L. Wright.
Henderson	Chester.	M. F. Ozier	Farmers & Merchants Bk.	R. E. McKinney.
Huntington	Carroll.	George T. McCall	Bk. of Huntington	J. McNiel Wright
Huntsville	Scott.	W. H. Buttram	At Harriman, First Natl. Bk.	W. H. Julian.
Jacksborough	Campbell.	E. H. Powers	At Coal Creek, Bk. of Anderson Co.	E. L. Foster.
Jackson	Madison.	McCorry & Bond	First Natl. Bk.	J. W. Vanden.
Jamestown	Fentress.	Smith & Smith	See Livingston	
Jasper	Marion.	W. D. Spears	At South Pittsburg, First Natl. Bk.	T. G. Garrett.
JONESBOROUGH	Washington.	S. J. Kirkpatrick	First Natl. Bk.	T. L. Earnest.
Kingston	Roane.	George L. Burke	Kingston Bk. & Trust Co.	S. P. Sparks.

THE LEGAL AND FINANCIAL LIGHTS OF AMERICA. 131

TENNESSEE—Continued.

County Seat.	County.	Name of Atty.	Name of Bank.	Cashier.
Knoxville	Knox.	Jesse L. Rogers	East Tennessee Natl. Bk.	S. V. Carter.
La Fayette	Macon.	I. L. Roark	La Fayette Bkg. Co.	J. W. Beckwith.
LAWRENCEBURGH	Lawrence.	W. R. King	Lawrence Bkg. & Trust Co.	J. M. Gilmore.
Lebanon	Wilson.	E. E. Beard	Bk. of Lebanon	S. G. Stratton.
Lewisburgh	Marshall.	P. C. Smithson	Bk. of Lewisburgh	W. D. Fox.
Lexington	Henderson.	John E. McCall	Bk. of Lexington	E. J. Tunberlake.
Linden	Perry.	T. W. Sims	See Centreville	
Livingston	Overton.	Knight & Hussey	Bk. of Livingston	H. S. Estes.
Loudon	Loudon.	G. W. Fox	Bk. of Loudon	R. H. Bell.
Lynchburgh	Moore.	W. D. L. Record	Farmers Bk.	J. W. Motlow.
McMinnville	Warren.	T. C. Lind	Peoples Natl. Bk.	Frank Colville.
Madisonville	Monroe.	McCroskey & McCroskey	Bk. of Madisonville	W. N. Magill.
Manchester	Coffee.	George W. Cross	Coffee Co. Bk.	J. G. Wilkinson.
Maryville	Blount.	McTeer & Gamble	Bk. of Maryville	Joseph Burger.
Maynardville	Union.	C. A. Culp	See Knoxville	
Memphis	Shelby.	Wm. M. Randolph & Sons	State Natl. Bk.	M.S.Buckingham
Morristown	Hamblen.	Shields & Mount Castle	First Natl. Bk.	George S. Crouch.
Mountain City	Johnson.	Jenkins & Donnelly	See Bristol	
MURFREESBORO'	Rutherford.	H. E. Palmer	First Natl. Bk.	H. H. Williams.
Nashville	Davidson.	Tillman & Tillman	Fourth Natl. Bk.	J. T. Howell.
Newburg	Lewis.	See Centreville	See Columbia	
Newport	Cocke.	McSween & Mims	Merchants & Planters Bk.	D. A. Mims.
Ooltewah	James.	H. H. McNab	See Chattanooga	
Paris	Henry.	T. N. Thomason	Commercial Bk.	Alex. B. White.
Pikeville	Bledsoe.	John C. Myers	Peoples Bk.	Sam. M. Pope.
Pulaski	Giles.	John T. Allen	Peoples Natl. Bk.	N. A. Crockett.
Ripley	Lauderdale.	John P. Gause	Ripley Bk.	W. L. Neel.
Rogersville	Hawkins.	Smith & Chesnutt	Rogersville Natl. Bk.	James Cooper.
Rutledge	Grainger.	A. S. Tate	See Morristown	
Savannah	Hardin.	D. W. Broyles	Bk. of Savannah	J. J. Williams.
Selmer	McNairy.	D. W. Herring	McNairy Co. Bk.	J. R. Adams.
Sevierville	Sevier.	J. R. Penland	Bk. of Sevierville	M. B. McMahan.
Shelbyville	Bedford.	Wm. B. Bates	Peoples Natl. Bk.	J. D. Hutton.
Smithville	DeKalb.	Nesmith & Smallman	Potter's Bk.	T. B. Potter.
Sneedville	Hancock.	A. J. Tyler	See Rogersville	
Somerville	Fayette.	H. C. Moorman	Fayette Co. Bk.	A. J. Rooks.
Sparta	White.	M. A. Cummings	First Natl. Bk.	J. N. Walling.
Spencer	Van Buren.	J. R. Simmons	See Sparta	
Springfield	Robertson.	A. E. Garner	Springfield Natl. Bk.	J. Y. Hutchison.
Tazewell	Claiborne.	W. A. Owens	See Rogersville	
Tiptonville	Lake.	W. W. Cochran	See Troy	
Trenton	Gibson.	Neil & Deason	Exchange Bk.	J. E. Carthel.
Troy	Obion.	J. G. Smith & Son	Bk. of Troy	Paul Ingram.
Wartburg	Morgan.	S. M. Vance	At Harriman, First Natl. Bk.	W. H. Julian.
Waverly	Humphreys.	Thomas Bowman	Waverly Bk. & Trust Co.	W. H. Meadow.
Waynesboro	Wayne.	Morrison & Harding	See Savannah	
Winchester	Franklin.	Bankes & Embrey	Bk. of Winchester	F. A. Pattie.
Woodbury	Cannon.	James A. Jones	Bk. of Woodbury	W. C. Covington.

TENNESSEE—Continued.
DIGEST OF TENNESSEE COMMERCIAL LAWS.

Assignments.—Assignments for the benefit of creditors are allowed, but without preference.

Attachments.—Attachments may be granted where the debtor or defendant resides out of the State; where he is about to remove or has removed himself or property from the State; where he has removed or is removing himself out of the county privately; where he conceals himself, so that the ordinary process of law cannot be served upon him; where he absconds or is absconding or concealing himself or property; where he has fraudulently disposed of or is about fraudulently to dispose of his property; where any person liable for any debt or demand, residing out of the State, dies, leaving property in the State.

Bank Laws.—Any company incorporated under the laws of Tennessee, having, by its charter, the right to receive money in trust or otherwise, has the power to receive deposits and loan same and its capital on any kind of commercial business paper or real estate, buy and sell exchange and all kinds of public or private securities and commercial paper. State banks may be chartered at any time in same manner as other private corporations, and, if they so choose, may couple with the usual banking business, a safe deposit and trust company. They may do all acts usually performed by banks. Allow 3 per cent. interest on deposits, advance money on real and personal property, and sell same; and, if the safe deposit and trust feature is added, may take on deposit jewelry and other valuables, and guarantee the preservation and delivery of same; guarantee the titles to real estate and the payment of bonds and mortgages; execute trusts of every description, and own a vault and rent out boxes for the keeping of valuables, but shall not be liable for losses by fire, theft, or other excuse. Stockholders not liable except for payment of stock subscribed by each. Every six months banks must publish a statement of their condition. The Secretary of State is made a bank examiner, and required to examine each bank quarterly and report to the Comptroller, and each bank is subject to legislative inspection. There is no law regulating the class of bonds in which savings banks may invest.

Exemptions.—A homestead or real estate in the possession of, or belonging to, each head of a family, and the improvements, if any, thereon, to the value of in all $1,000, shall be exempt from sale under legal process during the life of such head of the family, and which shall inure to the benefit of his widow and children, and shall be exempt from sale in any way at the instance of any creditor or creditors.

Interest.—Legal rate is 6 per cent. A defendant sued for money may avoid the excess over legal interest by a plea setting forth the amount of the usury. If usurious interest has been paid it may be recovered by action at the suit of the party from whom it was taken.

Legal Holidays.—Sunday, January 1, February 22, first Monday in September (Labor Day), July 4, December 25, Thanksgiving and Good Friday, Decoration Day, Memorial Day and election days.

Limitation of Actions.—Upon bonds, notes, accounts and contracts generally, six years; judgments or decrees of courts of record, and other cases not expressly provided for, ten years.

Married Women.—Are without power to bind themselves or property by contract.

Notarial Fees.—Protest $1, each notice fifty cents.

TENNESSEE—Continued.

Notes and Bills of Exchange.—A verbal acceptance of bill of exchange communicated to one who accepts it on faith of such acceptance is valid. Bills of exchange, promissory notes, bank checks, and bonds for payment of money are negotiable. When negotiable paper is taken in payment of pre-existing debt, equities can be set up against the holder. Notary's certificate that he gave notice on protest of bill or note to drawer or indorser, is *prima facie* evidence that such notice was given as therein stated. All warehouse receipts for cotton, tobacco, grain, hemp, whiskey, or any kind of produce, wares, merchandise, or of any description of personal property, are negotiable in the same manner as bills of exchange, unless such receipts shall have the words "Not Negotiable" plainly written or stamped thereon. Damages recoverable on a protested bill of exchange drawn or indorsed in Tennessee, are three per cent. if it was drawn on a person or corporation in any of the United States or Territories thereof; fifteen per cent. if drawn on any person or corporation of or in any other State or place in North America bordering on the Gulf of Mexico, or of or in any of the West India Islands; twenty per cent. if drawn on any person or corporation of or in any other part of the world. Days of grace are not allowed on bills payable at sight. Paper maturing on a holiday becomes due on business day preceding.

Stay of Executions.—In Justices' Courts a stay of eight months is allowed on giving security.

Transfer of Corporation Stocks.—Shares may be transferred by presentation of old certificates at the office of the company properly endorsed. New shares will then be issued by the proper officer.

TEXAS.

County Seat.	County.	Name of Atty.	Name of Bank.	Cashier.
Abilene	Taylor.	Fred Cockrell	Abilene Natl. Bk.	George S. Berry.
Albany	Shackleford.	J. R. Warren	First Natl. Bk.	N.L.Bartholomew
Alpine	Brewster.	Vacant	See Pecos	
Amarillo	Potter.	Plemens & Veale	First Natl. Bk.	Walter Davis.
Anderson	Grimes.	Lindsay & Baker	At Navasota, First Natl. Bk.	James M. Shaw.
Anson	Jones.	C. M. Christenberry	Bk. of R. V. Colbert	
Archer	Archer.	F. E. Dyens	See Seymour	
Athens	Henderson.	Richardson,Watkins&Miller.	First Natl. Bk.	G. M. Wofford.
Austin	Travis.	West & Cochran	State Natl. Bk.	J. G. Palm.
Baird	Callahan.	Otis Bowyer	First Natl. Bk.	W. C. Powell.
Ballinger	Runnels.	Gulon & Truly	First Natl. Bk.	D. M. Baker.
Bandera	Bandera.	H. C. Duffy	See San Antonio	
Barstow	Ward.	See Pecos		
Bastrop	Bastrop.	J. B. Price	First Natl. Bk.	Chester Erhard.
Batesville	Zavalla.	See Eagle Pass		
Beaumont	Jefferson.	Greer & Greer	First Natl. Bk.	Frank Alvey.
Beeville	Bee.	Beasley & Flournoy	First Natl. Bk.	B. W. Klipstein.
Bellville	Austin.	A. Chesley	First Natl. Bk.	J. G. Wessendorf.
Belton	Bell.	A. J. Harris	Belton Natl. Bk.	J. Z. Miller.
Benjamin	Knox.	J. J. Brents	See Seymour	
Big Spring	Howard.	S. H. Cowan	First Natl. Bk.	E. O. Price.
Blanco	Blanco.	J. W. Bains	Bk. of Boon & Crist.	
Boerne	Kendall.	Eugene Digges	See San Antonio	
Bonham	Faunin.	Taylor, Galloway & McGrady.	First Natl. Bk.	A.B. Scarborough
Brackettville	Kinney.	Thomas & McDonald	See Del Rio	
Brady	McCulloch.	F. M. Newman	Commercial Bk.	W. D. Crothers.
Brazoria	Brazoria.	H. Masterson	At Velasco, Velasco Natl. Bk.	J. M. Moore.
Breckenridge	Stephens.	J. W Crudgington	Bk. of Ward & Black	
Brenham	Washington.	Searcy & Garrett	First Natl. Bk.	H. K. Harrison.
Brownsville	Cameron.	James B. Wells	First Natl. Bk.	J. D. Anderson.
Brownwood	Brown.	Jenkins & McCartney	Merchants Natl. Bk.	J. A. Austin.
Bryan	Brazos.	Ford & Nall	Merchants & Planters Bk.	J. P. Burrough.
Burnet	Burnet.	J. G. Cook	Bk. of W. H. Westfall & Co.	
Caldwell	Burleson.	A. W. McIver	Bk. of Wm. Reeves & Co.	
Cameron	Milan.	W. T. Hefley	First Natl. Bk.	T. F. Hardy.
Canadian	Hemphill.	H. E. Hoover	Canadian Valley Bk.	D. J. Young.
Canton	Van Zandt.	Kilgore & Lively	At Willspoint, Willspoint Bk.	J. M. Lybrand.
Canyon	Randall.	See Clarendon		
Carrizo	Zapata.	See Laredo		
CARRIZO SPRINGS.	Dimmit.	F. Vandervoorst	See Eagle Pass	
Carthage	Panola.	J. G. Hazlewood	Bk. of Carthage	
Castroville	Medina.	H. E. Hasse	Bk. of Joseph Couraud	
Center	Shelby.	R. S. Bryerly	See Nacogdoches	
Centerville	Leon.	S. W. Dean	See Franklin	
Childress	Childress.	Johnson & Fires	First Natl. Bk.	J. H. P. Jones.
Clairmont	Kent.	Belcher & Hendrix	See Haskell	
Clarendon	Donley.	Browning & Medden	Bk. of Clarendon	W. H. Patrick.

THE LEGAL AND FINANCIAL LIGHTS OF AMERICA. 135

TEXAS—Continued.

County Seat.	County.	Name of Atty.	Name of Bank.	Cashier.
Clarksville	Red River.	Lennox & Lennox	Red River Natl. Bk.	D. W. Cheatham.
Claude	Armstrong.	See Clarendon		
Cleburne	Johnson.	Poindexter & Padelford	Farmers & Merchants Natl. Bk.	S. B. Allen.
Cold Spring	San Jacinto.	A. R. Chapman	See Huntsville	
Coldwater	Sherman.	See Lipscomb		
Coleman	Coleman.	H. C. Randolph	Coleman Natl. Bk.	R. H. Alexander.
Colorado	Mitchell.	R. H. Looney	Peoples Natl. Bk.	W. T. Scott.
Columbus	Colorado.	J. W. Munson	Bk. of R. E. Stafford & Co.	Ike T. Pryor.
Comanche	Comanche.	Lindsey & Goodson	First Natl. Bk.	T. C. Hill.
Cooper	Delta.	Wood & Phillips	First Natl. Bk.	R. M. Walker.
Corpus Christi.	Nueces.	G. R. Scott & Bro.	Corpus Christi Natl. Bk.	Thos. Hickey.
Corsicana	Navarro.	R. S. Neblett	Corsicana Natl. Bk.	T. P. Kerr.
Cotulla	La Salle.	P. H. Clark	Cotulla Bk.	E. G. Hubbard.
Crockett	Houston.	Nunn & Nunn	First Natl. Bk.	H. F. Moore.
Crowell	Foard.	See Quanah		
Cuero	De Witt.	Bailey & Schleicher	First Natl. Bk.	Lee Joseph.
Daingerfield	Morris.	J. M. Moore	Natl. Bk. of Daingerfield	J. F. Jones.
Dallas	Dallas.	D. H. Morrow	City Natl. Bk.	E. O. Tenison.
Decatur	Wise.	R. E. Carswell	First Natl. Bk.	Ben. F. Allen.
Del Rio	Val Verde.	H. C. Carter	Bk. of John Woods & Son	
Denton	Denton.	Smith & Hill	Denton Co. Natl. Bk.	B. H. Davenport.
Dickens	Dickens.	See Haskell		
Dimmitt	Castro.	See Floydada		
Dumas	Moore.	See Canadian		
Eagle Pass	Maverick.	Winchester Kelso	First Natl. Bk.	W. A. Bonnet.
Eastland	Eastland.	Scott & Brelsford	Eastland Natl. Bk.	B. B. Kenyon.
Edna	Jackson.	W. A. McDowel	Bk. of Edna	J. W. Allen.
El Paso	El Paso.	W. B. Brack	State Natl. Bk.	J. C. Lackland.
Emma	Crosby.	See Haskell		
Emory	Rains.	W. M. Brook	At Mineola, Bk. of Mineola	S. Munzesheimer.
Fairfield	Freestone.	R. G. Anderson	See Palestine	
Floresville	Wilson.	Camp & Cocke	Bk. of A. B. Briscoe	D. C. McRae.
Floydada	Floyd.	H. Snodgrass	Floyd Co. Bk.	B. W. Ainsworth.
Fort Davis	Jeff Davis.	G. E. Pope	See Pecos	
Fort Stockton.	Pecos.	Howell Johnson	See Pecos	
Fort Worth	Tarrant.	Hyde Jennings	Fort Worth Natl. Bk.	N. Harding.
Franklin	Robertson.	Cochron & Kinnard	Bk. of Mitchell Bros. & Decherd	
FREDERICKSBURGH	Gillespie.	A. O. Cooley	Bk. of Fredericksburgh.	T. D. Smith.
Gail	Borden.	See Big Spring		
Gainesville	Cooke.	Potter & Potter	First Natl. Bk.	Wm. Worsham.
Galveston	Galveston.	Spencer & Kincald	Galveston Natl. Bk.	A. J. Compton.
Garden City	Glasscock.	See Big Spring		
Gatesville	Coryell.	S. B. Hawkins	City Natl. Bk.	J. S. Corley.
Georgetown	Williamson.	Brooks & John	First Natl. Bk.	F. W. Carothers.
Giddings	Lee.	J. L. Rousseau	First Natl. Bk.	I. J. Farris.
Gilmer	Upshur.	F. S. Eberhart	Gilmer Bk.	W. S. Sasser.
Glen Rose	Somervell.	J. J. Farr	See Cleburne	
Goldthwaite	Mills.	Tripett & Doughty	First Natl. Bk.	W. H. Trent.
Goliad	Goliad.	Browne & Burns	First Natl. Bk.	W. B. Campbell.

THE LEGAL AND FINANCIAL LIGHTS OF AMERICA.

TEXAS—Continued.

County Seat.	County.	Name of Atty.	Name of Bank.	Cashier.
Gonzales	Gonzales.	Burgess & Hopkins	Bk. of Miller & Sayers	W. J. Bright.
Graham	Young.	R. F. Arnold	Beckham Natl. Bk.	W. T. Stewart.
Granbury	Hood.	Riddle & Martin	First Natl. Bk.	Otho S. Houston.
Greenville	Hunt.	Perkins, Gilbert & Perkins.	Greenville Natl. Bk.	W. A. Williams.
Groesbeck	Limestone.	Farrar, Williams & Farrar	Groesbeck Natl. Bk.	D. Oliver.
Groveton	Trinity.	See Huntsville		
Guthrie	King.	See Haskell		
Hallettsville	Lavaca.	Paulus & Ragsdale	Lavaca Co. Natl. Bk.	F. Simpson.
Hamilton	Hamilton.	Eldson & Roberts	Hamilton Natl. Bk.	E. A. Pery.
Hansford	Hansford.	See Lipscomb		
Hartley	Hartley.	See Amarillo		
Haskell	Haskell.	Baldwin & Lomax	First Natl. Bk.	J. V. W. Holmes.
Haymond	Buchel.	See Del Rio		
Hemphill	Sabine.	A. D. Hamilton	See Nacogdoches	
Hempstead	Waller.	A. C. Tompkins	Farmers Natl. Bk.	Ed. F. Jones.
Henderson	Rusk.	W. C. Buford.	Bk. of A. Wettermark & Co.	
Henrietta	Clay.	W. G. Eustis	Farmers Natl. Bk.	F. B. Wyatt.
Hidalgo	Hidalgo.	Rentfro & Scott	See Corpus Christi	
Hillsborough	Hill.	Tarlton & Morrow	Farmers Natl. Bk.	John J. Warren.
Houston	Harris.	Ewing & Ring	First Natl. Bk.	W. H. Palmer.
Huntsville	Walker.	Benton Randolph	Gibbs Natl. Bk.	G. A. Wynne.
Jacksborough	Jack.	Thomas S. Spooner	First Natl. Bk.	D. L. Knox.
Jasper	Jasper.	Seale & Powell	See Nacogdoches	
Jefferson	Marion.	W. T. Armistead	Natl. Bk. of Jefferson	W. T. Atkins.
Junction City.	Kimble.	W. A. Williamson	See Macon	
Karnes City	Karnes.	Graves & Wilson	Buchel, Wagner & Co.	C. L. Burghard.
Kaufman	Kaufman.	Huffmaster & Huffmaster	First Natl. Bk.	Wood Nash.
Kerville	Kerr.	W. G. Garrett	Charles Schreiner	L. A. Schreiner.
Kountz	Hardin.	See Beaumont		
Lagrange	Fayette.	Brown. Lane & Jackson	First Natl. Bk.	Jno. B. Holloway.
Lampasas	Lampasas.	Matthews & Browning	First Natl. Bk.	J. F. White.
La Plata	Deafsmith.	See Amarillo		
Laredo	Webb.	M. H. Lane	Milmo Natl. Bk.	Miles T. Cogley.
Liberty	Liberty.	M. D. Rayborn	See Houston	
Linden	Cass.	F. S. Eberhard	See Daingerfield	
Lipscomb	Lipscomb.	H. E. Hoover	Bk. of Lipscomb	Wm. H. Parker.
Livingston	Polk.	James E. Heil	See Houston	
Llano	Llano.	Moore & Linden	Iron City Natl. Bk.	M. M. Hargis.
Lockhart	Caldwell.	Storey & Storey	First Natl. Bk.	J. M. Jolley.
Longview	Gregg.	Otho F. Lane		
Lubbock	Lubbock.	See Haskell		
Lufkin	Angelina.	H. G. Lane		
Madisonville	Madison.	J. F. Randolph	See Nacogdoches	
Marfa	Presidio.	H. H. Kilpatrick	See Franklin	
Marlin	Falls.	Martin & Eddings	See Pecos	
Marshall	Harrison.	M. R. Geer	First Natl. Bk.	B. C. Clark.
Mason	Mason.	M. Fulton	First Natl. Bk.	W. C. Field.
Matador	Motley.	See Quanah	First Natl. Bk.	E. M. Reynolds.
Matagorda	Matagorda.	See Edna		

THE LEGAL AND FINANCIAL LIGHTS OF AMERICA. 137

TEXAS—Continued.

County Seat.	County.	Name of Atty.	Name of Bank.	Cashier.
McKinney	Collin.	Smith & Evans	First Natl. Bk.	T. H. Emerson.
Memphis	Hall.	W. M. Pardue	Bk. of Memphis	Byron Jones.
Menardville	Menard.	J. A. Snook	See Mason	
Mentone	Loving.	See Pecos		
Meridian	Bosque.	Wm. N. Knight	First Natl. Bk.	J. W. Rudasill.
Midland	Midland.	R. H. Zane	First Natl. Bk.	W. E. Connell.
Mobeetie	Wheeler.	L. O. Miller	Bk. of J. L. Dickerson	C. H. Philbrick.
Montague	Montague.	J. M. Chambers	First Natl Bk.	W. M. Dugan.
Montgomery	Montgomery.	B. H. Powell	See Houston	
Mt. Pleasant	Titus.	S. P. Pounders	First Natl. Bk.	C. C. Carr.
Mt. Vernon	Franklin.	Glass & McLean	Mt. Vernon Bk.	
Nacogdoches	Nacogdoches.	George H. Matthews	First Natl. Bk.	W. G. Ratcliff.
New Bramfels	Comal.	J. D. Guinn	First Natl. Bk.	Herman Clemens.
Newton	Newton.	L. B. Clunk	See Beaumont.	
Oakville	Live Oak.	See Beeville		
Ochiltree	Ochiltree.	See Lipscomb		
Odessa	Ector.	See Midland		
Orange	Orange.	D. W. Solliday	First Natl. Bk.	W. W. Reid.
Ozona	Crockett.	See San Angelo		
Paducah	Cottle.	See Quanah		
Paint Rock	Concho.	G. H. Garland	See Ballinger	
Parnell	Roberts.	See Canadian		
Palestine	Anderson.	Gregg & Gardner	First Natl. Bk.	Lucius Gooch.
Palo Pinto	Palo Pinto.	M. L. Garrett	Cunningham Bros.	Jno. H. Eaton.
Panhandle	Carson.	Frank Lester	Panhandle Bk.	J. C. Paul.
Paris	Lamar.	Denton & Long	First Natl. Bk.	J. F. McReynolds
Pearsall	Frio.	T. N. Spann	See San Antonio	
Pecos	Reeves.	Frank E. Hunter	Pecos Valley Bk.	W. D. Johnson.
Pittsburgh	Camp.	S. D. Snodgrass	First Natl. Bk.	W. C. Hargrove.
Plainview	Hale.	See Floydada		
Pleasanton	Atascosa.	W. H. Smith	See Karnes City	
Port Lava	Calhoun.	W. H. Woodward	See Victoria	
Quanah	Hardeman.	Smith & Martin	Bk. of C. H. Harwell & Co.	
Quitman	Wood.	W. B. Harris	See Gilmer	
Rayner	Stonewall.	Balcher & Hendrix	See Haskell	
Refugio	Refugio.	See Beeville		
Richmond	Fort Bend.	Thomas E. Mitchell	Bk. of J. H. P. Davis & Co.	C. A. Beasley.
Rio Grande	Starr.	F. D. Yoden	See Brownsville	
Robert Lee	Coke.	See Ballinger		
Roby	Fisher.	Crane & Kiefer	See Sweetwater	
Rockport	Aransas.	E. A. Stevens	First Natl. Bk.	J. M. Hoopes.
Rock Springs	Edwards.	See Kerrville		
Rockwall	Rockwall.	N. C. Edwards	Rockwall Co. Natl. Bk.	Frank Jones.
Rusk	Cherokee.	M. J. Whitman	First Natl. Bk.	A. A. Simmons.
San Angelo	Tom Green.	Cochran & Hill	San Angelo Natl. Bk.	Jno. Carragher.
San Antonio	Bexar.	Berry & Culberson	San Antonio Natl. Bk.	F. Herff, Jr.
San Augustine	San Augustine	Wilson & Blount	See Nacogdoches	
San Diego	Duval.	James O. Luby	See Corpus Christi.	
San Marcas	Hayes.	Sterling & Fisher	Glover Natl. Bk.	E. L. Thomas.

138   THE LEGAL AND FINANCIAL LIGHTS OF AMERICA.

TEXAS—Continued.

County Seat.	County.	Name of Atty.	Name of Bank.	Cashier.
San Patricio	...San Patricio.	See Corpus Christi		
San Saba	........San Saba.	Allison & Reeber	Bk. of Ward, Murray & Co.	
Sequin	.........Guadelupe.	John Ireland	Bk. of E. Nolte & Sons	Walter Nolte.
Seymour	........Baylor.	Newton & Dalton	First Natl. Bk.	G. S. Plants.
Sherman	........Grayson.	Dillard & Muse	Merchants & Planters Natl. Bk.	C. B. Dorchester.
Sherwood	......Irion.	See San Angelo		
Silverton	........Briscoe.	See Floydada		
Snyder	..........Scurry.	C. C. Johnson	Citizens Bk.	Lee Boren.
Sonora	..........Sutton.	See Mason		
Stanton	........Martin.	See Big Spring		
Stephenville	...Erath.	Martin & George	First Natl. Bk.	J. S. Hyatt.
SULPHUR SPRINGS	Hopkins.	J. A. B. Putnam	First Natl. Bk.	Phil. H. Foscue.
Sweet Water	...Nolan.	Cowan & Fisher	Bk. of Thos. Trammell & Co.	R.L.McCaulley.
Tascora	.........Oldham.	See Amarillo		
Texarkana	.....Bowie.	Jacob M. Carter	Texarkana Natl. Bk.	W. R. Grim.
Texline	..........Dallam.	See Amarillo		
THROCKMORTON	..ThrockmortonW. T. Andrews		See Haskell	
Tilden	..........McMullen.	See Beeville		
Tulia	............Swisher.	See Floydada		
Tyler	............Smith.	Marsh & Butler	City Natl. Bk.	W. L. Cain.
Uvalde	..........Uvalde.	J. N. Garner	First Natl. Bk.	B. A. Randle.
Vernon	..........Wilbarger.	Elliott & Sitterly	Bk. of A. C. Neal & Co.	
Victoria	.........Victoria.	Samuel B. Dabney	First Natl. Bk.	Theodore Buhler.
Waco	............McLennon.	Williams & Evans	Citizens Natl. Bk.	L. B. Black.
Wallisville	....Chambers.	Hugh Jackson	See Houston	
Waxahachie	..Ellis.	G. C. Crose	Citizens Natl. Bk.	T. A. Ferris.
Weatherford	..Parker.	G. A. McCall	Merchants & Farmers Natl. Bk.	H. L. Brevard.
Wellington	....CollingsworthSee Clarendon			
Wharton	.......Wharton.	G. G. Kelley	Bk. of R. T. Ervin & Co.	
Wichita Falls	.Wichita.	James & Sherrod	City Natl. Bk.	Frank Dorsey.
Woodville	.....Tyler.	A. E. Adams	See Beaumont	
Not Organized	.Andrews.			
"	Bailey.			
"	Cochran.			
"	Crane.			
"	Dawson.			
"	Encinal.			
"	Foley.			
"	Gaines.			
"	Garza.			
"	Gray.			
"	Hockley.			
"	Hutchinson.			
"	Lamb.			
"	Lynn.			
"	Parmer.			
"	Schleicher.			
"	Sterling.			
"	Terry.			

TEXAS—Continued.

| County Seat. | County. | Name of Atty. | Name of Bank. | Cashier. |

Not Organized. Upton.
" Winkler.
" Yoakum.

DIGEST OF TEXAS COMMERCIAL LAWS.

Assignments.—Assignments of all a debtor's estate for distribution among all his creditors may be made. Insolvent debtors may make assignments for benefit of such creditors only as will accept their pro rata in discharge of all liability, provided the creditor receives as much as one-third of the amount due him.

Attachments.—Attachments may be issued when defendant is not a resident of the State, or is a foreign corporation, or is acting as such ; that he is about to remove permanently out of the State, and has refused to pay or secure the debt due the plaintiff ; that he secretes himself so that the ordinary process of law cannot be served upon him; that he has secreted his property for the purpose of defrauding his creditors; or, that he is about to secrete his property for the purpose of defrauding his creditors; or that he is about to remove his property out of the State without leaving sufficient remaining for the payment of his debts; or that he is about to remove his property, or a part thereof, out of the county where the suit is brought, with intent to defraud his creditors; or that he has disposed of his property, in whole or in part, with intent to defraud his creditors; or that he is about to dispose of his property with intent to defraud his creditors; or that he is about to convert his property, or a part thereof, into money for the purpose of placing it beyond the reach of his creditors; or that the debt is due for the property obtained under false pretenses.

Bank Laws.—No statutes regulating operations of banks. There is no provision for official examination of affairs of any existing state banks, nor are such banks required to make any statement of their condition.

Exemptions.—A suburban homestead consisting of not more than 200 acres of land, which may be in one or more parcels with the improvements thereon, without regard to value, an urban homestead consisting of lot or lots not to exceed in value $5,000 at the time of designation as the homestead, without reference to value of any improvements, provided that same shall be used for the purpose of a home, or as a place to exercise the calling or business of the head of a family, are exempt.

Interest.—Legal rate is 6 per cent.; conventional, 10 per cent. Double the amount of usury paid may be recovered at any time within two years after the payment thereof.

Legal Holidays.—Sunday, January 1, February 22, March 2, April 21, July 4, December 25, and all days appointed by the President of the United States, or by the Governor, as days of fasting or thanksgiving, and every day on which an election is held throughout the State, are declared holidays.

Limitation of Actions.—Trespass, conversion, debt where the indebtedness is not evidenced by a contract in writing; stated or open account other than such mutual

TEXAS—Continued.

and current accounts as concern the trade of merchandise, between merchant or merchants, their factors or agents, two years. Debt when evidenced by or founded upon any contract in writing; for penalty or damages on the penal clause of any bond to convey real estate; action by one partner against his co-partner for the settlement of partnership accounts, or upon mutual and current accounts concerning merchandise, between merchant or merchants, their factors or agents; the cause of action shall be deemed to have accrued for the cessation of the dealings in which they were interested together, four years.

Married Women.—All property acquired by the wife in any way before marriage, or by gift, devise, or descent thereafter, with all revenues therefrom, are her separate property; the husband during marriage has control of the separate property of the wife. A married woman cannot contract as a partner in business nor embark her separate means in trade.

Notarial Fees.—Protest, $2.50, and fifty cents for each notice.

Notes and Bills of Exchange.—Unless otherwise provided, commercial paper will be considered payable at the residence of the maker or acceptor, or other person bound. Days of grace allowed on all negotiable instruments. Bill or note maturing on a legal holiday becomes due on business day preceding. Attorney's fees may be stipulated for in note and recovered in case of suit. The liability of any drawer or indorser may by fixed by instituting suit against the acceptor or maker, before first term of district of county court. to which suit can be brought, or before second term, showing good cause why not brought at first term; within jurisdiction of justice, suit must be brought within sixty days. Such liability may also be fixed by protest, according to the custom of merchants. The holder of a protested draft or bill, drawn by a merchant in this State, upon his agent or factor without the State, may recover ten per cent. damages thereon, besides interest and costs.

Stay of Executions.—Three months allowed on all cases in Justices' Courts, provided defendant gives good security for its payment.

Transfer of Corporation Stocks.—Shares of stock may be transferred in such manner as the by-laws prescribe, but only on the books of the corporation.

UTAH.

County Seat.	County.	Name of Atty.	Name of Bank.	Cashier.
Ashley	Uinta.	Richard Veltman	See Salt Lake City	
Beaver	Beaver.	J. W. Christian	See Richfield	
Bluff	San Juan.	See Richfield		
Box Elder	Box Elder.	J. M. Coombs	Bk. of Brigham City	J. D. Peters.
Castle Dale	Emery.	See Manti		
Coalville	Summit.	See Salt Lake City		
Farmington	Davis.	Wilson & Wilcox	Davis Co. Bk.	A. L. Clark.
Filmore	Millard.	James A. Melville	See Richfield	
Junction	Piute.	See Richfield		
Heber	Wasatch.	Wm. Briggs	See Provo City	
Kanab	Kane.	See Richfield		
Logan	Cache.	J. C. Walters	First Natl. Bk.	Ripley S. Lyon.
Manti	San Pete.	J. E. Cochran	Manti City Savings Bk.	P. P. Dyreng.
Moab	Grand.	See Nephi		
Morgan	Morgan.	T. H. Phillips	At Kaysville, Barnes Bkg. Co.	R. W. Barnes.
Nephi	Juab.	Henry Adams	First Natl. Bk.	W.W. Aimstrong.
Ogden	Weber.	A. R. Heywood	First Natl. Bk.	James Pingree.
Panguitch	Garfield.	See Richfield		
Parowan	Iron.	J. W. Brown	See Richfield	
Price	Carbon.	Fred Erickson	At Mt. Pleasant, Mt. Pleasant Commercial & Savings Bk.	Ferd Erickson.
Provo City	Utah.	King & Houtz	Provo Commercial & Savings Bk.	J. R. Twelves.
Randolph	Rich.	See Logan		
Richfield	Sevier.	I. J. Stewart	James M. Peterson Bk.	J. S. Christiansen.
Salt Lake City	Salt Lake.	Marshall & Royle	Bk. of Commerce	S. F. Walker.
St. George	Washington.	F. L. Doggett	See Richfield	
Tooele	Tooele.	See Salt Lake City		
Not Organized.	Wayne.			

DIGEST OF UTAH COMMERCIAL LAWS.

Assignments.—Assignments by insolvents for the benefit of creditors are made and administered as at common law, there being no statute law in respect to such assignments. Preferences are therefore allowed, and accepting a dividend from the assignee does not operare to discharge debtor from further liability.

Attachments.—Writ of attachment may be issued when defendant is not a resident of this Territory; stands in defiance of an officer or conceals himself so that process cannot be served upon him; has assigned, disposed of, or concealed, or is about to assign, dispose of, or conceal any of his property, with intent to defraud his creditors; has departed, or is about to depart from the Territory, to the injury of his creditors; fraudulently contracted the debt or incurred the obligation respecting which the action is brought.

Bank Laws.—Six or more persons, two-thirds of whom must be residents of this Territory, may associate themselves together as a bank of discount and deposit or as a

UTAH—Continued.

savings bank. When $100,000 at least shall have been subscribed, and 20 per cent. of the capital shall have been paid to the treasurer of the association in cash, the the subscribers may adopt articles of association and elect five or more directors; provided, that in towns having from 10,000 to 20,000 inhabitants the capital of the bank must be at least $50,000; in towns of less than 10,000 inhabitants the capital must be at least $25,000. The articles of association must set forth that the object of the subscribers is to avail themselves of the privileges of this act; the amount of the capital stock and the number of shares; the names and places of residence of the stockholders, and the number of shares held by each; the number and kind of officers who are to manage the affairs of the bank, and the names of those who are to act for the first year. These articles must be sworn to by three or more of the subscribers, and must show among other things that 20 per cent. of the capital has been paid in. The articles must be filed in the office of the Clerk of the Probate Court, or in that of the Clerk of the District Court, who is thereupon required to issue a certificate showing that the articles of association have been filed, and this certificate and a copy of the articles must be filed in the office of the Secretary of the Territory, who must issue a certificate of incorporation. It shall have power, among other things, to exist for fifty years. The Secretary of the Territory is Bank Examiner *ex-officio*, and is required at least once a year to examine any bank and make a detailed report of its condition.

Exemptions.—The statute provides that if the debtor be the head of family there shall be exempt a homestead to be selected by the debtor, consisting of lands not exceeding in value the sum of $1,000 for the judgment debtor, and the further sum of $500 for his wife, and $250 for each other member of the family. If the homestead selected is of greater value than is exempted, the judgment debtor has option to permit same to be partitioned or to be sold and to receive in money the value of the homestead.

Interest.—Legal rate 8 per cent., but parties may agree in writing for any rate of interest on any contract. There is no usury law.

Legal Holidays.—Sunday, January 1, February 22, the first Saturday in April (Arbor Day), May 30, July 4 and 24, the first Monday in September (Labor Day), December 25, and Thanksgiving and fast days.

Limitation of Actions.—Within five years: on a judgment or decree rendered in any court of the United States, or of any State or Territory within the United States, for *mesne* rents and profits of real property. Within four years on a contract, obligation, or liability founded on an instrument or writing, except judgments of a court of the United States, or of a State or Territory within the United States. Within two years, on a contract, obligation or liability not founded on an instrument of writing, open account for goods, etc. No limitation against actions to recover money or other property deposited with bank, banker, trust company, savings or loan society.

Notarial Fees.—Protest $1.50 and thirty-five cents for each notice.

Notes and Bills of Exchange.—Bills of exchange, promissory notes, bank notes, checks, bonds, and certificates of deposit are negotiable instruments and are governed by the statutes of the Territory. Notice of dishonor may be given by the holder or any party to the instrument who may be called on to pay it, and must be in writing. Days of grace are not allowed. Paper falling due on a holiday becomes due the next preceding business day except when such preceding day is also a holiday, in which event it becomes due on the next succeeding business day.

UTAH—Continued.

Damages instead of interest to time of dishonor are allowed on dishonored bills drawn or negotiated within this Territory as follows: One dollar upon each $100 specified in the bill, if drawn on any person within this Territory; if drawn on any person without this Territory but within the United States, two and one-half dollars upon each $100 of said principal sum; if drawn on any person in any place in a foreign country, five dollars upon each $100 of said principal sum.

Stay of Executions.—Not more than sixty days on small cases before Justices' Courts.

Transfer of Corporation Stocks.—Stock is personal property and may be transferred in such manner as provided in the charter or by-laws.

VERMONT.

County Seat.	County.	Name of Atty.	Name of Bank.	Cashier.
Bennington...Bennington.		Chas. H. Darling	First Natl. Bk.	L. A. Graves.
Burlington....Chittenden.		Hamilton S. Peck	Howard Natl. Bk.	F. E. Burgess.
Chelsea.........Orange.		J. K. Darling	Natl. Bk. of Orange Co.	O. B. Copeland.
Guildhall......Essex.		Harry Blodgett	At Island Pond, Island Pond Natl. Bk.	L. A. Cobb.
Hyde Park....Lamoille.		H. M. McFarland	Lamoille Co. Natl. Bk.	E. L. Noyes.
Middlebury...Addison.		C. M. Wilds	Natl. Bk. of Middlebury	C. E. Pinney.
Montpelier....Washington.		Frederick L. Laird	First Natl. Bk.	A. G. Eaton.
Newfane........Windham.		M. Davidson	At Battleboro, Vermont Natl. Bk.	George C. Averill.
Newport........Orleans.		C. A. Prouty	Natl. Bk. of Newport	Robert Y. Wright.
North Hero....Grand Isle.		Wilson & Hall	See St. Albans	
Rutland........Rutland.		Edward Dana	Clement Natl. Bk.	O. F. Harrison.
St. Albans......Franklin.		A. A. Hall	Weldem Natl. Bk.	J. C. Stranahan.
St. Johnsbury.Caledonia.		W. P. Stafford	First Natl. Bk.	Homer E. Smith.
Woodstock....Windsor.		W. E. Johnson	Woodstock Natl. Bk.	H. C. Johnson.

DIGEST OF VERMONT COMMERCIAL LAWS.

Assignments.—Assignments of all property may be made for benefit of all creditors.

Attachments.—Attachment may be made, on mesne process, of both personal and real property.

Bank Laws.—Any number of persons, not less than five, at least three-fourths of whom shall be residents of the State, may associate to establish banks of discount, deposit and circulation. The aggregate amount of the capital stock must not be less than $50,000, nor more than $500,000. No association can commence the business of banking until its entire capital stock is paid in. Examinations of the condition of a bank may be had by order of a chancellor, upon application of creditors or shareholders whose debts amount to $1,000, stating the cause, verified by affidavit. The treasurer of every savings institution and trust company is required, on or before the 10th of July of each year, to report to the Inspector of Finance, showing accurately its condition at the close of business on the 30th of June. This report is to include the name of the institution, place of business, amount of deposits, number of depositors, and all other particulars relative to the condition of the institution.

Exemptions.—The law exempts a homestead to the amount of $500.

Interest.—Legal rate, 6 per cent. Usury forfeits double amount of interest taken.

Legal Holidays.—Sunday, January 1, July 4, May 30, December 25, Thanksgiving and fast days.

Limitation of Actions.—Actions for the recovery of lands or other possessions must be begun within fifteen years after the cause of action first accrues. Actions of covenant shall be brought within eight years. Actions on contracts, accounts, trespass and replevin, six years. Action to recover on a note must be brought within six years after becoming due, unless the note is witnessed, in which case action may be began at any time within fourteen years.

VERMONT—Continued.

Married Women.—If a married woman does business in her own name, a Court of Equity will enforce her contracts made in the course of such business against her separate estate.

Notarial Fees.—Protest, $1.00, and postage on notices.

Notes and Bills of Exchange.—Notes and bills of exchange are not entitled to grace. Negotiable paper need not be made payable at any particular bank or place. Notes payable on demand are considered overdue after sixty days from date. Whenever any bill or note shall fall due on a holiday, the same shall be considered as due on the next following business day.

Stay of Executions.—No general stay laws exist.

Transfer of Corporation Stocks.—On the books of the corporation.

146   THE LEGAL AND FINANCIAL LIGHTS OF AMERICA.

VIRGINIA.

County Seat.	County.	Name of Atty.	Name of Bank.	Cashier.
Abington	Washington.	Fulkerson, Page & Hunt.	Bk. of Carpenter & Bell	
Accomack	Accomack.	J. W. G. Blackstone	At Onancock, First Natl. Bk.	E. A. Herbst.
Alexandria	Alexandria.	Francis L. Smith	First Natl. Bk.	Chas. R. Hooff.
Amelia	Amelia.	H. Meade	See Richmond	
Amherst	Amherst.	C. L. Scott	Bk. of Amherst	F. J. Harris.
Appomatox	Appomatox.	H. D. Flood	At Pamplin, Farmers & Merchants Savings Bk. First Natl. Bk.	W. D. Thornton Chas. L. Mosby.
Bedford City	Bedford.	M. P. Burks		
Berryville	Clarké.	Marshall McCormick	Bk. of Clarke Co.	John R. Nunn.
Bland	Bland.	Sam. W. Williams	At Pulasky City, Pulasky Natl. Bk.	W. F. Nicholson.
BOWLING GREEN	Caroline.	A. B. Chandler	At Fredericksburg, Natl. Bk. of Fredericksburg Bk. of Mecklenburg	J. A. Taylor. E. W. Overbey.
Boydton	Mecklenburgh	Finch & Faulkner		
Brentsville	PrinceWilliam	Meredith & Thornton	See Warrenton	
Buckingham	Buckingham.	E. W. Hubbard	See Farmville	
CHARLOTTESVILLE	Albermarle.	Woods & Fishburne	Peoples Natl. Bk.	B. C. Flannagan.
Chatham	Pittsylvania.	Joseph Whitehead	Chatham Savings Bk.	E. S. Reid.
Chesterfield	Chesterfield.	P. V. Cogbill	See Richmond	
CHRISTIANSBURGH	Montgomery.	Phlegar & Johnson	Bk. of Christiansburgh	Chas. J. Wade.
Clintwood	Dickenson.	F. P. Phipps	At Richlands, Bk. of Richlands	Allen Cuculli.
Courtland	Southampton.	Prince & Sebrell	At Franklin, Bk. of Vaughan & Co.	C. C. Vaughan, Jr.
Covington	Allegheny.	J. T. Delaney	Covington Natl. Bk.	J. E. Rollins.
Culpeper	Culpeper.	Rixey & Barbour	Farmers Natl. Bk.	C. J. Rixey.
Cumberland	Cumberland.	S. F. Coleman	See Farmville	
Dinwiddie	Dinwiddie.	W. R. McKinney	At Blackstone, Citizens Bk.	J. M. Hurt.
Eastville	Northampton	O. F. Mears	At Onancock First Natl. Bk.	O. L. Parker.
Emporia	Greeneville.	Wm. M. Powell	See Lawrenceville	
Fairfax	Fairfax.	Moore & Love	See Alexandria	
Farmville	PrinceEdward	A. D. Watkins	Planters Bk.	Wm. G. Venable.
Fincastle	Botetourt.	J. H. H. Figgart	Bk. of Fincastle	James Godwin.
Floyd	Floyd.	V. M. Sowder	Farmers Bk.	Winfield Scott.
Front Royal	Warren.	Giles Cook, Jr.	Front Royal Natl. Bk.	J. A. Sommerville
Gate City	Scott.	H. S. K. Morison	Bk. of Gate City	Isaac P. Kane.
Gloucester	Gloucester.	F. L. Taylor	At West Point, West Point Bkg. Co.	W. V. Wilkinson.
Goochland	Goochland.	A. K. Leak	See Richmond	
Grundy	Buchanan.	F. H. Evans	At Richlands, Bk. of Richlands	Allen Cucullu.
Hampton	ElizabethCity	A. S. Segar	Bk. of Hampton	G. M. Peek.
Hanover	Hanover.	Geo. P. Haw	See Richmond	
HARRISONBURGH	Rockingham.	Sipe & Harris	First Natl. Bk.	L. C. Myers.
Heatsville	Northumber- land.	Warner Ball	See Richmond	
Hillsville	Carroll.	Walter S. Tipton	Citizens Bk.	R. G. Wilkinson.
Independence	Grayson.	C. C. Porterfield	See Hillsville	
Isle of Wight	Isle of Wight.	R. S. Thomas	At Smithfield, Bk. of Smithfield	A. S. Barrett.
Jonesville	Lee.	H. J. Morgan	Powells Valley Bk.	C. E. Couk.
King & Queen	King & Queen	C. B. Jones	See Richmond	
King George	King George.	W. A. Rose	At Fredericksburg, Natl. Bk. of Fredericksburg See Richmond	J. A. Taylor.
King William	King William	B. Taylor		
Lancaster	Lancaster.	H. S. Gresham	See Richmond	
Lawrenceville	Brunswick.	R. Turnbull	Bk. of Lawrenceville	Chas. E. May.

THE LEGAL AND FINANCIAL LIGHTS OF AMERICA. 147

VIRGINIA—Continued.

County Seat.	County.	Name of Atty.	Name of Bank.	Cashier.
Lebanon	Russell.	H. A. Routh	At Richlands, Bk. of Richlands	Allen Cucullu.
Leesburgh	Loudoun.	Ed. Nichols	Peoples Natl. Bk.	H. A. Thompson.
Lexington	Rockbridge.	W. T. Shields	Bk. of Rockbridge	W. C. Stuart.
Louisa	Louisa.	W. E. Bibb	See Charlottesville	
Lovingston	Nelson.	Caskie & Coleman	See Amherst	
Lunenburgh	Lunenburgh.	W. E. Mellette	See Nottoway	
Luray	Page.	Walton & Bro.	Page Valley Bk.	Chas. S. Landram
Madison	Madison.	James Hay	See Culpeper	
Marion	Smyth.	B. F. Buchanan	Bk. of Marion	E. H. Copenhaver
Martinsville	Henry.	H. Z. Mullins	Farmers Bk.	G. W. Coan.
Mathews	Mathews.	John B. Donovan	At West Point, West Point Bkg. Co.	W. V. Wilkinson.
Monterey	Highland.	C. P. Jones	See Staunton	
Montrose	Westmoreland	C. C. Baker	See Richmond	
New Bern	Pulaski.	J. C. Wyson	At Pulaski City, Pulaski Natl. Bk.	M. F. Nicholson.
New Castle	Craig.	P. V. Jones	Bk. of New Castle	H. W. Yoder.
New Kent	New Kent.	R. T. Lacy	See Richmond	
Newport News	Warwick.	Garnett & Lett	First Natl. Bk.	J. A. Willett.
Nottoway	Nottoway.	W. H. Mann	At Blackstone, Citizens Bk.	Joseph M. Hurt.
Orange	Orange.	John G. Williams	State Bk. of Orange	M. G. Field.
Palmyra	Fluvanna.	Pettit & Leake	See Charlottesville	
Pearisburgh	Giles.	A. R. Heflin	At Radford, Bk. of Radford	G. S. Baskerville.
Portsmouth	Norfolk.	O. Hatton	Bk. of Portsmouth	J. L. Bilisoly.
Powhatan	Powhatan.	W. M. Flanagan	See Richmond	
Prince George	Prince George	J. J. Cocke	At Petersburg, Petersburg Sav. & T. Co. See Portsmouth	G. J. Seay.
Princess Anne	PrincessAnne	J. M. Keeling	Merchants Natl. Bk.	J. F. Glenn.
Richmond	Henrico.	Leake & Carter	Merchants & Farmers Bk.	G. H. T. Greer.
Rocky Mount	Franklin.	Dillard & Lee	At Lynchburg, Peoples Natl. Bk.	J. W. Ivey.
Rutsburgh	Campbell.	Wm. M. Murrel	Farmers Natl. Bk.	W. H. Ruthrauff.
Salem	Roanoke.	R. H. Logan	See Richmond	
Saluda	Middlesex.	R. McCandish	Charlotte Bkg. & Ins. Co.	F. C. Thornton.
Smithville	Charlotte.	Wm. C. Carrington	Planters & Merchants Bk.	Henry Easley.
South Boston	Halifax.	Henry Edmund	At Fredericksburgh, Natl. Bk. of Fredericksburg See Culpeper	J. A. Taylor.
Spottsylvania	Spottsylvania	A. B. Rawlings		
Stafford	Stafford.	Thomas P. Wallace	See Orange	
STANNARDSVILLE	Greene.	Field & Thomas	Natl. Valley Bk.	H. A. Walker.
Staunton	Augusta.	Patrick & Gordon	Patrick Co. Bk.	W. B. Rucker.
Stuart	Patrick.	W. C. Lawson	See Richmond	
STURGEON POINT	Charles City.	D. G. Tyler	Farmers Bk. of Nansemond	Wm. H. Jones, Jr.
Suffolk	Nansemond.	E. E. Holland	See Newport News	
Surry	Surry.	George T. Clark & Son	At Smithfield, Bk. of Smithfield	A. S. Barrett
Sussex	Sussex.	C. L. Cocke	See Richmond	
TAPPAHANNOCK	Essex.	Thomas Croxton	Bk. of Clinch Valley	Henry Preston.
Tazewell	Tazewell.	Chapman & Gillespie	See Staunton	
Warm Springs	Bath.	J. W. Stephenson	Bk. of Gaines & Bro.	W. H. Gaines.
Warrenton	Fauquier.	A. D. Payne	See Richmond	
Warsaw	Richmond.	Jones & Son	See Warrenton	
Washington	Rappahannock	E. T. Jones	See Newport News	
WILLIAMSBURGH	James City.	E. C. Peachy	Shenandoah Valley Natl. Bk.	John W. Rice.
Winchester	Frederick.	John J. Williams		

VIRGINIA—Continued.

County Seat.	County.	Name of Atty.	Name of Bank.	Cashier.
Wise	Wise.	E. M. Fulton	See Jonesville	
Woodstock	Shenandoah.	Walton & Walton	Shenandoah Co. Bk.	M. Coffman.
Wytheville	Wythe.	C. B. Thomas	Bk. of Wytheville	J. G. Brown.
Yorktown	York.	See Newport News		

PRINCIPAL CITIES, NOT COUNTY SEATS.

Danville	Pittsylvania.	Withers & Withers	Citizens Bk.	James T. Catlin.
Lynchburg	Campbell.	W. V. Wilson, Jr.	Peoples Natl. Bk.	J. W. Ivey.
Norfolk	Norfolk.	John B. Jenkins	Norfolk Natl. Bk.	Caldwell Hardy.
Roanoke	Roanoke.	Penn & Cocke	First Natl. Bk.	J. W. Shields, Jr.

DIGEST OF VIRGINIA COMMERCIAL LAWS.

Assignments.—There is no insolvent law, but an insolvent debtor may make a voluntary assignment for the benefit of creditors, and may prefer certain creditors to others.

Attachments.—Attachments issue against a foreign corporation; a non-resident of this State having estate or debts owing him within the county or corporation in which the action is, or is sued with defendant residing therein; a defendant who is removing, or is about to remove out of the State with intent to change his domicile; a defendant who is removing, intends to remove, or has removed the specific property sued for, or his own estate, or the proceeds of the sale of his property, or a material part of such estate or proceeds out of this State, so that process of execution on a judgment, when obtained in said action, will be unavailing; a defendant who is converting, or is about to convert, or has converted his property of whatever kind, or some part thereof, into money, security or evidences of debt; a defendant who has assigned or disposed of, or is about to assign or dispose of his estate or some part thereof.

Bank Laws.—The circuit and corporation courts have power to charter any bank except a bank of circulation, which become effective only from the time they are lodged in the office of the Secretary of Commonwealth. Every such bank has power to prescribe, by its Board of Directors, by-laws regulating the manner in which its stock shall be transferred, its general business conducted, and the privileges granted to it by law exercised and enjoyed. The affairs of such bank shall be managed by a Board of Directors, consisting of not less than five persons, a majority of whom shall be citizens of the State, and each director is required to own at least $100 of the capital stock of the bank of which he is director. The Board of Directors shall meet at least once a month. The directors shall be elected at the annual meeting of the stockholders. Every such bank must make statements to the Auditor of Public Accounts, identically as the national banks are required to make to the Comptroller of the Currency, and must publish such statements in a condensed form, as published by said national banks, and the Auditor is required to call for such statements, whenever the Comptroller of the Currency calls on the national banks for such statements.

VIRGINIA—Continued.

Exemptions.—A householder, the head of a family, is entitled to have real and personal property exempt to the value of $2,000. And in case of householder or head of a family, all wages not exceeding $50 a month are exempt. The homestead claimed to be exempt must be described in a writing signed by the householder and duly admitted to record in the county or corporation wherein the property claimed is located.

Interest.—Six per cent.; all contracts for more are void, except as to principal sum.

Legal Holidays.—Sunday, January 1, January 19 (General Lee's birthday), February 22, July 4, December 25, Thanksgiving, fasting and prayer, Labor Day.

Limitation of Actions.—Upon any contract by writing under seal, within ten years; upon an award, or upon a contract by writing, signed by the party to be charged thereby, or by his agent, but not under seal, within five years ; if it be upon an oral contract, express or implied, for articles charged in a store account, although such articles be sold on a written order, within two years ; and if it be on any other contract, within three years.

Notarial Fees.—Protest $1, seal $1, and for each notice ten cents.

Notes and Bills of Exchange.—On all negotiable notes and bills payable at a future day, grace is allowed according to custom of merchants. No grace on sight drafts. Where a bill of exchange, drawn or indorsed within this State is protested, the party liable for the principal of such bill shall, in addition, pay damages upon the principal at the rate of three per cent. if the bill is payable out of Virginia, and within the United States, and ten per cent. if payable without the United States. All bills, notes, checks and other negotiable instruments maturing on a legal holiday shall become due on the secular or business day next preceding.

Stay of Executions.—Not more than sixty days on small cases before Justices' Courts.

Transfer of Corporation Stocks.—Shares of stock may be transferred on the books of the company by delivery of the certificate of stock, and a power of attorney authorizing the transfer.

WASHINGTON.

County Seat.	County.	Name of Atty.	Name of Bank.	Cashier.
Asotin	Asotin.	George W. Bailey	At Union Town, First State Bk.	S. Hilliard.
Cascades	Skamania.	W. H. Metcalf	See Vancouver	
Cathlamet	Wahkiakum.	J. B. Polwath	At Kelso, Kelso State Bk.	T. S. Rolston.
Chehalis	Lewis.	Millett & Harmon	First Natl. Bk.	J. Y. Coffman.
Colfax	Whitman.	Hanna,McCroskey&Ettinger.	Second Natl. Bk.	J. J. Humphrey.
Colville	Stevens.	Samuel Douglass	Bk. of Colville	C. W. Winter.
Conconully	Okanogan.	Vacant	See Colville	
Coupeville	Island.	Thomas Cranney	See Port Townsend	
Dayton	Columbia.	J. A. Kellogg	Columbia Natl. Bk.	F. W. Guernsey.
Ellensburgh	Kittitass.	Snively & Lloyd	Ellensburg Natl. Bk.	J.T.M.Stoneroad.
FridayHarbor	San Juan.	J. A. Gould	San Juan Co. Bk.	J. A. Gould.
Goldendale	Klickitat.	G. N. Maddock	First Natl. Bk.	O. D. Sturgess.
Kalama	Cowlitz.	A. H. Imus	Cowlitz Co. Bk.	J. P. Atkin.
Montesano	Cheballs.	George D. Schofield	Bk. of Montesano	Chas. H. Lamp.
Mt. Vernon	Skagit.	Frank Quimby	First Natl. Bk.	C. S. Moody.
North Yakima	Yakima.	Jones & Newman	Yakima Natl. Bk.	J. D. Cornett.
Olympia	Thurston.	Daniel Gaby	Capital Natl. Bk.	W. J. Foster.
Pasco	Franklin.	F. P. Speck	See Walla Walla	
Pomeroy	Garfield.	S. G. Cosgrove	First Natl. Bk.	G. L. Campbell.
Port Angeles	Clallam.	George C. Hatch	Bk. of Clallam Co.	C. E. Mallette.
Port Orchard	Kitsap.	G. H. Elder	See Seattle	
Pt. Townsend	Jefferson.	Carroll & Rohde	Merchants Bk.	N. C. Strong.
Ritzville	Adams.	P. D. Oliphant	Adams Co. Bk.	Benjamin Martin.
Seattle	King.	Carr & Preston	First Natl. Bk.	Lester Turner.
Shelton	Mason.	H. S. Tremper	State Bk. of Shelton	J. D. Riley.
Snohomish	Snohomish.	Coleman & Hart	First Natl. Bk.	Wilson M. Snyder
South Bend	Pacific.	Rice & Davis	First Natl. Bk.	R. A. Carney.
Spokane	Spokane.	McBroom & McBroom	Traders Natl. Bk.	C. E. McBroom.
Sprague	Lincoln.	D. Higgins	First Natl. Bk.	W. B. Lottman.
Tacoma	Pierce.	Thomas Carroll	Pacific Natl. Bk.	L. R. Manning.
Vancouver	Clarke.	E. E. Coovert	First Natl. Bk.	E. L. Canby.
Walla Walla	Walla Walla.	B. L. & J. L. Sharpstein	Beker-Boyer Natl. Bk.	H. E. Johnson.
Waterville	Douglas.	W. A. Rencan	First Natl. Bk.	A. E. Case.
Whatcom	Whatcom.	Chas. I. Roth	At Fairhaven, Citizens Bk.	H. W. Kinney.

DIGEST OF WASHINGTON COMMERCIAL LAWS.

Assignments.—Insolvent debtor may be discharged from debts upon executing an assignment of all his property for benefit of his creditors, if done in good faith, and without fraud.

Attachments.—Attachments may be issued when the defendant is a foreign corporation ; or is not a resident of this State ; or conceals himself so that the ordinary process of law cannot be served upon him ; or has absconded or absented himself from his usual place of abode in this State, so that the ordinary process of law cannot be served upon him ; or has removed or is about to remove any of his property from

THE LEGAL AND FINANCIAL LIGHTS OF AMERICA. 151

WASHINGTON—Continued.

this State, with intent to delay or defraud his creditors ; or has assigned, secreted or disposed of, or is about to assign, secrete or dispose of any of his property, with intent to delay or defraud his creditors, or is about to convert his property or a part thereof, into money, for the purpose of placing it beyond the reach of his creditors ; or has been guilty of a fraud in contracting the debt, or incurring the obligation for which the action is brought ; or that the damages for which the action is brought are for injuries arising from the commission of some felony.

Bank Laws.—Two or more persons may be chartered as a bank by subscribing articles of incorporation in triplicate , one of which must be filed with the Secretary of the Treasury, one with the County Auditor of the County where the bank is to be located, and the other is retained by the corporation. The minimum capital stock is $25,000, divided into shares of $100 each. The whole must be subscribed for, and three-fifths must be paid in before the bank begins business, the remainder being subject to the call of the trustees. Stockholders are individually ratably liable for all the debts accruing while they remain stockholders to the extent of the par value of their stock in addition to the amount invested therein. On the first Monday in June of each year the bank is required to file with the Auditor a report of its affairs.

Exemptions.—To every householder being the head of a family, a homestead to the value of $1,000 is exempt (a homestead may consist of a house and lot or lots, or a farm) ; also personal property to the value of $750. A homestead may be mortgaged.

Interest.—Legal rate of interest is 8 per cent. per annum, and any rate agreed upon is legal. Judgments bear the legal rate of interest. There is no usury law.

Legal Holidays.—Sunday, January 1, February 22, Decoration Day, July 4, September 1, December 25, Thanksgiving, Days of general and special election for State and National officers, Labor Day.

Limitation of Actions.—Upon a contract in writing, or liability, express or implied, arising out of a written agreement ; or for the rents and profits or for the use and occupation of 'real estate, must each be commenced within six years. Actions on a contract, express or impelied, not in writing, for relief, on the ground of fraud, and for torts generally, must be commenced within six years.

Married Women.—No law.

Notarial Fees.—Protest $2.50.

Notes and Bills of Exchange.—Promissory notes payable to order or bearer have the same effect and are negotiable in like manner as inland bills of exchange, according to the custom of merchants. Three days of grace are allowed on bills of exchange payable at sight, and all negotiable promissory notes, orders or drafts payable at a future day certain, unless there is an express stipulation to the contrary. Paper maturing on a legal holiday becomes due the day before. No person within the State shall be charged as an acceptor of a bill of exchange, unless his acceptance shall be in writing, signed by himself or his authorized agent. If such acceptance be written on a paper other than the bill, it shall not bind the acceptor, except in favor of a person to whom such acceptance shall have been shown, and who, on the faith thereof, shall have the bill for a valuable consideration. Every holder of a bill, presenting the same for acceptance, may require that the acceptance be written on the bill ; a refusal to comply with such request shall be deemed a

WASHINGTON—Continued.

refusal to accept, and the bill may be protested for non-acceptance. In all promissory notes or similar instruments, in writing, an attorney's fees may be allowed when specially contracted to be paid by the terms of the note.

Transfer of Corporation Stocks.—Transferable in such manner as shall be prescribed by the by-laws of the company, by no transfer shall be valid except as between the parties thereto until the same shall have been entered upon the books of the company so as to show the names of the parties by and to whom transferred the numbers and designation of shares, and the date of transfer.

THE LEGAL AND FINANCIAL LIGHTS OF AMERICA.   153

WEST VIRGINIA.

County Seat. County.	Name of Atty.	Name of Bank.	Cashier.
BERKELEY SPRINGS Morgan.	J. H. Siler	Bk. of Berkeley Springs	A. M. Mendendall.
Beverley.........Randolph.	L. D. Strader	See Phillippi	
Braxton.........Braxton.	L. M. Wade	At Sutton, Sutton Bk.	T. M. Berry.
Buckhannon..Upshur.	G. M. Fleming	Traders Natl. Bk.	P. M. Boggess.
Charleston.....Kenawa.	George Baylor	Charleston Natl. Bk.	H. L. Prechard.
Charlestown..Jefferson.	T. C. Green	Bk. of Charlestown	Geo. A. Porterfield
Clarksburgh..Harrison.	A. C. Moore	Traders Natl. Bk.	C. Sprigg Sands.
Clay..............Clay.	C. Pierson	See Charleston	
Elizabeth ....Wirt.	T. A. Brown	At Ravenswood, Bk. of Ravenswood.	J. L. Armstrong.
Fairmont......Marion.	A. B. Fleming	First Natl. Bk.	J. E. Sands.
Fairview.......Hancock.	E. G. Smith	At New Cumberland, Citizens Bk.	James E. Brandon
Fayetteville....Fayette.	Isabell & Dillon	See Charleston	
Franklin.......Pendleton.	D. G. McChing	Farmers Bk. of Pendleton	Frank Anderson.
Glenville.......Gilmer.	Linn & Withers	See Weston	
Grafton.........Taylor.	W. R. D. Dent	First Natl. Bk.	L. Mallonee.
Grantsville.....Calhoun.	Linn & Hamilton	See Spencer	
Hamlin.........Lincoln.	A. F. Morris	See Charleston	
Hinton ....Summers.	Thompson & Lively	Bk. of Hinton	E. O. Prince.
Huntersville...Pocahontas.	H. S. Rucker	See Lewisburgh	
Huntington...Cabell.	Vinson & Thompson	Huntington Natl. Bk.	James K. Oney.
Jackson.........Jackson.	Warran Miller	Bk. of Ripley	H. F. Pfost.
Keyser..........Mineral.	F. M. Reynolds	Keyser Bk.	J. T. Carskadon.
Kingwood.....Preston.	Brown & Hyde	Bk. of Kingwood	J. W. Parks.
Lewisburgh...Greenbrier.	Alex. F. Mathews	Bk. of Lewisburgh	J. W. Mathews.
Logan...........Logan.	John B. Wilkinson	At Williamson, Bk. of Williamson.	Hiram Williamson
Madison........Boone.	J. E. Stollings	See Charleston	
Martinsburgh.Berkely.	Flick & Westenhaver	Peoples Natl. Bk.	F. E. Wilson.
Middlebourne Tyler.	Engle & Riggle	At Sistersville, Tyler Co. Bk.	A. C. Jackson.
Moorefield......Hardy.	Benjamin Dailey	South Branch Valley Natl. Bk.	J. W. Gilkeson.
Morgantown .Monongalia.	Cox & Baker	Bk. of Monongahela Valley	E. H. Combs.
Moundsville...Marshall.	J. L. Parkinson	Marshall Co. Bk.	H. W. Hunter.
NEW MARTINSVILLE Wetzel.	W. S. Wiley	Wetzel Co. Bk.	J. E. Bartlett.
Oceana..........Wyoming.	L. L. Chambers	At Williamson, Bk. of Williamson.	Hiram Williamson
Parkersburgh Wood.	Vandervort & Moats	Citizens Natl. Bk.	C. H. Shattuck.
Perryville .....McDowell.	W. P. Payne	At Bramwell, Bk. of Bramwell	Isaac T. Mann.
Petersburgh...Grant.	Reynolds & Forman	See Moorefield	
Phillippi.......Barbour.	Dayton & Dayton	Tygarts Valley Bk.	J. F. Mallown.
Point Pleasant Mason.	Tomlinson & Wiley	Merchants Natl. Bk.	C. C. Bowyer.
Princeton......Mercer.	Johnston & Hale	Princeton Bkg. Co.	H. Scott.
Raleigh ....Raleigh.	J. H. McGinnis	See Hinton	
Ritchie..........Ritchie.	Thomas E. Davis	See West Union	
Romney . ...Hampshire.	H. B. Glikerson	Bk. of Romney	J. T. Vance.
St. George......Tucker.	Lipscomb & Lipscomb	At Piedmont, Davis Natl. Bk.	U. B. McCandlish
St. Mary's ......Pleasants.	August M. Campbell	See Parkersburgh	
Spencer.........Roane.	Wells & Pendleton	Bk. of Spencer	John Claypool.
Summersville. Nicholas.	R. A. Kincaid	See Charleston	
Union............Monroe.	Logan & Patton	Bk. of Union	James W. McNeer.
Wayne..........Wayne.	B. J. Pritchard	See Huntington	

WEST VIRGINIA—Continued.

County Seat.	County.	Name of Atty.	Name of Bank.	Cashier.
Webster	Webster.	C. P. Door	See Buckhannon	
Wellsburgh	Brooke.	John C. Palmer	Wellsburgh Natl. Bk.	E. W. Paxton.
Weston	Lewis.	Andrew Edmiston	Citizens Bk.	D. W. Bailey.
West Union	Doddridge.	J. V. Blair	West Union Bk.	P M. Robinson
Wheeling	Ohio.	W. P. Hubbard	Bk. of Wheeling	Joseph Seybold.
Winfield	Putnam.	J. H. Nash	See Charleston	

DIGEST OF WEST VIRGINIA COMMERCIAL LAWS.

Assignments.—Assignments can be made for the benefit of creditors without preference.

Attachments.—Attachments will issue when defendant is a foreign corporation, or is a non-resident, or has left or is about to leave the State with intent to defraud his creditors ; or so conceals himself that a summons cannot be served upon him, or is removing or is about to remove his property, or a part thereof, out of this State with like intent ; or is converting or about to convert his property, or a part thereof, into money or securities with like intent ; or has assigned or disposed of his property, or a part thereof, or is about to do so with like intent ; or has property or rights in action, which he conceals ; or that he fraudulently contracted the debt or incurred the liability.

Bank Laws.—State banks may be chartered. Stockholders are liable to extent of stock held by them, and an equal additional amount for debts accruing while they are such stockholders. Such double liability does not extend to stockholders in other corporations than banks. Embezzlement is larceny and punishable as such. Fraudulent false entries by bank officer, felony. Title and trust companies are authorized to do a general banking business. The State Bank Examiner is required, between April and November, to examine the condition of each bank and publish a statement in the county where the bank is located.

Exemptions.—A resident husband or parent, or the infant children of deceased parents, may have personal property not exceeding $200 in value, exempt from forced sales ; and since 1872, such husband or parent, or the guardian of such infants, may have recorded a claim of homestead, not exceeding $1,000 in value, as exempt from, liability for debts. except such as were incurred for the purchase of such property, or for permanent improvements or taxes thereon. Any resident mechanic, artisan, or laborer, whether a husband, or parent, or not, may hold the working tools of his trade or occupation exempt to the extent of $50, but not so as in any case to allow more than $200 exemption of personal property to one person.

Interest.—Legal rate is 6 per cent. Though a higher rate may be agreed upon, the ex cess may be avoided on a plea of usury, except by an incorporated company. Corporations are authorized to borrow money at higher rates. Illegal interest paid may be recovered within five years.

Legal Holidays.—Sunday, January 1, February 22, July 4, December 25, or a day of national thanksgiving, Labor Day.

WEST VIRGINIA—Continued.

Limitation of Actions.—Store account, three years ; accounts concerning trade between merchants, five years; contract, not in writing, or in writing and not under seal, five years ; contracts under seal, twenty years ; contracts in writing, whether under seal or not, ten years.

Notarial Fees.—Protest $1.00 and ten cents for each notice and postage.

Notes and Bills of Exchange.—Every promissory note or check for money payable in this State at a particular bank, or at a particular office thereof, for discount and deposit, and every inland bill of exchange payable in this State, shall be deemed negotiable. Three days of grace are allowed. Commercial paper falling due on a holiday is payable on the preceding day. When a bill of exchange drawn or indorsed within this State is protested for non-acceptance or non-payment, there shall be paid by the party liable for the principal of such a bill, in addition to what else he is liable for, damages upon the principal at the rate of three per cent., if payable out of the State and within the United States, and ten per cent., if payable without the United States.

Stay of Executions.—Under $50, two months ; $50 to $100, five months ; over $100, six months.

Transfer of Corporation Stocks.—On the books, but if stock is transferred by delivery of certificate with power of attorney authorizing the transfer on the books, (which power of attorney is usually endorsed on certificate) the title is vested in the transferee not only as between the parties themselves, but also as against the creditors of, and subsequent purchaser from the former owner.

WISCONSIN.

County Seat.	County.	Name of Atty.	Name of Bank.	Cashier.
Alma	Buffalo.	Robert Lees.	Exchange Bk.	Hunner&Ginzkey
Antigo	Langlade.	J. H. Trever.	Bk. of Antigo	E. E. Buckman.
Appleton	Ontagamie.	F. W. Harriman.	First Natl. Bk.	Herman Erb.
Ashland	Ashland.	Tompkins & Merrill.	Ashland Natl. Bk.	N. I. Willey.
Baraboo	Sauk.	R. D. Evans	Bk. of Baraboo	J. Van Orden.
Barron	Barron.	J. F. Coe	Bk. of Barron	J. F. Coe.
Bayfield	Bayfield.	W. W. Downs	Lumbermans Bk.	A. H. Wilkinson.
BLACK RIVER FALLS	Jackson.	B. J. Castle	First Natl. Bk.	W. H. Richards.
Chilton	Calumet.	John E. McMullen	German Exchange Bk.	Henry Kersten.
CHIPPEWA FALLS	Chippewa.	Jenkins & Jenkins	Lumbermans Natl. Bk.	S. B. Nimmons.
Crandon	Forrest.	John Barnes	See Rhinelander	
Darlington	Lafayette.	Wilson & Martin	First Natl. Bk.	T. C. L. Mackay.
Dartford	Green Lake.	J. C. McConnell	At Princeton, Princeton State Bk.	J. E. Leimer.
Dodgeville	Iowa.	Jenks & Jones	Dodgeville Bk.	S.W. Reese&Son.
Durand	Pepin.	W. E. Plummer	Bk. of Durand	J. E. Wise.
Eagle River	Vilas.	N. A. Coleman	Bk. of Eagle River	McKenzie&Morey
Eau Claire	Eau Claire.	J. C. Gores	Bk. of Eau Claire	C. W. Lockwood.
Elkorn	Walworth.	J. B. Wheeler	First Natl. Bk.	Fred. W. Isham.
Ellsworth	Pierce.	J. W. Hancock	Bk. of Ellsworth	Orin Lord.
Florence	Florence.	J. E. Abbott	State Bk. of Florence	E. E. Wilcox.
Fond du Lac	Fond du Lac.	E. S. Bragg	Fond du Lac Natl. Bk.	G. A. Knapp.
Friendship	Adams.	J. A. Gunning	See Mauston	
Grand Rapids	Wood.	Gardiner & Gaynor	First Natl. Bk.	E. T. Harmon.
Grantsburg	Burnett.	T. Grettum	See Shell Lake	
Green Bay	Brown.	Greene & Vroman	Kellogg Natl. Bk.	H. B. Baker.
Hayward	Sawyer.	John F. Riordam	Sawyer Co. Bk.	R. L. McCormick
Hudson	Saint Croix.	Humphrey & Arnquist	First Natl. Bk.	D. C. Fulton.
Hurley	Iron.	Foster & Bushnell	Iron Exchange Bk.	W. S. Reynolds.
Janesville	Rock.	Smith & Phelps	Rock Co. Natl. Bk.	A. P. Burnham.
Jefferson	Jefferson.	George Grimm	Jefferson Co. Bk.	John Reinel.
Juneau	Dodge.	K. C. Lewis	Citizens Bk.	Theo. P. Demmy.
Kenosha	Kenosha.	Cavanagh & Fisher	First Natl. Bk.	Chas. C. Brown.
Kewaunee	Kewaunee.	Wing & Wattawa	Bk. of Kewaunee.	John Pecka.
La Crosse	La Crosse.	Benjamin F. Bryant	La Crosse Natl. Bk.	Geo. W. Burton.
Lancaster	Grant.	Bushnell, Watkins & Moses.	State Bk. of Grant Co.	Joseph Pock.
Madison	Dane.	George W. Bird	First Natl. Bk.	Wayne Ramsey.
Manitovoc	Manitovoc.	Nash & Nash	Manitovoc Savings Bk.	Louis Schuette.
Marinette	Marinette.	J. B. Fairchild	Stephenson Natl. Bk.	L. A. McAlpine.
Mauston	Juneau.	H. W. Barney	Jeff. T. Heath & Co.	
Medford	Taylor.	G. W. Adams	State Bk. of Medford	C. L. Alverson.
Menomonie	Dunn.	Hunt & Freeman	First Natl. Bk.	W. C. McLean.
Merrill	Lincoln.	Curtis & Reed	First Natl. Bk.	J. W. Ladd.
Milwaukee	Milwaukee.	N. Pereles & Sons	First Natl. Bk.	F. J. Kipp.
Monroe	Green.	P. J. Clawson	First Natl. Bk.	C. W. Twining.
Montello	Marquette.	John Barry	Bk. of Montello	M. H. Barry.
Neillsville	Clark.	O'Neill & Marsh	Neillsville Bk.	Joseph Morley.

THE LEGAL AND FINANCIAL LIGHTS OF AMERICA. 157

WISCONSIN—Continued.

County Seat.	County.	Name of Atty.	Name of Bank.	County.
Oconto	Oconto.	W. H. Webster	Oconto Natl. Bk.	Wm. K. Smith.
Osceola Mills.	Polk.	Chas. H. Oakley	Bk. of Osceola	H. C. Harding.
Oshkosh	Winnebago.	Bouck & Hilton	Natl. Bk. of Oshkosh	Chas. Schriber.
Phillips	Price.	M. Barry	State Bk. of Phillips	E. H. Winchester.
Portage	Columbia.	W. S. Stroud	First Natl. Bk.	E. A. Gowran.
PORT WASHINGTON	Ozaukee.	H. B. Schwin	German American Bk.	Odler & Clark.
PRAIRIE DU CHIEN.	Crawford.	D. Webster	Bk. of Prarie du Chien	E. I. Kidd.
Racine	Racine.	Hand & Fleet	Manufacturers Natl. Bk.	B. B. Northrop.
Rhinelander	Oneida.	Alban & Barnes	First Natl. Bk.	W. E. Ashton.
RICHLAND CENTRE.	Richland.	Miner & Miner	Richland Co. Bk.	J. H. Yearman.
Shawano	Shawano.	J. C. Dickinson	Shawano Co. Bk.	F. W. Humphrey.
Sheboygan	Sheboygan.	F. R. Williams	Bk. of Sheboygan	Julius Kroos.
Shell Lake	Washburn.	L. H. Mead	Shell Lake Savings Bk.	Lewis Larsen.
Sparta	Monroe.	C. M. Masters	Bk. of Sparta	H. E. Canfield.
Stevens Point.	Portage.	James O. Raymond	First Natl. Bk.	W.B.Buckingham
Sturgeon Bay.	Door.	R. P. Cody	Bk. of Sturgeon Bay	James Keogh.
Superior	Douglas.	Pickering & Hartley	Bk. of Superior	John A. Bardon.
Viroqua	Vernon.	C. J. Smith	Bk. of Viroqua	E. H. Craig.
Waukesha	Waukesha.	Ryan & Merton	Waukesha Natl. Bk.	H. M. Frame.
Waupaka	Waupaka.	Irving P. Lord	Natl. Bk. of Waupaka	W. B. Baker.
Wausau	Marathon.	Silverthorn, Hurley, Ryan & Jones.	First. Natl. Bk.	A. H. Grout.
Wautoma	Waushara.	L. L. Soule	At Plainfield, Bk. of H. N. Drake	
West Bend	Washington.	Frisby & Miller	Bk. of West Bend	E. Franckenberg.
Whitehall	Trempealeau.	H. A. Anderson	Bk. of John O. Melby & Co.	Anton O. Melby.

DIGEST OF WISCONSIN COMMERCIAL LAWS.

Assignments.—An assignment carries all the property, real and personal, of the assignor, excepting his exemptions. Wages of employes for three months are preferred by law, and for six months may be preferred by insolvent. All other claims pro rata, and other preferences void the assignment.

Attachments.—Attachment is authorized when the defendant has absconded or is about to abscond the State, or is concealed therein to the injury of his creditors, or keeps himself concealed therein with intent to avoid service of summons ; has assigned, conveyed, disposed of or concealed his property, or some part of it, or is about to do so, with intent to defraud his creditors ; has removed or is about to remove any of his property out of the State with intent to defraud his creditors ; fraudulently contracted the debt or incurred the obligation respecting which the action is brought ; or is a non-resident of the State or is a foreign corporation, or if a domestic corporation, that all of the proper officers to serve summons upon are non-resident or cannot be found, or do not exist.

Bank Laws.—Any number of persons may associate themselves together to form a bank of discount, deposit and circulation with an aggregate capital of not less than $25,-000 or more than $500,000. Such bank must be located in a city, village or township containing at least 200 hundred voters. It cannot issue circulating notes ex-

WISCONSIN—Continued.

ceeding the capital, and must have at least $15,000 actually paid in and employed in the banking business. The State Treasurer is ex-officio Banking Comptroller, and issues bank notes to the banks in sums not exceeding the amount of the United States or State bonds deposited with him in trust as security for the payment of said notes, and the directors or stockholders of the bank must give bonds with sureties resident in Wisconsin to the amount of one-fourth of the notes issued. A correct list of the shareholders of each bank is required to be filed in the office of the Register of Deeds of the county where the bank is located, and also in the office of the Comptroller on the first Monday of January and July annually, at which time a report must also be made under oath by the President or Cashier to the Comptroller concerning the bank's affairs, which it is his duty to publish in a newspaper at the capital of the State. He must also transmit to the Legislature a summary of the condition of all banks in the State, and must publish a statement of the financial condition of every bank, which must be furnished him by its officers. Stockholders are liable only to the amount of the shares respectively held by them. Private banking is permitted, without State control or interference, apart from the usual civil and criminal liabilities and remedies, except that the name of the person or firm must be displayed. Most banking not under National charters is so conducted.

Exemptions.—Exemption from execution extends to forty acres of agricultural lands, or one-fourth acre of village or city property, to be selected by debtor, together with dwelling house and its appurtenances. Proceeds of sale of homestead are exempt for two years while held in good faith with intent to procure another therewith.

Interest.—Legal rate is 6 per cent. with right of contract in writing as high as 10; penalty for higher rate is a forfeiture of all interest. Any person having paid excessive interest may recover back treble the excess paid by action brought within one year after payment. Corporations are barred from pleading the defense of usury.

Legal Holidays.—Sunday, January 1, February 22, May 30, June 10, July 4, December 25, Thanksgiving, Labor Day, every general election day and any day appointed by the Governor or the President for Thanksgiving.

Limitation of Actions.—Within twenty years: actions upon any judgment of a Court of Record, sitting without this State, and actions upon sealed instruments accruing within this State not hereafter mentioned. Within ten years : actions upon sealed instruments accruing without this State, excepting those hereinafter mentioned. Within six years: actions upon judgments of Courts not of Record, upon any contract for payment of money, sealed or unsealed, issued by any town, county, city, village or school district ; upon any other contract, obligation or liability created by statute, excepting penalties and forfeitures, where no other limitation is provided by law. No evidences of debt issued by any bank are barred by statute.

Married Women.—All property of the wife's at marriage with all revenues therefrom, together with what she acquires after marriage by inheritance, gift, grant, devise or bequest, from any person other than her husband, is her separate estate. She may sue and be sued alone when the action concerns her separate property or business.

Notarial Fees.—Protest $1.00 and twenty-five cents for each notice and postage.

Notes and Bills of Exchange.—The common law prevails as to the negotiability, protest, and rights and liabilities of the various parties to them. Warehouse receipts are negotiable unless expressed not to be. Municipal bonds are not negotiable,

WISCONSIN—Continued.

unless expressly authorized to be. Days of grace have been abolished by statute. Bills of exchange and promissory notes are protested for non-acceptance or non-payment, and written notice thereof given to the drawer, maker and each endorser, immediately on making protest, by personal delivery or by mail, postage prepaid. Damages on foreign bills, five per cent. One action may be brought against all parties liable on a note or bill. Negotiable paper maturing on a holiday becomes due on the next preceding secular day.

Stay of Executions.—On Justices' judgments only ; under $10, one month ; $10 to $30, two months ; $30 to $50, three months ; over $50, four months.

Transfer of Corporation Stocks.—Shares of stock may be transferred by indorsement and delivery, which will transfer the title to a bona fide purchaser or pledgee for value as against all parties, saving the right of the corporation to treat the holder of record as the holder in fact until such transfer is recorded upon the books of the corporation, or a new certificate is issued. If the Secretary refuses to make proper transfers on the books, the Circuit Court may grant an order requiring it.

WYOMING.

County Seat.	County.	Name of Atty.	Name of Bank.	Cashier.
Buffalo	Johnson.	Charles H. Burritt	First Natl. Bk.	W. J. Thorn.
Casper	Natrona.	C. B. Bradley	Bk. of W. H. Denecke & Co.	W. A. Denecke.
Cheyenne	Laramie.	Potter & Burke	Stock Growers Natl. Bk.	J. D. Freeborn.
Douglas	Converse.	F. H. Harvey	First Natl. Bk.	H. R. Paul.
Evanston	Uinta.	Clark & Beard	Bk. of North & Stone	Charles Stone.
Green River	Sweetwater.	L. J. Palmer	Morris Mercantile Co.	
Lander	Fremont.	J. S. Vidal	First Natl. Bk.	S. C. Parks, Jr.
Laramie City	Albany.	R. S. Corthell	Albany Co. Natl. Bk.	E. Crumrine.
Newcastle	Weston.	R. H. Vosburgh	Bk. of Newcastle	Meyer Frank.
Rawlins	Carbon.	Craig & Chatterton	First Natl. Bk.	J. C. Davis.
Sheridan	Sheridan.	John P. Arnott	First Natl. Bk.	A. S. Burrows.
Sundance	Crook.	Stoots & Harper	Bk. of John W. Rogers	
Not Organized	Bighorn.			
"	National Park Reservation.			

DIGEST OF WYOMING COMMERCIAL LAWS.

Assignments.—Any debtor may make a general assignment of all his property in trust for the benefit of his creditors. No preferences allowed.

Attachments.—Attachment may be had where the debtor is a foreign corporation, or a non-resident of Wyoming, or is about to become a non-resident thereof; has absconded with intent to defraud his creditors; has left the county of his residence to avoid the service of summons; so conceals himself that service of summons cannot be had upon him; is about to remove his property, or a part thereof, out of the jurisdiction of the Court, with intent to defraud his creditors; is about to convert his property, or any part thereof, into money, for the purpose of placing it beyond the reach of his creditors; has property or rights of action which he conceals; has assigned, removed, or disposed of his property, or a part thereof with intent to defraud his creditors; fraudulently or criminally contracted the debt for which suit is brought.

Bank Laws.—Banks may be incorporated with capital not less than $10,000 in towns of 1,000 or less; not less than $25,000 in towns from one thousand to two thousand; not less than $50,000 in towns from 2,000 to 5,000; not less than $100,000 in towns over 5,000. Savings associations may incorporate. Loan and trust companies may incorporate. All banks are required to make full statements at the end of each quarter, showing their resources and liabilities. The statement is required to be filed in the office of the County Clerk of the County in which the bank does business, and in the office of the Auditor of the State. In the case of a corporation, the report must be published in a newspaper.

Exemptions.—Every householder in Wyoming, being the head of a family, is entitled to a homestead not exceeding in value the sum of $1,500, which is exempt from execution and attachment arising from any debt, contract, or other obligation entered into or incurred, but is exempt only where occupied as such by the owner-thereof, or the person entitled thereto, or his or her family.

WYOMING—Continued.

Interest.—Legal rate is 12 per cent., but any rate may be agreed upon in writing. No usury laws.

Legal Holidays.—Sunday, January 1, February 22, May 30, July 4, Thanksgiving, December 25, Election Day.

Limitation of Actions.—For the recovery of title, or possession of real estate, ten years; upon a specialty, or any agreement, contract or promise in writing, five years. But on all foreign claims, judgments, or contracts, expressed or implied, contracted or incurred before the debtor becomes a resident of this State, within two years from the time the debtor shall have established his residence within this State. Upon contracts not in writing, expressed or implied, within eight years.

Notarial Fees.—Protest $1.00, seal fifty cents and for each notice fifty cents.

Notes and Bills of Exchange.—Notes and bills of exchange are subject to a State law which substantially enacts the law merchant. Grace is allowed on negotiable instruments, except waived in note. Paper maturing on a holiday becomes due the day preceding. Damages on protested bills, 12 per cent.

Transfer of Corporation Stocks.—Shares of stock may be transferred in any manner provided by the by-laws of the corporation.

DIPLOMATIC SERVICE OF THE UNITED STATES.

To what country accredited.	Name and rank.	Residence.
Argentine Republic	Wm. I Buchanan, E. E. & M. P.	Buenos Ayres.
	George W. Fishback, Sec. of Leg	Buenos Ayres.
Austria-Hungary	Bartlett Tripp, E. E. & M. P.	Vienna.
	Lawrence Townsend, Sec. of Leg	Vienna.
	Capt. Joseph II. Dorst, Mil. Att.	Vienna.
	Lt. C. E. Vreeland, Nav. Att.	Vienna.
Belgium	James S. Ewing, E. E. & M. P.	Brussels.
	Lt. Floyd W. Harris, Mil. Att.	Brussels.
Bolivia	Thomas Moonlight, E. E. & M. P.	La Paz.
Brazil	Thomas L. Thompson, E. E. & M. P.	Rio de Janeiro.
	William Crichton, Sec. of Leg	Rio de Janeiro.
Chile	Edward H. Strobel, E. E. & M. P.	Santiago.
	Charles R. Simpkins, Sec. of Leg	Santiago.
China	Charles Denby, E. E. & M. P.	Peking.
	Charles Denby, Jr., Sec. of Leg	Peking.
	Edward K. Lowry, 2d Sec. of Leg	Peking.
	Fleming D. Cheshire, Int.	Peking.
	Com. Francis M. Barber, Nav. Att.	Peking.
Colombia	Luther F. McKinney, E. E. & M. P.	Bogotá.
	Jacob Sleeper, Sec. of Leg. & C. G.	Bogotá.
Costa Rica, Nicaragua and Salvador	Lewis Baker, E. E. & M. P.	Managua.
	John F. Baker, Sec. of Leg	Managua.
Denmark	John E. Risley, E. E. & M. P.	Copenhagen.
Ecuador	James D. Tillman, E. E. & M. P.	Quito.
France	James B. Eustis, Ambassador E. & P.	Paris.
	Henry Vignaud, Sec. of Leg	Paris.
	Newton B. Eustis, 2d Sec. of Leg	Paris.
	Major Sanford C. Kellogg, Mil. Att.	Paris.
	Lt. R. P. Rodgers, Nav. Att.	Paris.
Germany	Theodore Runyon, Ambassador E. & P.	Berlin.
	John B. Jackson, Sec. of Embassy	Berlin.
	Herbert G. Squiers, 2d Sec. of Embassy	Berlin.
	Lt. Robert K. Evans, Mil. Att.	Berlin.
	Lt C. E. Vreeland, Nav. Att.	Berlin.
Great Britain	Thomas F. Bayard, Ambassador E. & P.	London.
	James R. Roosevelt, Sec. of Embassy	London.
	David D. Wells, 2d Sec. of Leg	London.
	Maj. William Ludlow, Mil. Att.	London.
	Lt. Com. William S. Cowles, Nav. Att.	London.
Greece, Roumania, and Servia	Eben Alexander, E. E. &. M. P. &. C. G.	Athens.
Guatemala and Honduras	Pierce M. B. Young, E. E. & M. P.	Guatemala.
	D. Lynch Pringle, Sec. of Leg. & C. G.	Guatemala.
Haiti	Henry M. Smythe, Min. Res. & C. G.*	Port-au-Prince.
Hawaiian Islands	Albert S. Willis, E. E. & M. P.	Honolulu.
	Ellis Mills, Sec. of Leg. & C. G.†	Honolulu.
Honduras and Guatemala	Pierce M. B. Young, E. E. & M. P.	Guatemala.
Italy	Wayne McVeagh, Ambassador E. & P.	Rome.
	Larz Anderson, Sec. of Embassy	Rome.
	Capt. George F. Scriven, Mil. Att.	Rome.
	Lt. C. E. Vreeland, Nav. Att.	Rome.
Japan	Edwin Dun, E. E. & M. P.	Tokyo (Yedo).
	J. R. Herod, Sec. of Leg	Tokyo (Yedo).
	Stephen Bonsal, 2d Sec. of Leg	Tokyo (Yedo).
	Ransford Stevens Miller, Jr., Int.	Tokyo (Yedo).
	Com. Francis M. Barber, Nav. Att.	Tokyo (Yedo).
Korea	John M. B. Sill, Min. Res. & C. G.	Seoul.
	H. N. Allen, Sec. of Leg.‡	Seoul.
	Pang Kyeng Hi, Int.	Seoul.
	Ye Ho Yung, Int.	Seoul.
Liberia	William H. Heard, Min. Res. & C. G.	Monrovia.

THE LEGAL AND FINANCIAL LIGHTS OF AMERICA. 163

Mexico.............................Matt W. Ransom, E. E. & M. P......................Mexico.
                                   E. C. Butler, Sec. of Leg............................Mexico.
                                   Capt. Charles G. Dwyer, Mil. Att.....................Mexico.
Netherlands........................William E. Quinby, E. E. & M. P....................The Hague.
Nicaragua, Costa Rica, and Salvador...Lewis Baker, E. E. & M. P.........................Managua.
                                   John F. Baker, Sec. of Leg........................Managua.
Paraguay and Uruguay...............Granville Stuart, E. E. & M. P...................Montevideo.
Persia.............................Alexander McDonald, Min. Res. & C. G..............Teheran.
                                   ———, Int. to Leg. & C. G........................Teheran.
Peru...............................James A. McKenzie, E. E. & M. P...................Lima.
                                   Richard R. Neill, Sec. of Leg.....................Lima.
Portugal...........................George W. Caruth, E. E. & M. P....................Lisbon.
Roumania, Greece, and Servia.......Eben Alexander, E. E. & M. P. &. C. G............Athens.
Russia.............................Clifton R. Breckinridge, E. E. & M. P............St. Petersburg.
                                   H. H. D. Peirce, Sec. of Leg.....................St. Petersburg.
                                   Lt. R. P. Rodgers, Nav. Att......................St. Petersburg.
Salvador, Costa Rica, and Nicaragua....Lewis Baker, E. E. & M. P....................Managua.
                                   John F. Baker, Sec. of Leg.......................Managua.
Santo Domingo......................Henry M. Smythe, Chargé d'Affaires...............Port-au-Prince.
Servia, Greece, and Roumania.......Eben Alexander, E. E. & M. P. & C. G.............Athens.
Siam...............................John Barrett, Min. Res. & C. G...................Bangkok.
                                   ———, Int. to Leg. & C. G........................Bangkok.
Spain..............................Hannis Taylor, E. E. & M. P......................Madrid.
                                   H. Clay Armstrong, Jr., Sec. of Leg..............Madrid.
                                   1st Lieut. John H. H. Peshine, Mil. Att..........Madrid.
Sweden and Norway..................Thomas B. Ferguson, E. E. & M. P.................Stockholm.
Switzerland........................James O. Broadhead, E. E. & M. P.................Berne.
Turkey.............................Alex. W. Terrell, E. E. & M. P...................Constantinople.
                                   John W. Riddle Sec. of Leg.......................Constantinople.
                                   A. A. Gargiulo, Int..............................Constantinople.
Uruguay and Paraguay...............Granville Stuart, E. E. & M. P...................Montevideo.
Venezuela..........................Allen Thomas, E. E. & M. P.......................Caracas.
                                   W. W. Russell, Sec. of Leg.......................Caracas.
Egypt..............................Frederick C. Penfield, Agt. & C. G...............Cairo.

* Also Chargé d'Affaires to Santo Domingo.   † Also Consul-General at Honolulu.
‡ Also Deputy Consul-General.

THE LEGAL AND FINANCIAL LIGHTS OF AMERICA.

UNITED STATES CONSULAR SERVICE.

The letters C. G. indicate Consul-General; C.. Consul; V. C., Vice-Consul; C. A., Commercial Agent; D. C., Deputy Consul; Agt., Agent; Mar., Marshall; Int., Interpreter; C. C., Consular Clerk.

Place.   *Name and Title.*

ARGENTINE REPUBLIC.
Buenos Ayres..........Edward L. Baker..... ....C.
do................Lyman Wallace Chute....V. C.
Bahia Blanca.........Walter T. Jones..........Agt.
Cordoba...:...........John M. Thome ....V. C.
Rosario ....Willis E. Baker.............C.
do..............Augustus M. Barnes......V. C.

AUSTRIA-HUNGARY.
Budapest, Hungary....Edward P. T. Hammond.....C.
do............Louis Gerster........V. & D. C.
Fiume.............. .Giovanni Gelletich.........Agt.
Prague, Bohemia.......Carl Bailey Hurst.......... *C.
do..............Emil Kubinzky............V. C.
Reichenberg, Bohemia.George R. Ernst............C.
do..............Fritz Wagner........V. & D. C.
Haida. ....Anton Schlessing..........Agt.
Trieste, Austria........J. Edward Nettles............C.
do..............Basil Bryce...........V. & D. C.
Vienna, Austria........Max Judd.................C. G.
do.............Dean B. Mason........V. C. G.
Brunn ....Gustavus Schoeller........Agt.
Innsbruck...........August Bargehr............Agt.

BELGIUM.
Antwerp..............Harvey Johnson..............C.
do...............Louis Hees.........V. & D. C.
do..............Stanislas H. Haine........D. C.
Brussels................George W. Roosevelt........C.
do..............Gregory Phelan..... V. & D. C.
Charleroi ....J. Fisher Reese..............Agt.
Ghent................Henry C. Morris..............C.
do..............George Verhulst...........V.C.
Liege ....Henry W. Gilbert............C.
do...............John Gross..........V. & D. C.
Verviers..............Henry Dodt................Agt.

BOLIVIA.
La Paz................Gera·do Zalles.......... V. C.

BRAZIL.
Bahia................Richard P. McDaniel.........C.
do...............S. S. Schindler............V. C.
Aracaju ....Luiz Schmidt..............Agt.
Para ....George G. Mathews, Jr ......C.
do............Francisco B. da S. Aguiar.V. C.
Manaos ....George Lomas..............Agt.
Maranhão ... .Luiz F. da S. Santos.........V. C.
Pernambuco. ....John Malcolm Johnstone ....C.
do..............John Krause..............V. C.
Ceara ....William H. Murdock ......Agt.
Maceio........ .....Charles Goble..............Agt.
Natal....... ...... .Lyle Nelson................Agt.
Rio Grande do Sul......Joaquim M. Garcia.........V. C.
Porto Alegre.........A. H. Edwards............Agt.

Place.   *Name and Title.*

Rio de Janeiro.........William T. Townes.......C. G.
do...............John Taylor Lewis.V.&D.C.G.
do...............Reuben Cleary.........D. C. G.
Victoria...............Jean Zinzen..............Agt.
Santos ....Henry C. Smith.............C.
do.............. John A. Blair.............V. C.
Desterro.............Robert Grant............Agt.

CHILE.
Antofagasta...........Charles C. Greene.........V. C.
Arica ....David Simpeon.........V. C.
Coquimbo............William C. Tripler...........C.
do..V. C.
Iquique ....Joseph W. Merriam........C.
do........... ......Maximo Rosenstock......V. C.
Valparaiso .. ..James M. Dobbs............C.
do...............August Moller, Jr.........V. C.
Caldera ....John C. Morong.........:..Agt.
Coronel..............William Taylor............Agt.
Talcahuano..........John O. Smith............Agt.

CHINA.
Amoy.................Delaware Kemper............C.
do..V. C.
do.............James McD. Carrington...Mar.
do.............Tsin Ching Chung..........Int.
Takao..Agt.
Canton................Charles Seymour............C.
do..V. C.
do..............Hung Tsun Ki........Act'g Int.
Swatow...Agt.
Chin-Kiang ... .Alexander C. Jones..........C.
do..V. C.
do..............Wan Bing Chung..........Int.
do..............Nich S. Kin........Act'g Mar.
Fuchau..............J. Courtney Hixson..........C.
do..............Harry W. Churchill.......V. C.
do..............William C. Hixson.........Mar.
do. ....Timothy Hsü..............Int.
Hankow.............Jacob T. Child..... ....C.
do..V. C.
do..............M. A. Jenkins............Int.
do..............Jacob T. Child, Jr........Mar.
Niuchwang ....J. J. Fred. Bandinel.V. & D. C.
Ningpo ....John Fowler...............C.
do..V. C.
do..............Henry A. C. Emery...... Int.
Shanghai..............Thomas R. Jernigan......C. G.
do..............Isaac E. Avery....V. & D. C. G.
do..............Rufus F. Eastlack......D. C. G.
do..............George A. Shu*[illegible]*t........Mar.
do...... ....Walter S. Eme*[illegible]*.......Int.
Tien-Tsin ....Sheridan P. R*[illegible]*........C.
do..............Charles D. Tenn*[illegible]*......V. C.
do..............Arthur Ash.*[illegible]*........Mar.
do..............Charles D. Tenney..........Int.
Chefoo..............Arthur R. Donnelly.........Agt.

* Born of American parents temporarily residing abroad.

THE LEGAL AND FINANCIAL LIGHTS OF AMERICA. 155

Place.   *Name and Title.*

COLOMBIA.

Barranquilla ....John Bidlake................C.
do ... .Elias P. Pellet.......V. & D. C.
Rio Hacha ....T. V. Henriquez...........Agt.
Santa Maria..........Louis Von Veltheim.......Agt.
Bogotá................Jacob Sleeper..,. ......*C. G.
do................William G. Boshell.....V. C. G.
Bucaramanga.........Gustave Volkman.........Agt.
Cucuta.. ....Christian Andersen Möller..Agt.
Honda..... ....Henry Hallam.............Agt.
Cartagena.............Clifford Smyth.............C.
do................Augustus T. Hanabergh...V. C.
Colon (Aspinwall).. ...Josiah L. Pearcy...... .....C.
do............ ...Josiah L. Pearcy, Jr..V. & D. C.
Bocas del Toro.......David R. Hand ....Agt.
Medellin ....Thomas Herran..... ....C.
do................Luciano Santa-Maria.......V. C.
Panama................Victor Vifquain... ......C. G.
do..............Felix Ehrman............V. C. G.

COSTA RICA.

San José..............Harrison R. Williams........C.
do...............Walter J. Field............V. C.
Port Limon ....W. B. Unckles.............Agt.
Punta Arenas ....Max Diermissen. ....Agt.

DENMARK AND DOMINIONS.

Copenhagen............Robert J. Kirk................C.
do ....Olof Hansen...............V. C.
Dyrefjord, Iceland......N. Chr. Gram................Agt.
Elsinore............Alfred Christensen ....Agt.
St. Thomas, W. I......James H. Stewart...........C.
do ....Julius C. Lorentzen.......V. C.
Christiansted..........Andrew J. Blackwood .....Agt.
Fredericksted........William F. Moore..........Agt.

DOMINICAN REPUBLIC.

Puerto Plata...........Thomas Simpson..........C.
do............Washington Lithgow .....V. C.
Monte Christi........Isaac T. Petit..............Agt.
Samana..............Jean M. Villain........V. C. A.
Santo Domingo ....Archibald H. Grimke.........C.
do................Juan A. Read ....V. C.
Azua.........:.....John Hardy........ ....Agt.
Macoris.............Edward C. Reed............Agt.
Sanchez............Francis L. Wills...........Agt.

ECUADOR.

Guayaquil..........George G. Dillard.........C. G.
do...............Martin Reinberg.......V. C. G.
Bahia de Caraquez ..Zephyr Constantine ......Agt.
Esmeraldas ....Ferdinand Servat..........Agt.
Manta..............Pedro A. Moreira...........Agt.

FRANCE AND DOMINIONS.

Algiers, Africa.........Charles T. Grellet............C.
do................Victor A. Grellet ....V. & D. C.
Beni-saf............E. L. G. Milsom ....Agt.
Bone...............Elie G. F. Le Coat............Agt.

Place.   *Name and Title.*

Collo and Philippeville......... ......Marius Eyme.. ....Agt.
Oran...................Benjamin A. Courcelle.....Agt.
Bordeaux............John M. Wiley..............C.
do................John Preston Beecher.V.& D.C.
Pau.... ....J. Morris Poet...............Agt.
Calais................Charles W. Shepard.........C.
do ....V. C.
Boulogne-sur-Mer ....Paul Moleux..............Agt.
Cayenne, Guiana.......Leon Wacongne............C.
do.............Auguste Mathurin ....V. C.
Cognac..............Frederick Fitz Gerald........C.
do................Arch. W. Pollock....V. & D. C.
Gorée-Dakar, Africa ...Peter Strickland............C.
do.....................................V. C.
Grenoble ....C.
do.............Thomas W. Murton........V. C.
Guadeloupe Isl'd, W. I..Jacob E. Dart ....C.
do....................................D. & V. C.
Havre..............Charles W. Chancellor..... C.
do................Cicero Brown............ V. C.
do.............. Philip S. Chancellor.......D. C.
Cherbourg...........Emile Postel ....Agt.
Honfleur..............Henry M. Hardy............Agt.
Rennes.............Charles D. Huret............Agt.
St. Malo..............Raymond Moulton..........Agt.
Limoges................Walter T. Griffin ....C. A.
do................Auguste Jouhannaud...V. C. A.
Périgueux ....Agt.
Lyons................Frank E. Hyde..............C.
do.................Thos. Nicoll Browne.V. & D. C.
Dijon..............Lucien Bargy..............Agt.
Marseilles............Claude M. Thomas ....C.
do................Charles P. Pressly...V. & D. C.
Bastia................Simon Damiani ....Agt.
Cette...............L. S. Nahmens ....Agt.
Toulon..............Louis J. B. Jouve ....Agt.
Martinique, W. I......Julius G. Tucker...........C.
do................Simon Henry Davidt.V.& D. C.
Nantes................Reavel Savage..............C.
do ....Hiram D. Bennett........V. C.
Angers.............Jules Henri Luneau. ......Agt.
Brest...... ....A. Pitel....................Agt.
Lorient................Edouard Broni.............Agt.
Nice ....Wilburn B. Hall............C.
do................Alexander Vial...........V. C.
Cannes..............Philip T. Riddett..........Agt.
Mentone......... ......Auge Clericy............Agt.
Monaco ....Emile de Loth............ Agt.
Nouméa, N. C..........L. Le Mescam..........V. C. A.
Paris.................Samuel E. Morss.........C. G.
do................Clyde Shropshire..V. & D. C. G.
do.... ....Edw.P. MacLean..D.C.G.& C.C.
do...............Hubbard T. Smith..........C. C.
Rheims ....Henry P. du Bellet..........C.
do................Charles W. Ramsay.......V. C.
Troyes ....Gaston Baltet..............Agt.
Roubaix ....Stephen H. Angell..........C. A.
do ....Gaston Thiery............V. C. A.
Candry ....Hans Dietliker...............Agt.
Dunkirk.............Benjamin Morel ....Agt.
Lille ....C. Dubois Gregoire........Agt.

* The Consul-General is also Secretary of Legation.
† Born of American parents temporarily residing abroad.

THE LEGAL AND FINANCIAL LIGHTS OF AMERICA.

Place.	Name and Title.
Rouen	Horatio R. Bigelow..........C.
do	E. M. J. Delleplane.......V. C.
Dieppe	Raoulle Bourgeois..........Agt.
Saigon, Cochin China	Edward Schneegans.....C. A.
do	V. C. A.
St. Bartholomew, W. I.	R. Burton Dinzey.........C. A.
do	Julian O. Florandin....V. C. A.
St. Etienne	Charles W. Whiley, Jr.......C.
do	Hastings Burroughs.....V. C.
St. Pierre, Miquelon	George J. Steer........C. A.
do	George H. Frecker......V. C. A.
Tahiti, Society Islands	J. Lamb Doty................C.
do	John Hart...... ....V. C.
Tunis, Africa	Alfred Chapellé...........V. C.

GERMANY.

Place.	Name and Title.
Aix la Chapelle	William C. Emmet...........C.
do	Peter Knetgens.......V. & D. C.
Annaberg	Theodore M. Stephan........C.
do	Franz Max Jaeger...V. & D. C.
Elbenstock	Carl Borngraeber..........Agt.
Bamberg	Louis Stern............C. A.
do	Albert Kiessling.......V. C. A.
Barmen	Henry F. Merritt...........C.
do	Wilhelm R. Schaefer.....V. C.
do	Richard E. Jahn........D. C.
Solingen	Richard E. Jahn..........Agt.
Berlin	Charles de Kay........C. G.
do	F. C. Zimmerman..V. & D. C. G.
do	Frederick von Versen..D. C. G.
do	Charles H. Day ....C. C.
Guben	Wm. C. Dreher..........Agt.
Bremen	George Keenan...... ......C.
do	Georg W. Wätjen........V. C.
do	John H. Schnabel.......D. C.
Brake & Nordenhamm	Wilhelm Clemens........Agt.
Bremerhaven-Geestemunde	Wm. B. Murphy..........Agt.
Breslau	Frederick Opp..............C.
do	Max Loewenthal ....V. C.
Brunswick	Edward W. S. Tingle ......C.
do	Julius Seckel........V. & D. C.
Chemnitz	James C. Monaghan ....C.
do	Joseph F. Monaghan......V. C.
Cologne	William D. Warner..........C.
do	V. C.
Crefeld	Charles Jonas..............C.
do	Flavel Scott Miues..V. & D. C.
Dresden	William S. Carroll.........C. G.
do	William Knoop ..V. & D. C. G.
do	Hernando de Soto......D. C. G.
Zittau	Alfred Krauss............Agt.
Dusseldorf	Peter Lieber.... ....C.
do	Emil Hoette..............V. C.
Essen	F. Asthorver, Jr.... .....Agt.
Frankfort	Frank H. Mason..........C. G.
do	Alvesto S. Hogue.V. & D. C. G.
Cassel	Gustav C. Kothe...... . Agt.
Langen Schwalbach	Ernest Grebert...........Agt.
Freiburg, Baden	Jacob H. Thierlot........C. A.
do	V. C. A.
Fürth	Henry C. Carpenter.......C. A.
do	Fred. J. Hirschmann...V. C. A.
Glauchau	George Sawter,...........C. A.
do	V. C. A.
Hamburg	William Henry Robertson....C.
do	Charles H. Burke...,V. & D. C.
do	David H. Burke.............D. C.
Kiel	August Sartori............Agt.
Lübeck	Jacob Meyer, Jr............Agt.
Ritzebüttel and Cuxhaven	Johann G. F. Starcke......Agt.
Hanover	Edward P. Crane.............C.
do	Alex. Moritz Simon.V. &. D. C.
Kehl	Edward I. Prickett..........C.
do	Theodore Krüger.........V. C.
do	Ernest Therion..........D. C.
Leipsic	Otto Doederlein.............C.
do	Frederick Nachod...V. & D. C.
do	Rudolph Fricke..........D. C.
Gera	Charles Neuer...........Agt.
Madgeburg	Julius Muth................C.
do	Robert Welchsel, Jr......V. C.
Mannheim	Max Goldfinger............. C.
do	Carl Funck..............V. C.
Neustadt	Leopold Blum............Agt.
Mayence	Perry Bartholow..........C.
do	Peter Melchers......V. & D. C.
Munich	Ralph Steiner......... . ....C.
do	J. Leonard Corning..V. & D. C.
Augsburg	G. Oberndorf.............Agt.
Nuremberg	William J. Black.............C.
do	Sigmund Dunkelsbühler..V. C.
do	Sigmund Dunkelsbühler..D. C.
Plauen	Thomas Willing Peters...C. A.
do	Oscar Gottschalk..V. & D. C. A.
Markneukirchen	& Agt.
Sonneberg	Dwight J. Partello ....C.
do	Alvin Florschutz....V. & D. C.
Coburg	Emil Albrecht...........Agt.
Stettin	Frederick W. Kickbusch.....C.
do	Paul Grischow......V. & D. C.
Danzig	Philipp Albrecht........ ..Agt.
Königsberg	Conrad H. Gädeke........Agt.
Stuttgart	Alfred C. Johnson..........C.
do	William Hahn........V. C.
Weimar	Thomas Ewing Moore....C. A.
do	Paul Teichmann.......V. C. A.

GREAT BRITAIN AND DOMINIONS.

Place.	Name and Title.
Aden, Arabia	William W. Masterson........C
do	Judas Messa..............V. C.
Hodedia	John R. Mueller.........Agt.
Amherstburg, Ont	John Patton..............C.
do	James H. M. Florey..V. & D.C.
Antigua, W. I.	Richard M. Bartleman........C.
do	Samuel Galbraith.........V. C.
Anguila	Wager Rey..............Agt.
Dominica	William Stedman........Agt.
Montserrat	Richard Hannam..........Agt.
Portsmouth	Alex. Charles Reviere.....Agt.

THE LEGAL AND FINANCIAL LIGHTS OF AMERICA. 167

Place.	Name and Title.
Auckland, N. Z	John Darcy Connolly ....C.
do	Leonard A. Bachelder.....V. C.
Christ Church	Albert Cuff................Agt.
Dunedin	W. G. Neill................Agt.
Monganui	Robert Wyles..............Agt.
Wellington	Thomas Cahill............Agt.
Barbados, W. I	George T. Tate............C.
do	Arthur B. St. Hill........V. C.
St. Lucia	William Peter.............Agt.
St. Vincent	W. J. Shearman............Agt.
Bathurst, Africa	Henry Goddard............V. C.
Belfast, Ireland	James B. Taney..............C.
do	V. D. & C.
do	Louis Mantell...........D. C.
Ballymena	John G. Ballentine........Agt.
Londonderry	P. T. Rodgers.............Agt.
Lurgan	F. W. Magahan.............Agt.
Belize, Honduras	Albert E. Morlan...........C.
do	Phillip S. Woods........V. C.
Belleville, Ont	Michael J. Hendrick........C.
do	William N. Ponton........V. C.
Deseronto	Charles A. Millener.......Agt.
Napanee	William Templeton.......Agt.
Picton	Jacob F. Beringer.........Agt.
Trenton	Stephen J. Young..........Agt.
Bermuda (Hamilton)	Marshall Hanger............C.
do	James B. Heyl......V. & D. C.
Birmingham, England	George F. Parker...........C.
do	Frederick M. Burton......V. C.
do	Ernest Harker............D. C.
Kidderminster	James Morton..............Agt.
Redditch	H. C. Browning............Agt.
Wolverhampton	John Neve................Agt.
Bombay, India	Henry J. Sommer, Jr........C.
do	Samuel Comfort..........V.C.
Karachi	W. Flower Hamilton......Agt.
Bradford, England	Claude Meeker............C.
do	Thomas L. Renton..V. & D. C.
do	Richard B. Nicholls.....D. C.
Bristol, England	Lorin A. Lathrop...........C.
do	Gerard Mosely......V. & D. C.
Gloucester	Arnold Henry Palin.......Agt.
Brockville, Ont	James A. Demarest..........C.
do	William W. Wood..V. & D. C.
Calcutta, India	Van Leer Polk...........C. G.
do	William W. Bryant,V.&D.C.G.
Akyab	David R. Cameron........Agt.
Bassein	John Young..............Agt.
Chitagong	R. A. Mactaggart.........Agt.
Madras	Henry Scott..............Agt.
Moulmein	W. J. Davidson...........Agt.
Rangoon	Charles Gairdner.........Agt.
Cape Town, Africa	...........................C.
do	Clifford H. Knight.....V. C.
Bloemfontein	Ernst R. Landgraf........Agt.
Durban	J. Perrott Prince........Agt.
East London	William H. Fuller........Agt.
Johannesburg	J. C. Manion............ .Agt.
Kimberley	Gardner Williams.........Agt.
Port Elizabeth	John A. Chaband..........Agt.
Simonstown	John R. Black, Jr........Agt.
Cardiff, Wales	Anthony Howells...........C.

Place.	Name and Title.
Cardiff, Wales	William Harris......V. & D. C.
Llanelly	William Howell............Agt.
Milford Haven	George S. Kelway........Agt.
Newport	William E. Heard........Agt.
Ceylon, India	William Morey.............C.
do	Elmer Lake Morey...V. & D. C.
Jaffna	William M. S. Twynam....Agt.
Point de Galle	.........................Agt.
Charlottetown, P. E. I	Dominic J. Kane.........C.
do	John T. Crockett....V. & D. C.
Alberton	Albert Glidden ....Agt.
Georgetown	Archibald J. McDonald....Agt.
Souris	Caleb C. Carlton.........Agt.
Summerside	John Gaffney.............Agt.
Chatham, Ont	Edwin F. Bishop............C.
do	Edwin Bell ....V. C.
Clifton, Ont	George W. Nichols..........C.
do	James Butters ......V. & D. C.
St. Catharines	Leonard H. Collard.......Agt.
Coaticook, Quebec	Joel Linsley ....C.
do	George Pinkham....V. & D. C.
Hereford	John R. Nichols..........Agt.
Lineboro	Hoel S. Beebe............Agt.
Potton	Chandler Bailey..........Agt.
Stanstead	Horace S. Haskell........Agt.
Collingwood, Ont	James C. Quiggle ....C. A.
do	Chas. McDonnell..V. & D. C. A.
Barrie	Alfred E. H. Croswicke....Agt.
Lindsay	James M. Knowlson......Agt.
Owen Sound	William T. Robertson.....Agt.
Parry Sound	Walter R. Foot............Agt.
Cork (Queenstown)	Lucien J. Walker..........C.
do	James William Scott.....V. C.
Waterford	William H. Farrell........Agt.
Demerara, Guiana	Andrew J. Patterson........C.
do	James Spaight........V. & D. C.
Dublin, Ireland	Newton B. Ashby...........C.
do	Arthur Donn Piatt...V. & D. C.
Athlone	John Burgess.............Agt.
Limerick	George P. Mackenzie.....Agt.
Dundee, Scotland	John M. Savage............C.
do	Allan Baxter..........V. & D. C.
Aberdeen	Andrew Murray ....Agt.
Dunfermline, Scotland	James D. Reid...........C. A.
do	James Penman..........V. C. A.
Kirkcaldy	Andrew Innes............Agt.
Falmouth, England	Howard Fox...............C.
do	G. Henry Fox......V. & D. C.
Scilly Islands	John Banfield, Jr.........Agt.
Fort Erie, Ont	Ralph Johnson.............C.
do	Isaac H. Allen......V. & D. C.
Gaspé Basin, Quebec	Almar F. Dickson........C.
do	John Carter..............V. C.
Paspebiac	Daniel Bisson............Agt.
Gibraltar, Spain	Horatio J. Sprague ....C.
do	Richard L. Sprague ..V. & D. C.
Glasgow, Scotland	Allen B. Morse.............C.
do	William Gibson..........V. C.
do	James J. Inglis..........D. C.
Greenock	James A. Love..........Agt.
Troon	Andrew McMurray ......Agt.
Goderich, Ont	Robert S. Chilton........C. A.

168   THE LEGAL AND FINANCIAL LIGHTS OF AMERICA.

Place.	Name and Title.
Goderich, Ont.	William Campbell.....V. C. A.
Clinton	A. O. Pattison.............Agt.
Guelph, Ont.	Charles N. Daly ....C.
do	George A. Oxnard....V. & D. C.
Halifax, N. S.	Darius H. Ingraham......C. G.
do	George Hill.......V. & D. C. G.
Bridgewater	William H. Owen..........Agt.
Liverpool	James N. S. Marshall......Agt.
Lunenburg	Daniel M. Owen. ......Agt.
Hamilton, Ont.	Charles F. Macdonald......C.
do	Daniel B. Smith......V. & D. C.
Brantford	Frank B. Pollard..........Agt.
Galt	Milton P. Townshend.....Agt.
Paris	William W. Hume.........Agt.
Hobart, Tasmania	Alexander George Webster...C.
do	V. C.
Launceston	Lindsay Tulloch..........Agt.
Hongkong, China	William E. Hunt............C.
do	George B. Hunt.....V. & D. C.
do	Chin Poy Woo ....Int.
Huddersfield, England.	Frank C. McGhee ....C.
do	David J. Bailey......V. & D. C.
Hull, England...	........C.
do	Gordon B. Daniels...V. & D. C.
Kingston, Jamaica	Quincy O. Eckford...........C.
do	James L. Sykes......V. & D. C.
Black River	C. M. Farquharson.........Agt.
Milk River	A. A. Green ....Agt.
Port Morant	Lorenzo D. Baker, Jr......Agt.
Savannah-la-Mar	Ch. S. Farquharson........Agt.
Kingston, Ont.	Marshall H. Twitchell ......C.
do	Mat. H. Folger ......V. & D. C.
Gananoque	E. E. Abbott..............Agt.
Leeds, England	Norfleet Harris ....C.
do	William Ward............V. C.
do	Edmund Ward............D. C.
Leith (Edinburgh)..	Robert J. MacBride..........C.
do	Frederick P. Piatt...V. & D. C.
Galashiels	John Stalker..............Agt.
Levuka, Fiji Islands	Benjamin Morris....V. C. A.
Liverpool, England	James E. Neal...............C.
do	William J. Sulls......V. & D. C.
do	William Pierce............D. C.
Holyhead	John Jones...........Agt.
St. Helen's	John Hammill............Agt.
London, England	Patrick A. Collins........C. G.
do	John J. Collins....V. & D. C. G.
do	Francis W. Frigout.....D. C. G.
Dover	Francis W. Prescott........Agt-
London, Ont.	William H. Jacks............C.
do	Charles W. Davis....V. & D. C.
Malta (Island)	Daniel C. Kennedy....... C.
do	Joseph F. Balbi.... ......V. C.
Manchester, England.	William F. Grinnell..........C.
do	Ernest J. Bridgford......V. C.
Melbourne, Australia.	Daniel W. Maratta.......C. G.
do	Thos. W. Stanford.V.& D. C. G.
Adelaide	Charles A. Murphy ....Agt.
Albany	Frank R. Dymes..........Agt.
Freemantle	Edward Mayhew.........Agt.
Moncton, N. B.	James S. Benedict........C. A.
do	Geo. McSweeney.V. & D. C. A.

Place.	Name and Title.
Bathurst	Benedict C. Mullins........Agt.
Campbellton	Charles Murray........... Agt.
Newcastle	Robert R. Call............Agt.
Richibucto	George V. McInerney......Agt.
Montreal, Quebec	Wendell A. Anderson.....C. G.
do	Patrick Gorman..V. & D. C. G.
Coteau	Thomas Stapleton..........Agt.
Grenville	Alex. Pridham............Agt.
Hemmingford	Wellington W. Wark ......Agt.
Hinchinbrook	Samuel E. Ames............Agt.
Hochelaga and Longueuil	J. H. Turcotte.......Act'g Agt.
Huntingdon	John Dineen ....Agt.
Morrisburgh, Ont.	Albert Fowler............C. A.
do	Geo. F. Bradfield.V. & D. C. A.
Cornwall	David A. Flack...........Agt.
Nassau	Thomas J. McLain..........C.
do	Timothy Darling.........V. C.
Albert Town	Howard H. Farrington.....Agt.
Dunmore Town	Norman E. B. Monroe.....Agt.
Governor's Harbor	Charles A. Bethel..........Agt.
Green Turtle Cay	Edward W. Bethel........Agt.
Mathewtown.	Daniel D. Sargent ....Agt.
Newcastle, England	William S. Campbell.........C.
do	A. H. Dickinson ....V. C.
Carlisle	J. Hewetson Brown........Agt.
Old Hartlepool	Christian Neilson.........Agt.
Sunderland	Thomas A. Horan ....Agt.
Newcastle, N. S. W	C. A.
do	Stewart Keightley......V. C. A.
Brisbane	William J. Weatherill......Agt.
Townsville	William V. Brown....... ..Agt.
Nottingham, England	Asa D. Dickinson..........C.
do	William T. Cartwright....V. C.
Derby	Charles K. Eddowes........Agt.
Leicester	Samuel S. Partridge ....Agt.
Orillia, Ont.	James M. Rosse ....C. A.
do	Charles Corbould.V. & D. C. A.
North Bay, Nipissing.	Daniel J. McKeown........Agt.
Waubaushene	F. J. McCallum...........Agt.
Ottawa, Ont	John B. Riley..;.........C. G.
do	Julius G. Lay....V. & D. C. G.
do	Donnell Rockwell........C. G.
Arnprior	James Fowler ....Agt.
Palmerston, Ont	Loton S. Hunt..........C. A.
do	Wm. Mawhinney.V. &. D. C. A.
Wiarton	J. H. Tibeando............Agt.
Wingham	John Nicoll..............Agt.
Pictou, N. S.	Mark P. Pendleton..........C.
do	John R. Noonan...... . .V. C.
Antigonish	Rupert Cunningham......Agt.
Arichat	Peter Campbell...........Agt.
Cape Canso	Alfred W. Hart...........Agt.
Magdalen Islands	Robert J. Leslie..........Agt.
Port Hawksbury and Mulgrave	Alexander Bain.........Agt.
Pugwash and Wallace.	Conrad W. Morris........Agt.
Sydney	J. E. Burchell ....Agt.
Plymouth, England	Thomas W. Fox..........C.
do	V. C.
Dartmouth	George Hinston..........Agt.
Guernsey	William Carey............Agt.

THE LEGAL AND FINANCIAL LIGHTS OF AMERICA. 169

Place.	Name and Title.
Jersey....................E. B. Renouf................Agt.
Port Antonio, Jamaica..James Y. Walton..........C. A.
do...V. C. A.
Falmouth.........Charles A. Nunes............Agt.
Montego Bay..........G. L. P. Corinaldi...........Agt.
Port Maria............I. I. Lyon..................Agt.
St. Ann's Bay..........R. W. Harris..............Agt.
Port Hope, Ont.........Julian E. Gittings.........C. A.
do...............Ernest Evatt......V. & D. C. A.
Peterborough.......Edward E. Dodds..........Agt.
Port Louis, Mauritius..John P. Campbell ....C.
do..............A. Povah Ambrose.......V. C.
Port Rowan, Ont.......George B. Killmaster......C. A.
do...............William H. Meek ......V. C. A.
Port Sarnia, Ont........Arthur M. Clark ....C.
do................Charles S. Clark...V. & D. C.
Port Stanley, F. I......John H. Miller................C.
do................James Smith ....V. C.
Port Stanley and St.
Thomas, Ont..........George J. Willis...............C.
do................William H. King....V. & D. C.
Courtright............Fred W. Baby..............Agt.
Prescott, Ont..........Joseph Whalen................C.
do.............James Buckly......V. & D. C.
Quebec ....Philip B. Spence ....C.
do.............Robert McD. Stocking....V. C.
Point Levi.............Charles M. Barclay.........Agt.
Sault Ste. Marie, Ont...Charles McCall............C. A.
do.........Edward Biggings.V. & D. C. A.
Sheffield, England.......Bennington R. Bedle.........C.
do...............George Ernest Branson ..V. C.
do...............Frank M. Clark............D. C.
Barnsley ....Robert D. Maddison ....Agt.
Sherbrooke, Quebec....James R. Jackson..............C.
do................Edw. B. Worthington.V.&D.B.
Cookshire ....Charles C. Bailey..........Agt.
Megantic............Henry W. Albro...........Agt.
Sierra Leone, Africa....Robert P. Pooley ....C.
do................Cecil S. W. Pooley........V. C.
Singapore, S. S........E. Spencer Pratt..........C. G.
do.............Joaquim P. Joaquim...V. C. G.
Penang ....Frederick Lederer..........Agt.
Southampton, England.Warner S. Kinkead...........C.
do..............Joseph Dean.......V. & D. C.
do...............William C. Offutt..........D. C.
do................Henry W. Martin........C. C.
Portsmouth..........John Mal..................Agt.
Weymouth...............Richard Cox.............Agt.
St. Christopher, W. I....Leopold Moore *............C. A.
do...............Lewis H. Percival......V. C. A.
Nevis ....Charles C. Greaves..........Agt.
St. George's, Bermuda..Edward W. Willett.........C. A.
do...............William D. Fox.......V. C. A.
St. Helena (Island)......James B. Coffin................C.
do................Thomas E. Fowler......V. C.
St. Hyacinthe, Quebec.Charles Laberge............C. A.
do.............Francis Bartels....V. & D. C. A
Sorel ....Isale Sylvestre...............Agt.
Waterloo............Arthur S. Newell............Agt.
St. John, N. B..........John S. Derby...............C.
do...............Allen Derby......V. & D. C.
Campobello Island...John J. Alexander......... Agt.

Place.	Name and Title.
Fredericton ....James T. Sharkey.........Agt.
Grand Manan........William A. Fraser.........Agt.
St. George............Charles C. Ludgate........Agt.
St. John's, N. F..C.
do..............John Thomas Barron.....V. C.
St. John's, Quebec.....Thomas Keefe..............C.
do................John Donaghy......V. & D. C.
Farnham............William L. Hibbard.......Agt.
Lacolle...............Henry Hoyle..............Agt.
St. Stephen, N. B......Edgar Whidden..............C.
do............Charlie N. Vroom...V. & D. C.
McAdam Junction....James W. Green..........Agt.
St. Andrews.........George H. Stickney.......Agt.
Stanbridge, Quebec....Daniel G. Furman........C. A.
do..............Geo. M. Hastings.V. & D. C. A.
Clarenceville.........Edmund Macomber........Agt.
Frelighsburg.........William A. Reynolds......Agt.
Sutton.... ....Egbert R. Shepard..........Agt.
Stratford, Ont..........Luther M. Shaffer.............C.
do............Lewis H. Dingman..V. & D. C.
Swansea............David C. Davies.........C. A.
do................Arthur Sperry....V. & D. C. A.
Sydney, N. S. W........George W. Bell.............C.
do............Charles G. Ewing.........V. C.
do..............William H. Dawson........D. C.
Norfolk Island.........Isaac Robinson...........Agt.
Three Rivers, Quebec..Francois X. Belleau..........C.
do........Waters W. Braman, Jr....V. C.
Arthabaska.........Arthur Poitras.............Agt.
Toronto, Ont..........John W. Coppinger...........C.
do.............John B. Coppinger..V. & D. C.
Oshawa..............W. P. Sterricke.............Agt.
Trinidad, W. I.........William C. Foster............C.
do................Julian H. Archer..........V. C.
Grenada...............P. J. Dean................Agt.
Scarborough.........Edward Keens..........Agt.
Tunstall, England.....Wendell C. Warner............C.
do................John H. Copestake..V. & D. C.
Turks Island, W. I..C.
do.............William Stanley Jones....V. C.
Cockburn Harbor....John W. Tatem............Agt.
Salt Cay............Daniel F. Harriott..........Agt.
Vancouver, B. C.......William F. Peterson......C. A.
do..............Fred. J. Schofield.V. & D. C. A.
Union.................George W. Clinton..........Agt.
Victoria, B. C..........William P. Roberts............C.
do................Miles R. Eure.......V. & D. C.
Nanaimo ....William B. Dennison......Agt.
Wallaceburgh, Ont....Isaac G. Worden.........C. A.
do................Chas. B. Jackson.V. & D. C. A.
Windsor, N. S........Edward Young..............C.
do...................................V. & D. C.
Cornwallis..........Fenwick W. Rand........Agt.
Kempt..............John G Burgess..........Agt.
Parrsboro...........David A. Huntley.........Agt.
Port Joggins........William Moffat..........Agt.
Windsor, Ont.........Marshall P. Thatcher..........C.
do.............Joseph Prevost Carr.V. & D. C.
Winnipeg, Manitoba...Matthew M. Duffle............C.
do....................William Hall..............V. C.
Deloraine ....Albert M. Herron..........Agt.
Emerson.............Duncan McArthur..........Agt.

* Born of American parents temporarily residing abroad.

THE LEGAL AND FINANCIAL LIGHTS OF AMERICA.

Place.	Name and Title.
Fort William, Ont.	C. W. Jarvis............Agt.
Gretna............	Enoch Winkler..........Agt.
Lethbridge........	Thomas Curry...........Agt.
North Portal, Assiniboia............	W. H. Dorsey...........Agt.
Rat Portage, Ont.	George E. Frisbie........Agt.
Woodstock, N. B.	Grenville James..........C.
do............	John Graham............V. C.
Yarmouth, N. S.	Charles A. O'Connor......C.
do............	Ernest H. Armstrong.V.& D. C.
Annapolis........	Jacob M. Owen..........Agt.
Barrington.......	Thomas W. Robertson...Agt.
Digby...........	T. Howland White.......Agt.
Shelburne........	William B. Stewart......Agt.

GREECE.

Athens...........	Eben Alexander......‡C. G.
do............	George Horton..........C.
do............	Arthur C. McDowall....V. C.
Piræus..........	Arthur C. McDowall....Agt.
Syra............	Basil Padova...........Agt.
Volo............	Charles W. Borrell......Agt.
Patras...........	Edward Hancock.........C.
do............	....................V. C.
Corfu...........	Charles E. Hancock.....Agt.
Kalamata........	Denis A. Pantasopoulos..Agt.
Zante...........	Alfred L. Crowe........Agt.

GUATEMALA.

Guatemala.......	D. Lynch Pringle......*C. G.
do............	John North Todd.....V. C. G.
Champerico......	Florentine Souza........Agt.
Livingston.......	Frank C. Dennis........Agt.
Ocos............	J. Dawson Meza........Agt.
San José de Guatemala	Roger R. Vair..........Agt.

HAITI.

Cape Haitien......:	....................C.
do............	Theodore Behrmann.....V. C.
Gonaives........	Ethéart Dupny..........Agt.
Port de Paix.....	Albert Schumacher......Agt.
Port-au-Prince....	Henry M. Smythe.....†C. G.
do............	John B. Terres.......V. C. G.
do............	Alexander Battiste......D. C.
Aux Cayes.......	Henry E. Roberts.......Agt.
Jacmel..........	Jean Vital.............Agt.
Jeremie..........	L. Treband Ronzler.....Agt.
Miragoane.......	Francis W. Mitchell....Agt.
Petit Goâve......	F. Merantie............Agt.
St. Marc........	Charles Miot...........Agt.

HAWAIIAN ISLANDS.

Honolulu........	Ellis Mills..........*C. G.
do............	W.P.Boyd..V. & D.C. G. & C.C.
Hilo............	Charles Furneaux.......Agt.
Kahului.........	A. G. Dickine..........Agt.
Mahukona.......	Charles Jacob Falk.....Agt.

HONDURAS.

Ruatan..........	J. Eugene Jarnigan.......C.
do............	Philip S. Burchard......V. C.
Bonacca.........	William Bayly..........Agt.
Utilla...........	Robert Woodville.......Agt.

Place.	Name and Title.
Tegucigalpa......	William Myers Little......C.
do............	George Bernhard.......V. C.
Amapala........	William Heyden.........Agt.
Ceiba...........	Louis Bier.............Agt.
Macaome........	John E. Foster.........Agt.
Puerto Cortez....	William E. Alger.......Agt.
San Juancinto....	E. E. Dickason.........Agt.
San Pedro Sula...	J. M. Mitchell, Jr......Agt.
Truxillo.........	H. P. Boyce...........Agt.
Yuscaran........	Charles W. Benton.....Agt.

ITALY.

Castellamare di Stabia..	Henry G. Huntington....C. A.
do............	Robert Wickersham....V. C. A.
Sorrento........	Francesco Ciampa......Agt.
Catania.........	Louis H. Bruhl..........C.
do............	Jacob Ritter.........V. & D. C.
Florence........	Charles Belmont Davis....C.
do............	Spirito Bernardi....V. & D. C.
Bologna.........	Carlo Gardini..........Agt.
Genoa..........	James Fletcher..........C.
do............	Federico Scerni........V. C.
San Remo.......	Albert Ameglio.........Agt.
Leghorn........	Alexander S. Rosenthal....C.
do............	Emilio Masi........V. & D. C.
Carrara.........	Ulisse Boccacci.........Agt.
Messina.........	Charles M. Caughy.......C.
do............	Letterio Pirrone....V. & D. C.
Gioja...........	Luigi Giffoni..........Agt.
Milazzo.........	Pietro Siracusa........Agt.
Milan...........	Diovol B. Spagnoli.......C.
do............	S. N. D. Spagnoli..V. & D. C.
Naples..........	Frank A. Dean..........C.
do............	Jonathan Dean.....V. & D. C.
Bari............	Nicholas Schuck........Agt.
Rodi............	Tomaso del Giudice.....Agt.
Palermo.........	William H. Seymour......C.
do............	Felix Pirandello........V. C.
Carini..........	Francesco Crocchiolo....Agt.
Girgenti.........	Francis Ciotta.........Agt.
Licata..........	Arthur Verderame......Agt.
Trapani.........	Ignazio Marrone........Agt.
Rome...........	Wallace S. Jones.....C. G.
do............	C.M.Wood..V. & D. C. G & C.C.
Ancona.........	A. P. Tomassini........Agt.
Cagliari.........	Alphonse Dol..........Agt.
Civita Vecchia...	Gustav Marsanich......Agt.
Turin...........	William E. Mantius......C.
do............	Hugo Pizzotti........V. C.
Venice..........	Henry A. Johnson........C.
do............	Frederick Rechsteiner.V.&D.C.

JAPAN.

Kanagawa.......	Nicholas W. McIvor....C. G.
do............	John McLean....V. & D. C. G.
do............	G. H. Scidmore..D. C. G. & C. C.
do............	William B. Herbert......Mar.
do............	John McLean...........Int.
Nagasaki........	William H. Abercrombie....C.
do............	Herbert Blackburn......V. C.
do............	S. R. de Souza.........Int.
do............	John Frank Nevells......Mar.

†The Consul-General is also Minister Resident and Chargé d'Affaires to Santo Domingo.
*The Consul-General is also Secretary of Legation.
‡The Consul-General is also E. E. & M. P.

THE LEGAL AND FINANCIAL LIGHTS OF AMERICA. 171

Place.	Name and Title.
Osaka and Hiogo (Kobé)	James F. Connelly..........C.
do	Hunter Sharp............V. C.
do	George F. Smithers......D. C.
do	Edmond von Gehren......Agt.
do	Hunter Sharp............Mar.
do	W. Ebiharah..............Int.

KOREA.

| Seonl | John M. B. Sill..........†C. G. |
| do | Horace N. Allen ......*D. C. G. |

LIBERIA.

Monrovia	William H. Heard ......†C. G.
do	Beverly Y. Payne.........V. C.
Cape Coast Castle	George E. Emingsang......Agt.

LUXEMBURG.

| Luxemburg | Geo.H.Murphy.V.C.,C.A.&C.C. |

MADAGASCAR.

Tamatave	Edward Telfair Wetter.......C.
do	V. C.
Andakabe	Agt.
Majonga	Frank Harvey ....Agt.

MASKAT.

Maskat	C.
do	Archibald Mackirdy ......V. C.
do	Mahomed Fazel..........D. C.

MEXICO.

Acapulco	Edgar Battle..............C.
do	Herman Stoll.............V. C.
San Benito	L. R. Brewer............Agt.
Tehuantepec and Salina Cruz	James W. Jeffries.........Agt.
Chihuahua	Richard M. Burke..........C.
do	Rowland Anderson.......V. C.
Parral	James J. Long............Agt.
Durango	John S. McCaughan ....C.
do	Edward Williams.........V. C.
Toreon	Lenious F. Poston.........Agt.
Ensenada	C.
do	Anthony Godbe..........V. C.
La Paz	C.
do	James Viosca, Jr..........V. C.
Magdalena Bay	...Agt.
San José and Cape St. Lucas	Abraham Kurnitzky......Agt.
Matamoros	John B. Gorman............C.
do	J. Bielenberg.............V. C.
Camargo	Agt.
Mier	Henry Vizcayo ....Agt.
Santa Cruz Point	J. Bielenberg........Act'g Agt.
Mazatlan	Arthur de Cima...........C.
do	John P. de Cima, Jr .....V. C.
Merida	Robert L. Oliver............C.
do	John M. Gilkey......V. & D. C.
Campeachy	Gasper Trueba...........Agt.
Laguna de Terminos	German Hahn.............Agt.
Progreso	John Waddle............Agt.
Mexico	Thomas T. Crittenden ...C. G.
do	Wm. J. Crittenden..V. & D. C. G.

Place.	Name and Title.
Aguas Calientes	Alfred M. Raphall ....Agt.
Guanajuato	Dwight Furness............Agt.
Zacatecas	Edmond von Gehren......Agt.
Nogales	Frank W. Roberts...........C.
do	Reuben D. George...V. & D. C.
Guaymas	Agt.
Nuevo Laredo	Joseph G. Donnelly.......C. G.
do	John F. Valls......V. C. G.
do	Louis A. Coddington..D. C. G.
Garita Gonzales	John F. Valls............Agt.
Monterey	George D. Fitzsimmons....Agt.
Victoria	Murdock C. Cameron......Agt.
Paso del Norte	Louis M. Buford...........C.
do	Charles E. Wesche..V. & D. C.
Piedras Negras	Jesse W. Sparks..... ......C.
do	Samuel M. Simmons......V. C.
Ciudad Porfirio Diaz	Samuel M. Simmons.......Agt.
Sierra Mojada	Henry B. Hackley ....Agt.
Saltillo	John Woessner..............C.
do	V. C.
Tampico	John Maguire................C.
do	Neill E. Presaly..........V. C.
San Luis Potosi	Voelian C. Whitfield......Agt.
Tuxpan	John Drayton..............C.
do	V. C.
Veracruz	Charles Schaefer............C.
do	Louis W. Shouse..........V. C.
Coatzacoalcos	Frank W. Carpenter......Agt.
Frontera	Michael Girard........... Agt.

MOROCCO.

Tangier	John Judson Barclay......C. G.
do	John Judson Barclay, Jr.V.C.G.
Casa Blanca	John Cobb...............Agt.
Laraiche	Solomon Benatuil ....Agt.
Mazagan	Leon Roffé................Agt.
Mogador	George Broome............Agt.
Rabat	Jacob R. Benatar.........Agt.
Saffi	John Russi ....Agt.
Tetuan	Isaac L. Cohen ....Agt.

NETHERLANDS AND DOMINIONS.

Amsterdam	Edward Downes............C.
do	Albertus Vinke......V. & D. C.
Batavia, Java	Bradstreet S. Rairden........C.
do	V. C.
Macassar, Celebes	Karl Auer.................Agt.
Samarang	Frederick W. Beauclerk...Agt.
Sœrabaya	Agt.
Curaçao, W. I	Jervis Spencer..............C.
do	Jacob Wulster............V. C.
Buen Ayre	Lodewyk C. Boyé.........Agt.
Padang, Sumatra	Clemens Boon..........V. C.
Paramaribo, Guiana	Eli Van Praag............V. C.
Rotterdam	Lars S. Reque...............C.
do	John Visser..............V. C.
do	Aire H. Voorwinden......D. C.
Flushing	Peter Smith..............Agt.
Schidam	Leonard Koot............Agt.
St. Martin, W. I	Diedric C. Van Romondt.....C.
St. Eustatius	J. G. C. Every............Agt.

* Also Secretary of Legation.
† The Consul-General is also Minister Resident.

THE LEGAL AND FINANCIAL LIGHTS OF AMERICA.

Place.	Name and Title.
NICARAGUA.	
Managua..C.	
do................Henry E. Low..............V. C.	
Cerinto................Henry Palazio..............Agt.	
San Juan del Sur.....Charles Holmann..........Agt.	
San Juan del Norte....Thomas O'Hara...............C.	
do................Henry de Soto.............V. C.	
Bluefields.............J. Herbert Perkins..........Agt.	
PARAGUAY.	
Asuncion...............Samuel W. Thome............C.	
do................Eben M. Flagg............V. C.	
PERSIA.	
Teheran...............Alexander McDonald.....*C. G.	
do................John Tyler..............V. C. G.	
Bushire..............Tigrane J. Malcolm........Agt.	
PERU.	
Callao..................Leon Jastremski.............C.	
do ....John Eyre..................V. C.	
Chiclayo..............Alfred Solf.................Agt.	
Mollendo............Enrique Meier..............Agt.	
Paita.................John F. Hopkins, Jr......Agt.	
Piura...................Emilio Clark..............Agt.	
Truxillo.............Edward Gottfried..........Agt.	
Tumbez...............William Baldini............Agt.
PORTUGAL AND DOMINIONS.	
Fayal, Azores..........Colin C. Manning.............C.	
do................Moyses Benarus.....V. & D. C.	
Flores.................James McKay, Jr..........Agt.	
Graciosa..............José de C. C. Mello........Agt.	
St. Michael's ....William W. Nicholls ......Agt.	
San Jorge............Joaquin J. Cardozo........Agt.	
Terceira............Henrique de Castro........Agt.	
Funchal, Madeira .....Thomas C. Jones ....C.	
do................William J. G. Reid...V. & D. C.	
Lisbon ....John B. Wilbor............V. C.	
Faro ....F. L. Tavares..............Agt.	
Loanda, Africa........Frank Weston..............Agt.	
Oporto........ ....William Stuve.............Agt.	
Setubal ....Joaquin T. O'Neill........Agt.	
Mozambique, Africa....W. Stanley Hollis....... ....C.	
do......................................V. C.	
Beira................Charles A. Andrews ....Agt.	
Lourenco Marquez...James McIntosh............Agt.	
Santiago, C. V. Islands.T. S. Bergstrom ....V. C.	
Brava ....Joao J. Nunes.............Agt.	
Fogo ....C. J. Barbosa.............Agt.	
St. Vincent...........J. B. Guimaraes............Agt.	
ROUMANIA.	
Bucharest..............Eben Alexander.........†C. G.	
do................Wm. G. Boxshall......V. C. G.	

Place.	Name and Title.
RUSSIA.	
Archangel............Ferdinand Lindes......Act'g C.	
Batoum................James C. Chambers..........C.	
do................Harry R. Briggs ....V. C.	
Helsing'örs...C.	
do................Herman Donner..........V. C.	
Abo...................Victor Forselius......... ...Agt.	
Wiborg ....C. Edwin Ekstrom..........Agt.	
Moscow ....Adolph Billhardt............C.	
do................Thomas Smith............V. C.	
Odessa................Thomas E. Heenan...........C.	
do................John H. Volkmann......V. C.	
Rostaff and Taganrog.... ....William R. Martin...Act'g Agt.	
Riga....................Niels P. A. Bornholdt........C.	
do...V. C.	
St. Petersburg.........John Karel...............C. G.	
do................Paul Magnus..........V. C. G.	
Cronstadt............Peter Vigius....... ......Agt.	
Libau............ ....Hugo Smit................Agt.	
Revel ....Edmund Von Glehn. .....Agt.	
Warsaw..............Joseph Rawicz..............C.	
do.................................... ....V. C.	
SALVADOR.	
San Salvador..C.	
do................Guillermo J. Dawson.....V. C.	
Acajutla ....Otto Munchmeyer ....Agt.	
La Libertad..........Alfred Cooper..............Agt.	
La Union ....John B. Courtade..........Agt.	
SAMOA.	
Apia............. ....James H. Mulligan........C. G.	
do................William Blacklock.....V. C. G.	
Pagopago...Agt.	
SERVIA.	
Belgrade...............Eben Alexander..........†C. G.	
do................Elie Litzikas............V. C. G.	
SIAM.	
Bangkok ....John Barret .... *C. G.	
do................Edward V. Kellett.....V. C. G.	
SPAIN AND DOMINIONS.	
Alicante................William L. Giro...............C.	
do................John L. Giro..............V. C.	
Baracoa, Cuba.........Alfredo T. Triay...............C.	
do......... ..José Tur................ V. C.	
Barcelona.............Herbert W. Bowen...........C. G.	
do................Henry H. Rider..V. & D. C. G.	
Bilbao................Sydney I. Dyer..............Agt.	
Gijon ....Calisto Alvargonzalez.....Agt.	
Grao..................Theodore Mertens..........Agt.	
Palma Majorca......Ernesto Canut............Agt.	
Port Mahon..........P. B. Valls ....Agt.	
San Feliu de Guixols..José Sibils................Agt.	
San Sebastian........Julian de Salazar.........Agt.	

*The Consul-General is also Minister Resident.
†The Consul-General is also E. E. & M. P.

THE LEGAL AND FINANCIAL LIGHTS OF AMERICA. 173

Place.	Name and Title.
Santander	Faustino Adriozola........Agt.
Tarragona	Pelayo Montoya...........Agt.
Torrevieja	José Hodar................Agt.
Cadiz	Charles L. Adams............C.
do	John A. Parkinson........V. C.
Algeciras	Emilio S. Mensayas........Agt.
Huelva	John R. Catlin............Agt.
Jerez de la Frontera	William W. Wysor........Agt.
Port St. Mary's	George M. Daniels.........Agt.
Seville	Samuel B. Caldwell.......Agt.
Cardenas, Cuba	Joseph L. Hance.........C. A.
do	Francisco Cayro.......V. C. A.
Carthagena	Cirilo Molina.............C.
do	Alberto Molino..........V.C.
Cienfuegos, Cuba	Owen McGarr..............C.
do	Juan J. Casanova.......V. C.
Trinidad de Cuba	Daniel Quayle............Agt.
Zaza	P. D. Buzzi..............Agt.
Corunna	Julio Harmony ....C.
do	Raimundo Molina .... V. C.
Carril	Rogelio Fereiros..........Agt.
Corcubion	Plácido Castro.............Agt.
Ferrol	Nicasio Perez.............Agt.
Vigo	Camilo Molins.............Agt.
Vivero	Joaquín Muñiz...........Agt.
Denia	Andrew F. Fay.............C.
do	Ambrose Bordehore......V. C.
Garrucha	José Garcia Sucsa.......V. C.
do	.........................V. C. A.
Habana, Cuba	Ramon O. Williams......C. G.
do	Joseph A.SpringerV.C.G.&C.C.
do	Adolfo S. Dolz........D. C. G.
do	Joseph A. Springer......C. C.
Madrid	Ignacio F. Hernandez...V. C.
Malaga	David N. Burke............V. C.
do	Thomas R. Geary.........V. C.
Almeria Malaga	Herman F. Fischer.......Agt.
Granada	Eugene McCarthy........Agt.
Port of Marbella	Miguel Calzado........Agt.
Manila,PhilippineIsl'ds.Isaac M. Ell'ott..............C.
do	...........................V. C.
Cebu	G. E. A. Cadell............Agt.
Iloilo	George Shelmerdine......Agt.
Matanzas, Cuba	Alexander C. Brice ....C.
do	Henry Heidegger........V. C.
Nuevitas	..........................C. A.
do	Joaquin S. Adan.......V. C. A.
Gibara	José H. Beola..............Agt.
Sagua la Grande, Cuba..Walter B. Barker......C. A.
do	......................V. C. A.
San Juan, P. R.	John D. Hall..............C.
do	William H. Latimer.V. & D. C.
Aguadilla	Ang. Ganslandt.........Agt.
Arecibo	John J. Ball, Jr..........Agt.
Fajardo	J. Vaamonde Lopez......Agt.
Guayama	J. C. McCormick.........Agt.
Mayaguez	Manuel Badrena..........Agt.
Naguabo	Antonio Roig ....Agt.
Ponce	Felix W. Preston.........Agt.
Vieqnez	H. N. Longpré..........Agt.
San Juan de los Reme- James H. Springer.....V. C. A. dios, Cuba	

Place.	Name and Title.
Santiago de Cuba	Pulaski F. Hyatt...........C.
do	John T. Hyatt.......V. & D. C.
do	Louis M. Preval..........D. C.
Guantanamo	Paul Brooks..............Agt.
Manzanillo	W. Stakeman............Agt.
Santa Cruz	Walter Voigt.............Agt.
Teneriffe,CanaryIslands.................. C.
do	Philibert Lallier.........V. C.
Grand Canary	Thomas Miller ....Agt.
Lanzarotte	John G. Topham.........Agt.
Orotava	Peter S. Reid.............Agt.

SWEDEN AND NORWAY.

Bergen, Norway	Frederik G. Gade............C.
do	Johan C. Isdahl, Jr.......V. C.
Drontheim	Claus Berg ....Agt.
Stavanger	C. F. Falck................Agt.
Christiania, Norway...Gerhard Gade............C.
do	Lauritz F. Brown.........V. C.
Arendal	Christian Eyde...........Agt.
Christiansand	Ferd. Reinhardt...........Agt.
Gothenberg, Sweden...Otto H. Boyesen............C.
do	Urban Körner.............V. C.
Helsingborg	J. Palmeborg.............Agt.
Malmo	Peter M. Flensburg.......Agt.
Stockholm, Sweden	Thomas B. O'Neill.........C.
do	Axel Georgii..............V. C.

SWITZERLAND.

Basle	George Gifford..............C.
do	Lyman C. Bryan..........V. C.
Chauxdefonds	Henri Rieckel, Jr..........Agt.
Berne	John E. Hinnen...........V. C.
Geneva	Benjamin H. Ridgely........C.
do	Peter Naylor.............V. C.
Vevey	William Cuénod..........Agt.
Horgen	William F. Kemmler........C.
do	William Streuli..........V. C.
do	Ferdinand Leu...........D. C.
Lucerne	Ernest Williams..........Agt.
St. Gall	Irving B. Richman......C. G.
do	John H. Zollikofer....V. C. G.
Zurich	Eugene Germain.............C.
do	Emil J. Constam.........V. C.
Aarau	Remigius Sauerlaender.....Agt.
Winterthur	Heinrich Langsdorf........Agt.

TURKEY AND DOMIN- IONS.

Bagdad	..........................C.
do	Rudolph Hürner..........V. C.
Bassorah	.........................Agt.
Beirut, Syria	Thomas R. Gibson..........C.
do	Cor.stantine Khouri.....V. C.
Aleppo	Frederick Poché..........Agt.
Alexandretta	Daniel Walker............Agt.
Damascus	Nasif Meshaks...........Agt.
Haifa	Gottlieb Schumacher.......Agt.
Mersine	Stephen J. Coldam ....Agt.

THE LEGAL AND FINANCIAL LIGHTS OF AMERICA.

Place.	Name and Title.
Cairo, Egypt	Frederic C. Penfield......*C. G.
do	H. L. Washington.V. & D. C. G.
do	St. Leger A. Touhay......C. C.
Alexandria	James Hewat..............Agt.
Assioot	Bestauros W. Khayat......Agt.
Assouan	Agt.
Beni-Souef	Marcos Lucca..............Agt.
Candia, Crete	Agt.
Keneh	Abdel K. M. el Ammari....Agt.
Luxor	Aly Mourad................Agt.
Mansourah	Ibrahim Daoud............Agt.
Port Said	Richmond Broadbent......Agt.
Sohag and Akhmin	Abdel Shald..............Agt.
Suez	Alfred W. Haydn..........Agt.
Constantinople	Luther Short.............C. G.
do	William Albert........V. C. G.
do	John A. Bigelow..........Mar.
Dardanelles	Frank Calvert..............Agt.
Salonica	Pericles H. Lazarro........Agt.
Erzerum, Armenia	Robert S. Chilton, Jr......V. C.
Harpoot, Armenia	W. Dulany Hunter.V. C. & C. C.
Jerusalem, Syria	Edwin S. Wallace..............C.
do	Herbert E. Clark..........V. C.
Yafa	E. Hardegg ....Agt.
Sivas	Milo A. Jewett..............†C.
do	Eugene Rodigas.....V. & D. C.
Samsoun	G. C. Stephopoulo.........Agt.
Trebizonde	H. Z. Longworth ....Agt.
Smyrna	James H. Madden............C.
do	Ezra J. Davee ....V. C.
Mytilene	Michael M. Fottion........Agt.

Place.	Name and Title.
URUGUAY.	
Colonia	Benjamin D. Manton.........C.
do	Manuel Caballero.........V. C.
Montevideo	Edgar Schramm..............C.
do	Thomas W. Howard ......V. C.
Paysandu	John G. Hufnagel.........C. A.
do	George A. Hufnagel ...V. C. A.
VENEZUELA.	
La Guayra	Frank D. Hill................C.
do	Thomas D. Golding.......V. C.
Barcelona	Ignacio H. Balz............Agt.
Caracas	Winfield S. Bird............Agt.
Carupano	Juan A. Orsini.............Agt.
Ciudad Bolivar	Robert Henderson ....Agt.
Cumana	José G. N. Romberg.......Agt.
Maracaibo	Eugene H. Plumacher.......C
do	Edouard Beekman.. ......V. C.
do	William Volger............D. C.
Coro	Josiah L. Senior. ....Agt.
San Cristobal	Alexander Boué............Agt.
Tovar	M. Bodecker..............Agt.
Valera	Marquard Bodecker........Agt.
Puerto Cabello	Samuel Proskauer...........C.
do	William H. Volkmar......V. C.
Valencia	T. H. Grosewisch..........Agt.
ZANZIBAR.	
Zanzibar	R. Dorsey Mohun............C.

*The Consul-General is also Diplomatic Agent.
†Born of American parents temporarily residing abroad.

www.ingramcontent.com/pod-product-compliance
Lightning Source LLC
Chambersburg PA
CBHW031450160426
43195CB00010BB/921